KOREAN YEARBOOK OF INTERNATIONAL LAW

KOREAN YEARBOOK OF INTERNATIONAL LAW

Volume 11
2023

PARKYOUNGSA

THE KOREAN BRANCH OF THE INTERNATIONAL LAW ASSOCIATION

KOREAN YEARBOOK OF
INTERNATIONAL LAW

Copyright © The Korean Branch of the International Law Association 2024
Published by PARKYOUNGSA

PARKYOUNG Publishing&Company
210-ho, 53, Gasan digital 2-ro, Geumcheon-gu, Seoul, 08588, Korea
Tel 82-2-733-6771
Fax 82-2-736-4818

First published 20 December 2024
Printed in Seoul, Korea
ISBN 979-11-303-4815-5 93360
ISSN 2635-8484
For subscriptions to this Yearbook, please contact the sole distributor, PARKYOUNG Publishing&Company
210-ho, 53, Gasan digital 2-ro, Geumcheon-gu, Seoul, 08588, Korea
Tel 82-2-733-6771 Fax 82-2-736-4818 E-mail: pys@pybook.co.kr

THE KOREAN BRANCH OF
THE INTERNATIONAL LAW ASSOCIATION

PRESIDENT

Seokwoo Lee

HONORARY PRESIDENT

Jang-Hie Lee

PRESIDENT-ELECT

Gyooho Lee

VICE-PRESIDENTS

Changmin Chun

Min Jung Chung

Dongwon Jung

Young Seok Kim

Jihyun Park

SECRETARY-GENERAL

Seryon Lee

MEMBERS OF EXECUTIVE COUNCIL

CONTENTS

CONTEMPORARY PRACTICE AND JUDICIAL DECISIONS

EDITORIAL NOTE

It is our great pleasure to present Volume 11 of the Korean Yearbook of International Law. Above all, we would like to express our deep gratitude to the writers submitting valuable papers. With the active participation of experts, this yearbook can be truly special and unique.

This edition covers various topics of international law, from the law of the sea to international environmental law.

Professor Chang Wee LEE's article "Sovereignty over Dokdo as Seen through Japanese Historical Documents" examines historical Japanese documents that prove Korean sovereignty over Dokdo. LEE analyzes key documents from the 1667 Onshu Shichogakki to the 1877 Dajokan Directive, showing Japan historically acknowledged Dokdo was not its territory. The paper highlights two crucial pieces of evidence: the 1695 correspondence between the Tokugawa Shogunate and Tottori-han where Tottori admitted Dokdo was not its territory, and the 1877 Dajokan Directive where Japan's highest administrative body officially declared Dokdo had no relation to Japan. LEE argues these historical documents invalidate Japan's 1905 incorporation of Dokdo and suggests that resolving the dispute requires Japan to abandon its territorial claims.

Taking up a significant development in maritime law, Professor Seokyong LEE's article analyzes the recent ICJ judgment in Nicaragua v. Colombia (2023) where the Court ruled that under customary international law, a State's entitlement to continental shelf beyond 200nm cannot extend within 200nm of another State's baselines. This judgment effectively overrules the natural prolongation doctrine from the 1969 North Sea Continental Shelf cases. The article examines implications for Korea-Japan Joint Development Zone

(JDZ) in the East China Sea and explores options for the future as the JDZ Agreement approaches its potential termination. Professor LEE suggests maintaining the JDZ system could be preferable to new delimitation negotiations, given the conflict between Korea's natural prolongation theory and Japan's distance standard.

Delving into cultural heritage law, Jaehyun RYU and Sungjae HWANG's paper analyzes Korean courts' rulings on the Buseoksa Temple's Avalokiteshvara statue case from a private international law perspective. The paper examines the applicability of the UNESCO 1970 Convention, evaluates Korea's compliance with Article 20 of the Cultural Heritage Protection Act, and expresses hope that this case will encourage further research and efforts toward achieving restorative justice in international cultural heritage law.

In the wake of Korea's space achievements, Chang Wee LEE's paper "Recovering of Space Objects and Legal Status of Drop Area between Korea and Japan" analyzes recovery procedures and drop areas following Nuri's successful launch. The paper examines competing rights between coastal states and other states in the EEZ, jurisdiction and ownership of space objects, and the legal status of the intermediate zone in the East China Sea, while emphasizing the need for Korea-Japan cooperation.

Through detailed historical analysis, See-Hwan DOH's paper demonstrates how Japan utilized the Japanese Society of International Law and the concealed Temporary Investigation Committee to establish legal justifications for its invasion of Dokdo and colonization of Korea. The paper shows these organizations deliberately distorted international legal principles to support Japanese colonialism, particularly around the 1905 invasion of Dokdo and forced Korea-Japan Treaty. The author argues that Japan's continued claims stem from this colonial legacy.

At a critical juncture in climate policy, Professor Junha Kang traces the 30-year evolution of the Loss and Damage Fund from initial discussions to its formal establishment at COP 28. His analysis covers key concepts, institutional developments, and remaining challenges in operationalization. With particular attention to South Korea's position as a significant global emitter, Kang explores the complex dynamics between developed and developing nations in addressing climate-related losses.

Amid evolving jurisdictional challenges, Judge Soo-Jin CHO examines the ongoing development of a new convention on parallel proceedings at the Hague Conference. Her paper analyzes three crucial aspects: the scope of "related matters," approaches to resolving jurisdictional conflicts between civil and common law traditions, and mechanisms for judicial cooperation. Drawing from judicial experience, Cho advocates for core principles focused on pure parallel proceedings while emphasizing court-to-court communication.

With cross-border criminal cases on the rise, Judge Jung-Hwa YOU analyzes Korean criminal court decisions from 2020-2023 involving private international law issues. Through detailed case studies including embezzlement of a Singaporean company's assets and inheritance disputes involving U.S. citizens, the paper demonstrates how Korean courts determine applicable laws through conflict-of-laws rules when addressing civil law elements within criminal cases.

Against the backdrop of regional tensions, Professor Han Taek KIM examines the legal implications of recent satellite launches by both Koreas under international space law. The paper contrasts North Korea's violation of UN Security Council resolutions with South Korea's legitimate space development, while exploring broader questions of space security, militarization, and the evolving legal framework for military space activities.

Focusing on trade implications, Min Jung CHUNG examines proposed amendments to ban Japanese seafood imports following the Fukushima water discharge. Drawing on the WTO Appellate Body Report Korea-Radionuclides case, the paper assesses how future WTO challenges might differ, particularly regarding scientific evidence requirements under the SPS Agreement.

In a comprehensive review of recent disputes, Professor Sok Young CHANG examines two significant ISDS cases involving Korea: Lone Star v. Korea and Elliott v. Korea. The paper analyzes their proceedings, awards, and subsequent developments, noting the USD 216 million Lone Star award undergoing annulment proceedings and the USD 107.8 million Elliott award being challenged in UK courts.

Marking a major shift in adoption policy, Professor Gyooho LEE's article examines Korea's legislative preparations for implementing the HCCH 1993 Convention through two significant laws enacted in 2023. The article details how Korea is restructuring its adoption system through the International Adoption Act and Special Act on Domestic Adoption, effective July 19, 2025. These laws aim to strengthen state responsibility, separate international and domestic procedures, and align with international standards.

Throughout a diplomatically active year, Min Jung CHUNG analyzes 14 international law-related resolutions passed by Korea's National Assembly in 2023. The article notes significant increases in both quantity and scope compared to 2022, particularly in human rights-related resolutions and those concerning Japan. The paper details how these resolutions reflect Korea's diplomatic priorities and response to major international events.

Breaking new ground in public international law, Judge Eungi HONG examines four significant Korean court decisions from 2023. The article analyzes cases concerning state immunity in embassy property disputes, application of the Refugee Convention in criminal cases, state immunity in comfort women compensation claims, and interpretation of assault requirements in sexual offense cases considering international human rights standards.

Complementing public law developments, High Court Judge Jiyong JANG analyzes four pivotal private international law decisions from 2023. The cases examined include a sovereign immunity dispute involving diplomatic property, validity of exclusive international jurisdiction agreements in consumer contracts, application of CISG principles in international sales disputes, and determination of applicable law in cross-border cultural asset cases.

This volume of the Korean Yearbook of International Law features a diverse array of timely and impactful research from leading experts in international law. The papers cover crucial topics such as the Dokdo territorial dispute, maritime boundary delimitation, cultural heritage repatriation, space law, climate policy, and private international law developments in Korean courts. The insights and analyses presented will undoubtedly further the discourse on these important issues within the international legal community.

We are grateful to the contributing authors for their valuable scholarship. We look forward to continued growth and prominence of this publication as it serves to elevate global research in international law.

Junha Kang
Editor-in-Chief
Hongik University

Dahae Jung
Executive Editor
Legal Research Institute of Korea University

ARTICLES

Sovereignty over Dokdo as Seen through Japanese Historical Documents

Chang Wee LEE
Professor, University of Seoul

Key Words

Dokdo, Takeshima, Ulleungdo, terra nullius, territorial sovereignty, Grand State Council Directive, Dajokan Shirei

1. INTRODUCTION

As regards Dokdo, the Republic of Korea (hereinafter, "Korea") and Japan hold different views on the following three points: first, historical evidence of the sovereignty over Dokdo; second, the validity of Japan's 1905 occupation measure; and third, interpretation of a series of instruments-the Cairo Declaration through the 1951 San Francisco Peace Treaty.[1] The Dokdo issue could be analyzed legally in terms of these three aspects.

Historical evidence of the ownership of a particular island is important in the judicial settlement of disputes. However, historical records that do not form the basis of a legal claim to an island are not evidentiary, so obscure historical documents or maps are of little value in resolving territorial disputes. When dealing with a sovereignty issue of an island from the perspective of international law, historical evidence with legal foundation is considered mostly significant. We should interpret clear historical documents that can serve as a legal basis.

Territorial issues are conflicts between States in which international law and international politics interact in complex ways. The Dokdo issue should be approached in an integrated manner. To effectively counter Japan's claims to Dokdo, Korea needs evidence, legal interpretations, and a convincing logic about the island. It is important to respond to Japan's political claims in a firm and determined manner.

Korea and Japan's claims to Dokdo are summarized on the website of their respective foreign ministry. Under the heading of "Japan's Consistent Position on Territorial Sovereignty over Takeshima (Dokdo)," Japan emphasizes the following three points. First, Takeshima is indisputably an inherent territory of Japan in light of historical facts and based on international law. Second, Korea has been occupying Takeshima with no basis under international law. Any measures Korea takes regarding Takeshima based on such an illegal occupation have no legal justification. Third, Japan will continue to seek settlement of the dispute over the territorial sovereignty over Takeshima on the basis of international law in a calm and peaceful manner.[2]

These arguments of Japan are summarized in the "10 points to understand the Takeshima Dispute" on the website of the Japanese foreign ministry as follows: Japan has long recognized the existence of Takeshima, while Korea has not; Japan had established sovereignty over Takeshima by the mid-17th century at the latest; while Japan prohibited the passage to Ulleungdo, it did not ban the passage to Takeshima; Yong-bok Ahn's statements at the time were not credible, and Japan reaffirmed its sovereignty over the island through a cabinet decision in 1905; Dokdo was not recognized as the Korean territory in the San Francisco Peace treaty; it was designated as a bombing range for the U.S. forces in Japan; Korea illegally declared the "Syngman Rhee Line"; and Korea refused to bring the dispute before the International Court of Justice (ICJ).[3]

Korea's arguments about Dokdo are as follows: first, Dokdo had historically and clearly been the Korean territory, and this was confirmed several times by Yong-bok Ahn's visits to Japan and Japan's related official documents; second, the fact that Dokdo was the Korean territory was again confirmed by the 1900 Imperial Edict No. 41, and therefore Japan's acquisition measure of 1905 was null and void because the targeted island was not terra nullius at that time; and third, a series of measures from the Cairo Declaration during the Second World War to the 1951 San Francisco Peace Treaty after the end of the war show that Dokdo is Korean territory.[4]

In this context, the Korean government has made it clear that Dokdo, the easternmost island in the East Sea, is an integral part of the Korean territory historically, geographically, and under international law. Therefore, it claims that no territorial dispute exists regarding Dokdo, and it is not a matter to be dealt with through diplomatic negotiations or judicial settlement. The Korean government has stated that it exercises Korea's territorial sovereignty over Dokdo firmly as well as resolutely, and it will continue to defend Korea's sovereignty over the island.[5]

The issue of the sovereignty over Dokdo has been discussed many times between Korea and Japan, so there is no need to rehash old arguments here. This paper examines the territorial sovereignty issue of Dokdo by analyzing significant Japanese historical documents and sources that deal with the issue. Japanese old documents and sources on Dokdo will help us objectively evaluate the issue.

2. JAPANESE HISTORICAL DOCUMENTS AND SOURCES

2-1. Records of Observation in Oki Province (Onshu)

Japan also has historical records that justify Korea's sovereignty over Dokdo. In particular, between the 17th and 19th centuries, Japan produced a number of documents recognizing Korea's sovereignty over the island. The Japanese documents that mention Dokdo are not as old as the Korean documents.

One of the oldest Japanese documents that mention Dokdo is the Onshu Shichogakki, which clearly states that Dokdo is not part of Japan. The Onshu Shichogakki was written in 1667 during the Edo period by Kansuke Saito (斎藤勘介), a bureaucrat in the Izumo (出雲) region of Japan. This document is the oldest known geographic reference to the island of Oki.

> Records of Observation in Oki Province (Onshu)(隠州視聴合紀)[6]
> Onshu Province (On 隠, Province 州) is located in the north sea. Therefore, it is called Oki Island. If we sail northwest for two days and one night, we arrive at Matsushima (松島). If we sail for one more day, we arrive at Takeshima (竹島). (In slang, it is called Isotakeshima (磯竹島). It is abundant in bamboos, fish, and seals.)
> These two islands are uninhabited. Seeing Goryeo (from these islands) is like seeing Oki Island (隠岐) from Unshu (雲州: Izumo 出雲). Therefore, this Province constitutes the northwestern limit of Japanese territory.

The language at the end of the document makes it clear that the extent of Japanese territory ends at Oki. On this basis, Korea takes the position that Dokdo is excluded from Japanese territory. A reasonable interpretation of the records of the Onshu Shichogakki consolidates Korea's position.

Japan, however, has a different interpretation from that of Korea based on the fact that its own fishing boats already sailed to Ulleungdo in 1618, half a century before the Onshu Shichogakki was written in 1667. Japan argues that the Oya Jinkichi (大屋甚吉) and Murakawa Ichibei (村川市兵衛) families of Yonago (米子), the Hoki state (伯耆國) of Tottori-han (鳥取藩), received a navigation license for Ulleungdo from the shogunate through the lord of Tottori-han and traveled back and forth between Ulleungdo and Japan.

Japan claims that the document, which describes Ulleungdo and Dokdo as uninhabited islands, represents the territorial extent of human habitation as far as Okido. It also argues that the inclusion of Dokdo in the two islands is a misrepresentation because Dokdo is not visible from the Korean mainland. Japan's arguments are overly broad and not convincing at all.

2-2. License of Voyage to Takeshima (Ulleungdo) and Ban on Voyage to the Island

Japan's position on Dokdo was confirmed by the territorial conflict between the two countries that resulted from Yong-bok Ahn's two trips to Ulleungdo. The conflict, known as the "Ulleungdo Dispute" or the "Takeshima Affair" (Takeshima Ikken), culminated in the shogunate's banning of passage to Ulleungdo in 1696 and the recognition of Korea's sovereignty over the island.[7]

However, Japan claims that while it prohibited Japanese navigation to Ulleungdo, it did not prohibit navigation to Dokdo. In points 3 and 4 of the "10 points to understand the Takeshima Dispute," Japan emphasizes that the shogunate issued a navigation license to Ulleungdo in 1618 and then banned navigation to Ulleungdo except for Dokdo in 1696.

Japan argues that if the shogunate considered Ulleungdo and Dokdo to be foreign territories at the time, it would have banned passage to these islands in 1635 when it issued its directives to close

Japan from the outside world and to prohibit Japanese from traveling abroad. Japan, however, insists that no such ban was issued at the time.

License of Voyage to Takeshima (Ulleungdo)[8]

We have received the report that Murakawa Ichibei (村川市兵衛) and Oya Jinkichi (大屋甚吉),[9] residents of Yonago (米子) town, who had sailed from Yonago of Hoki state (伯耆國) to Takeshima, petitioned to voyage to the island again. Thereupon, we inform you that we have no objection and we hereby allow their voyage.

High consideration,

May 16

Nakai Shinanonokami Naomasa	(永井信濃守) 尚政
Inoue Gazuenokashira Masanari	(井上主計頭) 正就
Doi Ooinogashira Doshikaz	(土井大炊頭) 利勝
Sakai Utanokashira Tadayo	(酒井雅樂頭) 忠世

To Matsudaira Shintaro   (松平新太郎 殿)

In point 4, under the heading of "Although passage to Ulleungdo Island was banned in order to take into consideration the friendship with the Korean dynasty, passage to Dokdo was not banned," Japan states that it only prohibited navigation to Ulleungdo.

After realizing that negotiations with Korea had failed during the Ulleungdo Dispute, the shogunate decided to ban Japanese citizens from visiting Ulleungdo in January 1691. The shogunate instructed Tottori-han that passage by Japanese to Ulleungdo was now prohibited and ordered Tsushima-han (which served as the contact point with the Korean dynasty during the Edo period) to inform the Korean dynasty of the decision.

The shogunate explained that, as no Japanese had settled on Ulleungdo and that the distance from the Korean Peninsula was shorter than that from Hoki Province, Tottori-han, it was not wise to ruin a good relationship with a neighboring country for the sake of what was seen as a small unprofitable island and that it would be sufficient to ban passage to Ulleungdo because it had not been incorporated into Japan.

Ban on Voyage to Takeshima (Ulleungdo)[10]

In a previous year, when Matsudaira Shintaro (松平新太郎) was governing Inaba and Hoki states (因州伯州), Murakawa Ichibei (村川市兵衛) and Oya Jinkichi (大屋甚吉), residents of Yonago (米子) town, began to sail to Takeshima to catch fish, and they have continued fishing until now. But now, we hereby give the order to prohibit them from voyaging to the island. You shall bear it in mind.

High consideration,

January 28

Tsuchiya Sagami-no-kami	(土屋相模守)
Toda Yamashiro-no-kami	(戸田山城守)
Abe Bungo-no-kami	(阿部豊後守)
Okubo Kaga-no-kami	(大久保加賀守)

To Matsudaira, Lord of Hoki (松平伯耆守 殿)

However, Japan's argument is based on faulty reasoning and is neither reasonable nor convincing. First of all, the fact that the shogunate did not prohibit navigation to Ulleungdo and Dokdo in 1635 despite the Shogunate Decree does not support the claim that it recognized the islands as its territory. Japan's claim is also contrary to historical facts as the shogunate recognized the existence of Dokdo in December 1695 through several documents on questions and answers with Tottori-han.

And since the shogunate that banned navigation to Ulleungdo did not authorize navigation to Dokdo, the argument that it did not ban navigation to Dokdo does not hold water. The documents of the Oya and Murakawa families also recognized Dokdo as an integral part of Ulleungdo, and Japanese fishermen did not sail to Dokdo alone until

1900. Above all, the very fact that the shogunate issued a license of voyage to Ulleungdo shows that it recognized Dokdo as a foreign territory along with Ulleungdo.

2-3. Questions and Answers between the Shogunate and Tottori-han

As the conflict between Korea and Japan over Ulleungdo continued, the Tokugawa Shogunate inquired in 1695 about how long Dokdo and Ulleungdo had been part of Tottori-han.

Shogunate's Questions to Tottori-han on Ulleungdo[11]
- Since when has Takeshima (Ulleungdo), which belongs to Inshu and Hakushu,[12] been under the jurisdiction of the two states? Had it been brought under the jurisdiction of the two states before the fief was granted in the preceding dynasty or after that?
- How big is Takeshima approximately? Is it inhabited or not?
- Since when have people gone fishing there? Do they go there every year or seldom? How do they fish there? Do many boats go there?
- I heard that when Joseon people came there to fish three or four years ago, two of them were abducted to Japan as hostages. Did they come there often before? Or did they come only during those two years?
- Did the people of your states go to Takeshima during the last two years?
- When Joseon people came in previous years, how many boats and how many people were there?
- Is there any other island that belongs to the two states?
I send this letter to learn about the above points. The end.
December 24

Tottori-han responded to the Shogunate's questions that Ulleungdo and Dokdo were not part of Tottori-han. In its response, Tottori-han explains the geography of the islands, the process by which they were granted license of voyage, and how Korean and

Japanese fishermen came to meet there.

Reply of Tottori-han to the Shogunate's Questions[13]
- Takeshima (Ulleungdo) does not belong to Inaba or Hoki states (provinces). We have heard that Oya Kyuemon[14], Murakawa Ichibei, the residents of Yonago town of Hoki state sailed to the island, by order (of the Shogunate), when Matsushira Shintaro was the Lord of the states. We have also heard that they had sailed there before, but we don't know exactly about it.
- The perimeter of Takeshima is about eight or nine li, and there is no inhabitant there.
- The fishing season in Takeshima is February and March. Some boats leave Yonago for that island each year. Two boats go to that island to catch abalones and other fish.
- When Joseon people came to that island four years ago, i.e. in the shin year, the master mariners of our boats encountered them as we reported to you at that time. When Joseon people came again in the following yu year, the master mariners of our boats abducted them to Yonago. At that time as well, we reported the event to you and sent those Joseon people to Nagasaki. In the sul year, we reported that our boats inevitably anchored on that island because of a storm. They went there this year again, but they returned without anchoring on the island because there were many foreigners. On their way back home, they took some abalones on Matsushima. We hereby report this event to you.
- When Joseon people came in the shin year, six of their eleven boats were drifted by the storm, and the remaining five boats stayed at that island with 53 people on board. In the yu year, there were 42 people on three boats. This year, many boats and people from Joseon were seen there, but it was impossible to accurately count them because our boats could not anchor there.
- Neither Takeshima (Ulleungdo), Matsushima (Dokdo), nor any other island belong to the two states. The end.

The shogunate responded by banning Japanese navigation to

Ulleungdo and Dokdo. This report of Tottori-han constituted one of the bases upon which the Shogunate made a decision to recognize that Takeshima belonged to Korea.

2-4. Grand State Council (Dajokan) Directive

The Japanese government's push for modernization after the Meiji Restoration led to the abolition of the old prefectures (Han, 藩) and the establishment of new prefectures (Ken, 縣). In 1876, in conjunction with the Meiji Government's geographical publication project, the Ministry of Internal Affairs requested that Shimane Prefecture submit records and maps of Takeshima. On October 16, 1876, Shimane Prefecture submitted a map of Isotakeshima (磯竹島略圖) with a request to include "Takeshima (竹島: Ulleungdo) and one other island (一島)" as part of Shimane Prefecture's jurisdiction. In this case, one other island means Dokdo. The map of Isotakeshima clearly shows that the distance from Ulleungdo to Dokdo is 40 miles.

Question on the Land Registration of Takeshima (Ulleungdo) and the Other Island (Dokdo) in the Sea of Japan[15]

Officers of the Geography Department of the Ministry of Home Affairs made a tour to this prefecture to conduct research for compilation of the land register. They made a report of the research on Takeshima (Ulleungdo) and another island (Dokdo) in the Sea of Japan as described in the document Eul (乙), No. 28, attached hereunder.

The island is said to be discovered in the period of Eiroku (永祿). There is evidence that Oya Kyuemon and Murakawa Ichibei, merchants of Yonago town of the Hoki state of Tottori Province, sailed to that island with the license from the former Shogunate every year for seventy or eighty years from the 4th year of Genwa (元和) to the 8th year of Genroku (元祿). They brought animals and plants to sell in the domestic market.

Based on the ancient books and documents handed down to us, we first present the report on the island attached herewith together with a sketch of the island. If we had conducted a field survey on the entire island, we could have presented a report with a more detailed description. However, it is not determined whether the island belongs to this prefecture, it is located 100 li away toward the North Sea, the sea route is not well known, and it is difficult for a sailing boat to come back even in usual weather. For these reasons, we now submit this report prepared on the basis of the writings conserved in the two families Oya and Murakawa, and we will submit a detailed report in the future. In the light of the general situation, it would be preferable to attribute the islands to a west suburb of Sanin (山陰) in the northwest of Oki state. How shall we deal with these islands in drawing the map of this state and compiling the land register? We request an instruction on this matter.

> On behalf of the Prefect Sato Nobuhiro (佐藤信寛)
> October 16, the 9th year of Meiji
> Sakai Jiro (境二郎), Councillor of the Shimane Prefecture

To Okubo Doshimichi (大久保利通), Minister of Home Affairs

The Ministry of Internal Affairs ended the investigation with the conclusion that neither island belonged to Japan following the diplomatic negotiations between Korea and Japan. On March 17, 1877, the Ministry of Internal Affairs issued the "Inquiry into Takeshima (Ulleungdo) and one other island (Dokdo) in the Sea of Japan for compilation of the Land Registry" to the Grand State Council (Dajokan), the highest administrative body of the Japanese government. This was because the Ministry of Internal Affairs could not independently decide on territorial matters.

Inquiry into Takeshima (Ulleungdo) and One Other Island (Dokdo) in the Sea of Japan for Compilation of the Land Registry[16]

The Ministry of Home Affairs has conducted research to reply to the question submitted by the Shimane Prefecture on the subject of the jurisdiction over Takeshima (Ulleungdo) and one other island (Dokdo). The result of the research is described in the documents attached hereunder:

The summary of the documents made in the 5th year of Genroku, when Joseon People came to the island; Annex 1 The instruction of the Deliberation Committee of the Former Government; Annex 2 The Note delivered to the Interpreters; Annex 3 The Note from Joseon State; and Annex 4 Replying Note of Japan and the Verbal Note.

That is, it was said that the exchange of notes ended in the 12th year of Genroku (1699 CE), and it was decided that Japan has nothing to do with the island. However, since the determination of the territory is a serious matter, the Ministry submits this question, in case, and attaches herewith the relevant documents.

>   March 17, the 10th year of Meiji (1877)
>   Maeshima Hisoka (前島 密), Assistant Minister,
>   Acting for Okubo Doshimichi (大久保利通), Minister of Home
> Affairs
>
> To Iwakura Domomi (岩倉具視), Right Minister of the Grand State Council

On March 29, 1877, the Grand State Council (Dajokan) issued a directive to the Ministry of Internal Affairs. The directive states: "Regarding Takeshima (Ulleungdo) and one other island (Dokdo) … it must be known to all that Japan has nothing to do with these islands." This is so called Grand State Council (Dajokan) Directive. This is also known as the Dajokan Shirei (太政官指令) in Japanese, and it is an important document that officially confirms the position of the Japan's highest administrative body on Dokdo.[17]

Grand State Council (Dajokan) Directive[18]
On the subject of Takeshima (Ulleungdo) and one other island (Dokdo) mentioned in the document raising the question, it must be known to all that Japan has nothing to do with these islands.

March 29, the 10th year of Meiji (1877)

This document is significant in that the central government of Japan recognized the Shimane Prefecture's position that Ulleungdo and Dokdo were Korean territory. In particular, Japanese scholars have recognized that the Dajokan Directive cleared up the Meiji Government's confusion over Ulleungdo and Dokdo. Kazuo Hori (堀和生) and Seichu Naito (内藤正中) are two of the most prominent scholars who hold this view.[19]

However, Japan argues that these documents do not actively recognize Korea's sovereignty over Dokdo. Japan claims that the incorporation of a small uninhabited island (terra nullius) into the Japanese territory by the Shimane Prefecture Notice was justified under international law because it was said to be unrelated to Japan. Japan also claims that it reaffirmed Dokdo as Japanese territory many years ago. Japan's arguments are sometimes inconsistent. It is worth noting that Japan cites major international cases to support its claims.

3. RELATED INTERNATIONAL CASES

3-1. Minquiers and Ecrehos

This case concerns conflicting claims of sovereignty between France and the United Kingdom over two groups of islets and rocks in the English Channel near the French coast. The Minquiers and the

Ecrehos lie between the British island of Jersey and the French coast forming part of the Channel Islands. After the Norman Conquest of England in 1066, the King of England held Normandy, including the Channel Islands, in his capacity as Duke of Normandy, until 1204 when France reconquered the continental Normandy. French attempts to reoccupy the Channel Islands were unsuccessful, and France did not challenge British sovereignty over most of the Channel Islands. However, France claimed that England was not entitled to possess the Minquiers and Ecrehos groups after France reconquered Normandy in 1204. Both countries asserted claims of sovereignty over the islets and rocks, and founded their argument on an ancient and original title.[20]

The ICJ held that whether the kings of France had the original feudal title to the Minquiers and the Ecrehos groups was legally irrelevant in view of subsequent events. The Court also remarked that evidence of possession would be determinative of the question of sovereignty and found that evidence of possession by England far outweighed evidence of possession by France. The Court noted that in 1200 the King of England granted the Channel Islands to one of his barons, who subsequently granted the Ecrehos group to an ecclesiastical institution as his vassal. The Court rejected the French contention that this grant severed the Ecrehos Group from the rest of the Channel Islands. It was admitted that England exercised jurisdiction over the Ecrehos group in legal proceedings instituted during the early thirteenth century. Furthermore, English sovereignty over Jersey was always clear, and the Court found several examples, beginning in the early nineteenth century, of the exercise of governmental authority over the Ecrehos group by Jersey officials. The Court also found similar evidence with respect to the Minquiers group.[21] In consequence, the Court held that the two groups belonged to the United Kingdom.

Professor Kanae Taijudo of Japan argues that the Minquiers and

Ecrehos case is really similar to the Dokdo case. He points out that in both cases the state parties have argued that their inherent sovereignty over the islands came from historical bases. He justifies Japanese sovereignty over Dokdo, emphasizing that the Court found ancient historical materials to be inconclusive and instead focused on actual display of authority during the nineteenth and twentieth centuries. He also argues that the fact of Japan's effective occupation since 1905 provides a strong position to Japan.[22]

By contrast, professor Choung-Il Chee of Korea points out that the Minquiers and Ecrehos is totally different from Dokdo because Japan has argued Dokdo was terra nullius. The fact that Japan did not exercise its substantial administrative authority but just issued simple hunting and fishing permission is also different from the fact relating to the British measures in the Mingquiers and Ecrehos.[23] In addition, the ICJ relied for its decision on the view that the Minquiers group had been a dependency of Jersey and Guernsey which were part of the Channel Islands. This may be an advantage towards Korea because Korea stresses Dodko's status as a dependency of Ullungdo.

3-2. Ligitan and Sipadan

As regards the dispute over Pulau Ligitan and Pulau Sipadan, located in the Celebes Sea off the northeast coast of the island of Borneo, Indonesia and Malaysia brought the dispute before the ICJ on November 2, 1998, in accordance with the Special Agreement which was concluded on May 31, 1997.

The ICJ rendered its decision that the sovereignty over the two islands belonged to Malaysia. Having found that neither of the two countries has a treaty-based title to the islands, the Court considered the question whether the parties could hold title to the disputed islands by virtue of the effectivités. In this regard, the Court determined that, as Malaysia's activities were modest and diverse including legislative, administrative, and quasi-judicial acts, they showed a pattern revealing an intention to exercise State functions in the context of the administration of a wider range of islands.[24]

It should be noted that the Court ruled in favor of Malaysia attaching considerable importance to the effectivités. It is because this dispute shares a lot of similarities with the Dokdo issue between Korea and Japan. As both of the islands are quite remote from the mainlands, neither has been regarded as economically significant as large islands for a long time. So, the effectivités in respect to the islands should be examined closely in preparation for a possible dispute settlement between Korea and Japan. Also, we cannot emphasize the importance of this case too much as a leading case brought before the ICJ. This case is the first to be brought to international dispute settlement by a State of the ASEAN since the Temple of Preah Vihear case.

3-3. Pedra Branca, Middle Rocks, and South Ledge

As regards the dispute over Pedra Branca, Middle Rocks, and South Ledge in the entrance of the Singapore Straits, Malaysia and Singapore brought the dispute before the ICJ on July 14, 2003, in accordance with the Special Agreement which concluded on February 6, 2003.

The ICJ rendered its decision that the sovereignty over Pedra Branca belonged to Singapore. Having found that Malaysia had the ancient original title to the island, the Court considered the question whether it could hold the title to the disputed island continuously since then. In this regard, the Court determined that as Singapore's relevant activities were conducted à titre de souverain, they were more persuasive to the Court than Malaysia's acquiescence to them. The Court concluded that the sovereignty over Pedra Branca had been passed to Singapore.[25]

It should be noted that the Court ruled in favor of Singapore attaching considerable importance to the acts à titre de souverain. It is because this dispute shares a lot of similarities with the Dokdo issue between Korea and Japan. As both of the islands were uninhabited islands until the late nineteenth century, neither has been regarded as economically significant as large islands for a long time. So, the acts à titre de souverain in respect to the island should be examined closely in preparation for a possible dispute settlement between Korea and Japan. Also, we cannot emphasize the importance of this case too much as one of the leading cases brought before the ICJ. This case is the third to be brought to international dispute settlement by a State of the ASEAN since the Temple of Preah Vihear case.

4. CONCLUSION

Japan insists that in 1905 it formally confirmed its sovereignty over Dokdo, which had been alleged to be its own territory, by the Shimane Prefecture Notice. However, it is a well-known fact that, in order to acquire a certain area in the world by occupation, the object of occupation should be terra nullius under international law. So, it can be said that Japan's annexing its inherent territory is equivalent to adopting one's biological child redundantly.[26] In other words, it is not an exaggeration to say that Japan's claim is not only illogical but also self-contradictory.

As far as historical evidence and title is concerned, Korea's position on the sovereignty over Dokdo is much stronger and more persuasive to the world than that of Japan. Further, Korea's position on the island becomes clearer when interpreting a series of documents, including the Cairo Declaration, the Potsdam Declaration, the Japanese Instrument of Surrender, and the San Francisco Peace Treaty. The interpretation of these instruments is to reinforce Korea's position on Dokdo in the context of the historical documents reviewed above.

Because Dokdo is an undisputed territory of Korea, a legal resolution of the Dokdo issue is virtually impossible. Therefore, a legal settlement of the Dokdo issue should not be expected in the future. Instead, given the historical implications of the issue, the most feasible political and diplomatic solution would be for Japan to make a political decision to abandon its claims to the island and complete its maritime boundary delimitation with Korea. Taking into account the relationship between international law and international politics as a dual perspective on the Dokdo issue, Korea and Japan should consider the true resolution of the Dokdo issue and its implications.

Notes

1. Kentaro Serita, *Nihonno Ryodo(Japanese Territories)*, Chuokoron-Shinsha, 2002, pp.146~159.

2. https://www.mofa.go.jp/region/asia-paci/takeshima/index.html (last visit on November 30, 2023).

3. http://www.mofa.go.jp/mofaj/area/takeshima/gaiyo.html (last visit on November 30, 2023).

4. Chang Wee LEE, *History of Korea-Japan Relations in Terms of International Law and International Relations*, Bakyoungsa, 2022, pp.142~143.

5. The Korean Government's geographical rationale is not only based on the fact that the distance between Ulleungdo and Dokdo is closer than the distance between Japan and Dokdo, but also on the fact that Dokdo has historically been recognized as part of or attached to Ulleungdo (Korean Ministry of Foreign Affairs, *Dokdo Beautiful Island of Korea*, pp.4~5).

6. Korean Ministry of Foreign Affairs, *Dokdo Beautiful Island of Korea*, p.16.

7. https://dokdo.mofa.go.kr/kor/dokdo/reason.jsp (last visit on November 30, 2023).

8. Japanese Ministry of Foreign Affairs, 10 points to understand the Takeshima Dispute, p.8.

9. Oya Jinkichi (大屋甚吉) was also called Oya Kyuemon (大屋九右衛門).

10. Ban on Voyage to Takeshima (Ulleungdo), Sovereignty over Dokdo confirmed by Japan (https://dokdo.mofa.go.kr/kor/pds/part05_view06.jsp) (last visit on November 30, 2023); Northeast Asian History Foundation, *Korean Territory Dokdo*, 2015, pp.62~63.

11. Korean Ministry of Foreign Affairs, *Dokdo Beautiful Island of Korea*, pp.18~19.

12. Tottori Domain was constituted with Inshu (因州) and Hakushu (伯州). Inshu was also called Inaba state (因幡國) or Inaba Province (因幡州), Hakushu was called Hoki state (伯耆國) or Hoki Province (伯耆州). In the 17th century Japan, "state" and "province" were interchangeably used as units of local administration.

13. Northeast Asian History Foundation, *Korean Territory Dokdo*, 2015, pp.62~63; Reply of the Tottori-han to the Shogunate's Question, Sovereignty over Dokdo confirmed by Japan (https://dokdo.mofa.go.kr/kor/pds/part05_view01.jsp) (last visit on November 30, 2023).

14. Oya Kyemon (大屋九右衛門) is also called Oya Jinkichi (大屋甚吉).

15. Northeast Asian History Foundation, *Korean Territory Dokdo*, 2015, pp.66~67.

16. Northeast Asian History Foundation, *Korean Territory Dokdo*, 2015, pp.66~67.

17. https://dokdo.mofa.go.kr/kor/dokdo/reason.jsp (last visit on November 30, 2023).

18. Korean Ministry of Foreign Affairs, *Dokdo Beautiful Island of Korea*, pp.22~23; Northeast Asian History Foundation, *Korean Territory Dokdo*, 2015, pp.66~67.

19. Kazuo Hori, "Japan's Annexation of Takeshima in 1905," Proceedings of the

Korean Historical Research Association, 24, 1987, pp.103~104; Seichu Naito, *History of Japan-Korea Relations in Terms of Takeshima (Utsuryodo)*, Taga Shuppan, 2000, p.10.

20. Ronald H. Severaid and James C. Tuttle(ed.), *International Court of Justice Opinion Brief*, International Printing company, 1978, 8-1.

21. *Ibid.*, 8-1.

22. Kanae Taijudo, "Ryodo Mondai (Territory Problem)," *Jurist* No.647, 1977, pp.56~57.

23. Choung-Il Chee, "The Legal Status of Dok Island in International Law," *Korean Perspectives on Ocean Law Issues for the 21st Century*, 1999, pp.45~64.

24. *Sovereignty over Pulau Ligitan and Pulau Sipadan (Indonesia v. Malaysia)* (2002) *ICJ Rep.* pp.625~627, available on the Web site of the International Court of Justice at www.icj-cij.org.

25. *Sovereignty over Pedra Branca/Pulau Batu Puteh, Middle Rocks and South Ledge (Malaysia v. Singapotr)* (2008) *ICJ Rep.* paras.273~300, available on the Web site of the International Court of Justice at www.icj-cij.org.

26. A Korean diplomat further explains that Japan seems to be a kidnapper who maintains that an abducted child is his biological child (Seung-Mok Hong, "On the Ownership of Dokdo Island - Dialogue with a Foreign Scholar," *Korean Journal of International Law* Vol.48, No.2, 2003, p.233).

ICJ Judgment on the North Sea Continental Shelf Cases and Its Impacts on the Law of the Sea and Korea's Maritime Law and Policy

Seokyong LEE *
Emeritus Professor, Hannam University

Key Words

North Sea Continental Shelf cases, Maritime Delimitation, natural prolongation of the land territory, United Nations Convention on the Law of the Sea, Continental Shelf between Nicaragua and Colombia beyond 200 nm from the Nicaraguan Coast (Nicaragua v. Colombia 2023), East China Sea, JDZ Agreement

1. INTRODUCTION

As the conflicts over ocean resources and maritime jurisdictions grew, decisions of international courts or tribunals on the law of the sea issues became more and more important in international law. The International Court of Justice (ICJ) rendered one of its landmark judgments on February 20, 1969. North Sea Continental Shelf cases (hereinafter "North Sea cases") were submitted to the Court by the Special Agreement between Denmark and Germany, and another Agreement between the Netherlands and Germany. The States Parties to the cases requested the Court to decide on principles and rules of international law applicable to the continental shelf delimitation in the North Sea.

The Convention on the Continental Shelf, which was adopted at the First United Nations Conference on the Law of the Sea (UNCLOS I) in 1958, provides for an equidistance line method as the continental shelf delimitation principle. However, in the North Sea cases, the ICJ rejected the use of the equidistance method and found that delimitation is to be effected by agreement in accordance with equitable principles, taking account of all the relevant circumstances, in such a way as to leave as much as possible to each Party all those parts of the continental shelf that constitute a natural prolongation of its land territory into and under the sea.[1] The Court held that the basis of a coastal State's jurisdiction over the continental shelf is the natural prolongation of its land territory and that continental shelf delimitation is to be effected by agreement in accordance with equitable principles.

The contribution of international courts and tribunals to the development of international law consists mainly of interpretation and application of the existing international rules of law. However, the ICJ sometimes marked an epoch in cultivating a new area extending its role to be credited as a legislation by a judicial decision.[2] The ICJ judgment on the North Sea cases could be rated as one of those decisions, which has had enormous impact on international law of the sea and practices of governments. The principle of natural prolongation of the land territory and the equitable maritime delimitation principle stated by the ICJ in the North Sea cases have been weakened over time. However, the main points of the judgment are still influential.

This article will analyze the main points of the ICJ judgment on the North Sea cases and examine its implications on the international law of the sea focusing on the definition (outer limits) of the continental shelf and on maritime delimitation. Influences on law and practices of the Republic of Korea (hereinafter, "Korea") and Japan in the East China Sea will be analyzed. In particular, given the recent decision of the international court that a coastal State's rights over the continental shelf beyond 200 nm from its baseline cannot be extended beyond 200 nm from the baselines of another State, the future of the Korea-Japan Joint Development Zone will be reviewed.

2. PROCESS AND JUDGMENT

Article 4 of the North Sea Policing of Fisheries Convention of 1882 indicated that the North Sea lies between continental Europe and Great Britain, and is roughly oval in shape. The North Sea looks like an enclosed sea surrounded by British Isles, Germany, Denmark, Norway, the Netherlands, and Belgium. It is 970 ㎞ long and 580 ㎞ wide with an area of around 750,000 ㎢. The waters of the North Sea are shallow, and the whole seabed consists of continental shelf at a depth of less than 200 meters, except for the Norwegian Trough, which is 200-650 meters deep and 80-100 ㎞ wide. Part of this shelf had already been delimited by agreements between the United Kingdom and Norway, Denmark, and the Netherlands.[3]

By the Special Agreement concluded between Denmark and Germany, and another Agreement between the Netherlands and Germany, the Parties submitted to the ICJ differences concerning the delimitation of continental shelf in the North Sea. They requested the Court to decide on the principles and rules or international law applicable to the continental shelf delimitation between them in the North Sea beyond the partial boundary determined before.[4] The Court, considering that the three Governments agreed to ask the Court to join the two cases and that Denmark and the Netherlands were to be considered as one Party sharing the same interest, joined the proceedings in the two cases.

In the course of the written proceedings, Germany asked the

Court to delimit the contested continental shelf by the rule of just and equitable share rejecting the equidistance rule. In the oral proceedings, Germany requested the Court to adjudge and declare that the delimitation of the continental shelf is governed by the principle that each coastal State is entitled to a just and equitable share, that determining boundaries of the continental shelf by the equidistance method is not a rule of customary international law, and that the rule under Article 6(2) of the Continental Shelf Convention prescribing that, in the absence of agreement and unless another boundary is justified by special circumstances, the boundary shall be determined by the equidistance principle has not become customary international law.[5]

In the course of the written and oral proceedings, Denmark and the Netherlands asked the Court to delimit the contested continental shelf by the equidistance principle. In the oral proceedings, Denmark and the Netherlands requested the Court to adjudge and declare that the delimitation of the continental shelf is governed by the principles and rules of international law which were expressed in Article 6(2) of the 1958 Convention on the Continental Shelf and that, unless another boundary is justified by special circumstances, the boundary is to be determined by the principle of equidistance.[6]

Denmark and the Netherlands contended that the whole matter was governed by the rule of law, which was reflected in Article 6 of the 1958 Convention on the Continental Shelf. They regarded this "equidistance-special circumstances" rule was not merely a cartographical construction method to establish a boundary line but an expression of the essential element in law. They contended that, if the parties failed to reach an agreement to employ another method, continental shelf boundaries must be drawn by equidistant lines, unless special circumstances are recognized to exist.[7] Germany recognized the usefulness of the equidistance rule but denied its obligatory character. For Germany, the correct rule was giving each

State concerned a just and equitable share of the available continental shelf in proportion to the length of its coastline.[8]

The ICJ, by eleven votes to six, found as follows[9]:

(A) the use of the equidistance method of delimitation not being obligatory as between the Parties;

(B) there being no other single method of delimitation the use of which is in all circumstances obligatory; and

(C) the principles and rules of international law applicable to the delimitation as between the Parties of the areas of the continental shelf in the North Sea, which appertain to each of them, are as follows:

1) delimitation is to be effected by agreement in accordance with the equitable principles, and taking account of all the relevant circumstances, in such a way as to leave as much as possible to each Party all those parts of the continental shelf that constitute a natural prolongation of its land territory into and under the sea without encroachment on the natural prolongation of the land territory of the other;

2) if the delimitation leaves to the Parties areas that overlap, these are to be divided between them in agreed proportions or, failing agreement, equally, unless they decide on a regime of joint jurisdiction;

(D) in the course of the negotiations, the factors to be taken into account are 1) the general configuration of the coasts of the Parties and the presence of any special or unusual features; 2) the physical and geological structure, and natural resources of the continental shelf areas involved; 3) a reasonable degree of proportionality between the extent of the continental shelf areas appertaining to the coastal State and the length of its coast measured in the general direction of the coastline.

In summary, regarding the definition and outer limit of the

continental shelf, the ICJ ruled that the natural prolongation of land territory is the basis for the continental shelf. Regarding maritime delimitation, the Court ruled that delimitation is to be effected by agreement in accordance with the equitable principles taking account of the relevant circumstances in such a way as to leave as much as possible to each Party all those parts of the continental shelf that constitute a natural prolongation of its land territory.

3. ENTITLEMENT AND OUTER LIMIT OF THE CONTINENTAL SHELF

3-1. Truman Proclamation and the Convention on the Continental Shelf

The concept of the continental shelf originated from geology, but the definition and outer limits of the maritime zone have been under change with the development of marine science and technology. Geologically, the typical seabed adjacent to coasts are considered to be composed of three parts. The continental shelf proper is a part of the section which slopes down gradually to the depth where the angle of declination increases markedly. The section bordering the continental shelf which slopes down steeper is called a continental slope. Bordering the continental slope, the continental rise generally comprises the section which is composed mainly of sediments. These three sections form the continental margin, which covers about one-fifth of the whole sea floor.[10]

The 1945 Truman Proclamation of the United States was regarded as the first clear claim over the continental shelf and its resources. The Proclamation made it clear that the United States regards the natural resources of the subsoil and seabed of the continental shelf beneath the high seas but contiguous to the coasts of it as appertaining to the United States. This Proclamation sets out in definitive terms the nature of continental shelf as a natural and contiguous appurtenance of the land territory, in which the natural resources would be within the sole jurisdiction of the United States.[11] However, the Proclamation did not provide any criteria indicating the outer limits of its continental shelf. This claim was followed by other States, especially by the Latin American States. However, their claims were so diverse in scope and in character as the continental shelf could not be considered to have any definitive status in international law.[12]

When the International Law Commission (ILC) tried to draft articles for the high seas and continental shelf, the Committee of Experts of the Commission adopted Guidelines favoring the use of the equidistance method. Finally, the ILC decided to allow the equidistance method a residual character, so the application of the equidistance method was mandatory unless States agreed otherwise or special circumstances were present.[13] Article 1 of the 1958 Convention on the Continental Shelf provides that the term "continental shelf" refers to "the seabed and subsoil of the submarine areas adjacent to the coast but outside the area of the territorial sea, to a depth of 200 meters or, beyond that limit, to where the depth of the superjacent waters admits of the exploitation of the natural resources of the said areas." This definition followed the approach adopted at the ILC which defined the continental shelf by a 200 meters depth and exploitability of the natural resources of the seabed and subsoil. Geology and geomorphology of the continental shelf were not accepted as factors affecting the definition and extent of the concept. This definition based on the depth and exploitability faced with harsh criticism.[14]

3-2. North Sea Continental Shelf Cases

In its judgment on the North Sea Continental Shelf cases, the ICJ declared that a coastal State's sovereign right on the continental shelf derives from the fact that the continental shelf is the natural prolongation of the land territory into the sea. The Court said as follows:

> More fundamental than the notion of proximity appears to be the principle of the natural prolongation or continuation of the land territory or domain, or land sovereignty of the coastal State, into and under the high seas, via the bed of its territorial sea which is under the full sovereignty of that State. There are various ways of formulating this principle, but the underlying idea, namely of an extension of something already possessed, is the same, and it is this idea of extension which is, in the Court's opinion, determinant. Submarine areas do not really appertain to the coastal State because - or not only because - they are near it. They are near it of course; but this would not suffice to confer title any more than, according to a well-established principle of law recognized by both sides in the present case, mere proximity confers *per se* title to land territory. What confers the *ipso jure* title which international law attributes to the coastal State in respect of its continental shelf, is the fact that the submarine areas concerned may be deemed to be actually part of the territory over which the coastal State already has dominion, - in the sense that, although covered with water, they are a prolongation or continuation of that territory, an extension of it under the sea. From this it would follow that whenever a given submarine area does not constitute a natural - or the most natural - extension of the land territory of a coastal State, even though that area may be closer to it than it is to the territory of any other state, it cannot be regarded as appertaining to that state.[15]

The ICJ said that what confers the *ipso jure* title, in other words, which international law attributes sovereign rights to the coastal State, is the fact that the submarine areas concerned may be deemed to be part of the territory over which the coastal State already has dominion. Natural prolongation of the land territory confers legal title of the continental shelf to the coastal States. In the North Sea cases, both sides relied on the prolongation as a natural extension, but their interpretations were quite different. Denmark and the Netherlands identified natural prolongation with the closest proximity and argued that it justified the use of the equidistance method. For the Court, equidistance cannot be identified with the notion of natural prolongation or extension. Germany stressed that natural prolongation implied the notion of a just and equitable share, but the Court could not agree with the interpretation either.[16]

In the judgment, the ICJ emphasized the intrinsic affinities between the legal concept of the continental shelf and the geological concept of the continental shelf. The Court made it clear that the continental shelf is the natural prolongation of the land territory of the coastal State into and under the sea, giving rise to a notion of appurtenance. According to the Court, there are various ways of formulating this principle, but the idea, an extension of something already possessed, is the idea of extension, which is determinant. To be sure, the Court saw the continental shelf from a geological rather than a geographical perspective. As natural prolongation of the land territory of a coastal State consists of the continental shelf, continental slope, and continental rise, the legal doctrine invoked by the ICJ in the North Sea cases could be called "Continental Margin Doctrine."[17]

3-3. International Judicial Decisions

The ICJ's ruling in North Sea cases on the definition and outer limit of the continental shelf based on the principle of natural prolongation of the land territory, and the delimitation applying the principle of equity has had a great influence on the subsequent decisions of international courts and tribunals, and on practices of national governments.

In the Tunisia/Libya case (1972), the ICJ was asked to determine principles and rules of international law which were applicable to the delimitation between them. The Court considered the relevant articles of the Draft adopted at the UNCLOS III to incorporate new trends. The legal concept of the continental shelf was about to be modified by the provisions. The draft articles provided that the continental shelf of a coastal State comprises the seabedseabed and subsoil of the submarine areas that extend beyond its territorial sea throughout the natural prolongation of its land territory to the outer edge of the continental margin, or to a distance of 200 nm from the territorial sea baselines. According to this provision, natural prolongation of the land territory was the main criterion, and the distance of 200 nm could be the basis of the title in certain circumstances.[18]

The ICJ judgment on the Continental Shelf case between Libya and Malta was made at the time when EEZ was emerging as a new maritime jurisdiction. In its 1985 judgment, the World Court suggested changes in recognition of the coastal States' title to the continental shelf and in delimitation of the continental shelf between opposite or adjacent States. Malta was party to the 1958 Convention on the Continental Shelf, while Libya was not. Both Parties signed the 1982 UNCLOS Convention, but the Convention was not effective then. Thus, the Parties agreed that the dispute was to be governed by customary international law. As the UNCLOS Convention was adopted by an overwhelming majority of the States at the UNCLOS III, the Convention was considered to be an important evidence of customary international law.[19]

With regard to the legal basis of the title to the continental shelf, Libya asserted that the natural prolongation of the land territories of the Parties into and under the sea is the basis of the title to the areas of the continental shelf which appertain to each of them. For Libya, natural prolongation in the physical sense, involving geographical as well as geological and geomorphological aspects, was the fundamental basis of the legal title to the continental shelf areas. For Malta, the continental shelf of a State constitutes a natural prolongation of its land territory, but prolongation was no longer defined by reference to physical features, but by reference to a certain distance from the coasts. In Malta's view, the concept of natural prolongation had become a purely spatial concept. Malta stressed the natural prolongation principle from the perspective of "distance criterion," but, in fact, it asserted application of the equidistance method in maritime delimitation.[20]

Even though the present case relates only to the continental shelf delimitation, the Court considered the principles and rules of EEZ concept in this case. For the Court, it signified that greater importance must be attributed to elements such as distance from the Coast.[21] According to the UNCLOS Convention, there can be a continental shelf where there is no EEZ, but there cannot be an EEZ without a corresponding continental shelf. It follows that, for juridical and practical reasons, the distance criterion must now apply to the continental shelf as well as to the EEZ. According to the ICJ, this is not to suggest that the idea of natural prolongation is now superseded by the distance. However, it means that where the continental margin does not extend as far as 200 nm from the shore, natural prolongation is in part defined by distance from the shore, irrespective of the physical nature of the intervening seabed and subsoil.[22]

In Libya/Malta case, as the natural prolongation of the land territory into and under the sea was a primary basis of the title to the continental shelf, each Party made efforts to prove that the physical natural prolongation of its land territory extends into the area in which the delimitation is to be effected. If there exists a fundamental discontinuity between the shelves of States, then the boundary should lie along the general line of the fundamental discontinuity. The delimitation of the continental shelf must therefore respect the fundamental discontinuity or a "rift zone."[23] The Court considered that since the development of the law enables a State to claim that the continental shelf appertaining to it extends up to 200 nm from its coast, whatever the geological characteristics of the corresponding seabed and subsoil, there is no reason to ascribe any role to geological or geophysical factors within that distance either in verifying the legal title of the States concerned or in proceeding to a delimitation as between their claims. This is especially clear where verification of the validity of the title is concerned, since, in so far as those areas are situated at a distance of under 200 nm from the coasts in question, the title depends solely on the distance from the coasts of the claimant States of any areas of seabedseabed claimed by way of the continental shelf. The geological or geomorphological characteristics of those areas are completely immaterial.[24]

There were arguments whether there was a rift zone on the continental shelf between Libya and Malta. Having carefully studied evidence, the Court was not satisfied that it would be able to draw any sufficiently cogent conclusions from it as to the existence or not of the "fundamental discontinuity." The region has many geological or geomorphological features which may properly be described as "discontinuities." The Court rejected the so-called rift-zone argument of Libya, since the distance between the coasts of the Parties was less than 400 miles. So, for the Court, the feature referred to as the "rift zone" could not constitute a fundamental discontinuity in this case.[25]

3-4. United Nations Convention on the Law of the Sea

At the UNCLOS III Conference, there were suggestions not to maintain the continental shelf system in the new Convention. There was difficulty in reaching an agreement on the outer limits of the continental shelf, especially because of the conflicts between the States with a broad continental margin and States with narrow shelves.[26] However, the Conference decided to retain the continental shelf system in the new Convention. The Conference went through a very complex procedure in defining the new continental shelf. The supporters of the doctrine that the seabed and subsoil beyond the national jurisdiction should be a common heritage of mankind resisted the attempts to extend the coastal State jurisdictions.[27] What made negotiations more complicated was the advent of the new economic jurisdiction called EEZ. As this new jurisdiction was similar to the continental shelf in its extent and jurisdiction, uncertainties arose over the relationship between these two jurisdictions.

Article 76 of the 1982 Law of the Sea Convention introduced a new definition of the continental shelf utilizing the 200 nm distance and geological concept of a continental margin. Article 76 provides as follows:

Article 76 Definition of the Continental Shelf

1. The continental shelf of a coastal State comprises the seabed and subsoil of the submarine areas that extend beyond its territorial sea throughout the natural prolongation of its land territory to the outer edge of the continental margin, or to a distance of 200 nm from the baselines from which the breadth of the territorial sea is measured where the outer edge of the continental margin does not extend up to that distance.

3. The continental margin comprises the submerged prolongation of the land mass of the coastal State and consists of the seabed and subsoil of the shelf, the slope and the rise. It does not include the deep ocean floor with its oceanic ridges or the subsoil thereof.

4. (a) For the purposes of this Convention, the coastal State shall establish the outer edge of the continental margin wherever the margin extends beyond 200 nm from the baselines from which the breadth of the territorial sea is measured,

(b) In the absence of evidence to the contrary, the foot of the continental slope shall be determined as the point of maximum change in the gradient at its base.

5. The fixed points comprising the line of the outer limits of the continental shelf on the seabed, drawn in accordance with paragraph 4 (a)(i) and (ii), either shall not exceed 350 nm from the baselines from which the breadth of the territorial sea is measured or shall not exceed 100 nm from the 2,500 metre isobath, which is a line connecting the depth of 2,500 meters.

6. The outer limit of the continental shelf shall not exceed 350 nm from the baselines from which the breadth of the territorial sea is measured.

7. The coastal State shall delineate the outer limits of its continental shelf, where that shelf extends beyond 200 nm from the baselines from which the breadth of the territorial sea is measured, by straight lines not exceeding 60 nm in length, connecting fixed points, defined by coordinates of latitude and longitude.

8. Information on the limits of the continental shelf beyond 200 nm from the baselines shall be submitted by the coastal State to the Commission on the Limits of the Continental Shelf set up under Annex II on the basis of equitable geographical

representation. The Commission shall make recommendations to coastal States on matters related to the establishment of the outer limits of their continental shelf. The limits of the shelf established by a coastal State on the basis of these recommendations shall be final and binding.

The UNCLOS Convention's provisions on the definition of the continental shelf recognized the natural prolongation of the land territory and the 200 nm distance to be the legal basis for coastal States to exercise sovereign rights over the continental shelf. In fact, most of Article 76 of the Convention concerns the establishment of the outer limits of the continental shelf by natural prolongation. There is only one short provision on the 200 nm distance.

Despite its detail, the UNCLOS Convention provisions on the definition and outer limits of the continental shelf still leaves room for considerable uncertainty. There could be a conflict between the natural prolongation and 200 nm distance in deciding outer limits of the continental shelf of coastal States. However, the Convention does not have any provisions as to which of these two titles would be granted a superior status in the event of a conflict. So, Professor Oxman said that he could only confirm that the natural prolongation of the land territory was defined first.[28] The Convention established the 21-person Commission on the Limits of the Continental Shelf (CLCS). The Convention provides that information on the limits of the continental shelf beyond 200 nm from the baselines shall be submitted by the coastal State to the CLCS, and that CLCS render recommendations to the coastal States on matters related to the establishment of the outer limits of their continental shelf. To be sure, the CLCS is not in a position to determine legal title over the continental shelf.

3-5. Decisions of International Courts and Tribunals

The most sensitive issue regarding the continental shelf these days is whether the sovereign rights to an extended continental shelf based on the natural prolongation of a country's land territory can be recognized in waters within 200 nm from the coast of another country. This is a very important and complex issue because it concerns the priorities of the continental shelf and EEZ, and at the same time it concerns the competition between the natural prolongation and distance standard.

International courts and tribunals have showed a zigzag stance treating this question. In the Barbados/Trinidad and Tobago case, the ITLOS held that it had the jurisdiction, but in practice it did not exercise it because the maritime boundary it delimited did not extend beyond 200 nm from either party.[29] International judicial organs sometimes accorded primacy to the distance criterion over natural prolongation within 200 nm when delimiting overlapping entitlements to continental shelves and EEZs. The ICJ, in the Libya/Malta case, considering then the newly adopted the UNCLOS Convention, ruled that a coastal State's claim over the continental shelf beyond 200 nm which is based on the natural prolongation of the territory, cannot trump the rights of another State within 200 nm from its baselines.[30] In the decision on Mauritius/Maldives case, the Special Chamber of the International Tribunal for the Law of the Sea (ITLOS) had the opportunity to provide an answer to a similar question. The Special Chamber noted that, after drawing a single maritime boundary for the continental shelf and EEZ between the parties, there were in fact no areas remaining to be delimited which were within the 200 nm limit of either party. As it thought "neither Party may claim or exercise sovereign rights or jurisdiction with respect to the EEZ or the continental shelf within the 200 nm limit of the other Party on the latter's side of the boundary."[31]

In some cases, international courts and tribunals recognized the sovereign rights of States to the extended continental shelves. The ITLOS, in its 2012 judgment on Bangladesh/Myanmar case, and the Annex VII Tribunal, in its 2014 Award on Bangladesh v. India case, recognized the rights to the extended continental shelf. The Bangladesh/Myanmar case is significant especially because an international judicial organ addressed the question of continental shelf delimitation beyond 200 nm. In these cases, the international judicial organs decided to create wedge-shaped gray zones. The ITLOS determined that Bangladesh and Myanmar had entitlements to an extended continental shelf, and it continued the course of the adjusted equidistance line beyond the 200 nm limit. The use of an adjusted equidistance line produced a wedge-shaped area of a limited size located within 200 nm of the coast of Myanmar but on the Bangladesh side of the line delimiting continental shelves. A similar decision was made in the Bangladesh v. India case. These gray areas were the product of delimitation. Importantly, none of the three coastal States - India, Bangladesh, and Myanmar - disputed that an extended continental shelf margin existed in the Bay of Bengal. All three States had made full submissions to the CLCS and were waiting for recommendations. Furthermore, the ITLOS and the Annex VII tribunal were in no doubt, given the sediment thickness in the Bay of Bengal, that all three States could satisfy the criteria of article 76(4) and (5) of the Convention.[32]

In the Territorial and Maritime Dispute between Nicaragua and Colombia case (Nicaragua v. Colombia 2012), the ICJ took a more cautious approach declining to delimit maritime spaces beyond 200 nm from Nicaragua's coast. The Court, with respect to Nicaragua's claim for delimitation of a continental shelf extending beyond 200 nm, observed that "any claim of continental shelf rights beyond 200 nm must be in accordance with Article 76 of the UNCLOS and reviewed by the CLCS." Then Nicaragua had submitted to the CLCS only "Preliminary Information," which fell short of meeting the requirements for the Commission to be able to make its recommendations. The Court found that Nicaragua had not established that it had a continental margin extending far enough to overlap with Colombia's 200 nm entitlement to the continental shelf from Colombia's mainland coast. In the case, Nicaragua claimed entitlement to the outer continental shelf due to the presence of the "Nicaraguan Rise," a shallow area of the continental shelf extending from its mainland within 200 nm from the Colombia's coast. On the other hand, three judges indicated that the critical flaw in Nicaragua's claim was not procedural but a failure to produce sufficient evidence regarding the existence and extent of the Nicaraguan Rise.[33]

This issue was considered in depth in the ICJ judgment on the Continental Shelf between Nicaragua and Colombia beyond 200 nm from the Nicaraguan Coast (Nicaragua v. Colombia 2023). On September 16, 2013, Nicaragua filed an application instituting proceedings against Colombia relating to a dispute concerning the delimitation of the boundaries between the continental shelf of Nicaragua beyond the 200 nm limit from its baselines and the continental shelf of Colombia. Nicaragua requested the Court to adjudge and declare the precise course of the maritime boundary between Nicaragua and Colombia in the continental shelf, which appertain to each of them beyond the boundaries determined by the Court in the Nicaragua v. Colombia 2012 case. By an Order of October 4, 2022, the ICJ bifurcated the merits phase of the proceedings. The ICJ requested the parties to limit their oral pleadings "exclusively" to two questions: 1) Under customary international law, may a State's entitlement to a continental shelf beyond 200 nm from the baselines from which the breadth of its territorial sea is measured extends within 200 nm from the baselines of another State? 2) What are the criteria under customary international law for the determination of the limit of the continental shelf beyond 200 nm from the territorial sea baselines?[34] The first question was whether a State's entitlement to the continental shelf beyond 200 nm from the territorial sea baselines may extend within 200 nm from the baselines of another State. The Court concluded unambiguously that, under customary international law, a State's entitlement to a continental shelf beyond 200 nm from the territorial sea baselines may not extend within 200 nm from the baselines of another State.[35]

As a procedural issue, a question whether maritime space beyond 200 nm can be delimited before the CLCS has issued recommendations was raised. In fact, some States have not waited for a CLCS recommendation before delimiting their entitlements to the continental shelf beyond 200 nm by treaty. In the 2012 judgment by the ITLOS in Bangladesh/Myanmar case and the 2014 Award by the Annex VII Tribunal in Bangladesh v. India case, the Tribunals were of the opinion that a CLCS recommendation was not necessary before delimiting the continental shelf beyond 200 nm. The Tribunals determined that both parties had entitlements to an extended continental shelf, and it continued the course of the adjusted equidistance line beyond the 200 nm limit. The use of an adjusted equidistance line produced a wedge-shaped area of a limited size located within 200 nm of the coast of Myanmar but on the Bangladesh side of the line delimiting the parties' continental shelves. The gray areas were made as a consequence of delimitation.[36]

The Court's approach to customary international law has become a contentious issue in this case. Judge Tomka wrote perhaps the most sharply critical dissenting opinion. In it, he asked why the Court did not dismiss Nicaragua's claims to the outer continental shelf back in 2012 based on the customary rule it now identified. Under the doctrine of *iura novit curia,* the Court was assumed to know the law, and the customary rule that the Court identified probably already existed a decade ago.[37]

To reach the decision, the Court considered several factors. First, the ICJ suggested that, when analyzing the negotiation process of the UNCLOS III, and the relationship between the continental shelf and EEZ systems, it can be seen that the Convention gave more importance to the EEZ, which emphasizes distance, over the continental shelf, which stresses natural extension. The Court noted that the substantive and procedural conditions for determining the outer limits of the continental shelf beyond 200 nm were the result of a compromise reached during the final sessions of the UNCLOS III to avoid undue encroachment on the "common heritage of mankind." The text of Article 76 of the Convention suggested that the States participating in the negotiations assumed that the extended continental shelf would only extend into maritime areas that would otherwise be located in the Area. In this regard, the Court has emphasized that the main role of the CLCS consists of preventing the continental shelf from encroaching on the "area and its resources," which are "the common heritage of mankind." Furthermore, Article 82 (1) of the Convention has provisions for payments or contributions to be made through the International Seabed Authority in respect of the exploitation of "the non-living resources of the continental shelf beyond 200 nm from the baselines."[38]

Second, the legal régimes governing the EEZ and continental shelf of a coastal State within 200 nm from its baselines were considered. Within the EEZ, the rights with respect to the seabed and subsoil are to be exercised in accordance with the legal régime of the continental shelf. The Court stated in its 1985 judgment on the Libya/Malta case that "Although the institutions of the continental shelf and the EEZ are different and distinct, the rights which the EEZ entails over the seabed of the zone are defined by reference to the régime laid down for the continental shelf. Although there can be a continental shelf where there is no exclusive economic zone, there cannot be an exclusive economic zone without a corresponding continental shelf."[39] According to the Court, these facts showed that the UNCLOS Convention expects the EEZ (distance criterion) not the continental shelf (natural prolongation criterion) holds the dominant position.

However, for Judge Xue, although contemporary customary international law on the definition of the continental shelf was much influenced by the negotiations of the UNCLOS III, the fundamental basis of the continental shelf régime remains intact under the "package deal." Natural prolongation as the physical criterion for the determination of the continental shelf is not replaced by the distance criterion. So, there is no basis in customary international law to suggest that restrictions imposed on the extent and use of the continental shelf beyond 200 nm imply that the continental shelf is now under two régimes. Either based on the natural prolongation of its land territory or a distance of 200 nm, every coastal State is entitled to a single continental shelf. Judge Xue also pointed out that, it is true that the limitation on the continental shelf beyond 200 nm and the Article 82 mechanism are designed to protect the Area and its resources as the common heritage of mankind, but it is questionable whether the distance criterion was provided as the primary entitlement to a continental shelf within 200 nm to trump an overlapping entitlement based on natural prolongation.[40]

Third, the Court believed that there is sufficient State practice and *opinio juris* to conclude that a continental shelf entitlement beyond 200 nm may not extend within 200 nm of another State.[41] Colombia, in its pleadings, disclosed that the submissions turned in to the CLCS shows that the State practice of the "vast majority" of States (presumably 51 out of 55) did not claim extended continental shelf within 200 nm of another State's baselines. The Court considered that the practice of States not to assert outer limits of their extended continental shelf within 200 nm of the baselines of another State was indicative of the *opinio juris*. For the Court, the practice of States may be considered sufficiently widespread and uniform for the purpose of the identification of customary international law. In addition, given its extent over a long period of time, this State practice may be seen as an expression of *opinio juris*, a constitutive element of customary international law.[42]

However, the Court's decision on *opinio juris* and State practice inferred from the submissions to the CLCS raised some questions in relation to the character of the submissions and real intents of the States. Although it is true that many States did not include scientific information relating to areas within 200 nm of other States, there may be a variety of reasons including the objection procedure. As Nicaragua argued, the practice of States that refrained from asserting outer limits of their extended continental shelf that extend within 200 nm from the baselines of another State was to avoid the possibility of their submission giving rise to disputes with neighboring States.[43] As the submissions were only technical and scientific materials, they were not final and binding documents.[44] In this context, Judges Tomka and Xue questioned the sufficiency of State practice accepted by the Court. Although the State practice of the "vast majority" of States did not claim an extended continental shelf within 200 nm of another State's baselines, Judge Tomka identified "up to 20 States" with contrary practices. Some States in their submission claimed a continental shelf entitlement beyond 200 nm that extends within 200 nm from another State's baselines. In addition, several States have made claims before international courts and tribunals.[45] In Dissenting Opinion, Judge Robinson said, he acknowledged that CLCS submissions could be used as evidence of State practice as they were considered sufficiently widespread and uniform. However, he disagreed with the majority's conclusion that the practice before the CLCS "is indicative of *opinio juris*, even if such practice may have been motivated in part by considerations other than a sense of legal obligation (para. 77)." According to Judge Robinson, this conclusion is unsafe, because of the possibility that the practice in question was motivated by considerations other than a sense of legal obligation.[46]

The World Court concluded that, under customary international law, a State's entitlement to a continental shelf beyond 200 nm from the territorial sea baselines may not extend within 200 nm from the baselines of another State.[47] Therefore, even if a State can demonstrate that it is entitled to an extended continental shelf, the entitlement may not extend within 200 nm from the baselines of another State. And, regardless of the criteria that determine the outer limit of the extended continental shelf, there was no overlapping entitlements over the same maritime areas within 200 nm from the baselines of another State. So, the Court needed not to proceed with maritime delimitation in this case.[48] The Court determined that it is impossible for a State to assert rights over the continental shelf to areas beyond 200 nm from the baselines to areas which lie within 200 nm of the baselines of another State. In this context, this judgment could be called "overruling" the North Sea judgment in deciding the entitlement to the continental shelf.[49]

4. MARITIME DELIMITATION

4-1. Truman Proclamation and the Convention on the Continental Shelf

Truman Proclamation addressed in 1945 has been regarded as the first national act to proclaim a continental shelf and equitable delimitation. The Proclamation, which was followed by a series of similar claims by other States, said "in cases where the continental shelf extends to the shores of another State, or is shared with an adjacent State, the boundary shall be determined by the United States and the State concerned in accordance with equitable principles." On the other hand, Whittemore Boggs, a Geographer of the United States Department of State, developed a more sophisticated equidistant line method, under which every point of which is equidistant from the nearest point or points on the opposite shores of the lake, river or strait.[50]

In 1950s, the International Law Commission (ILC) considered seriously the scope of the continental shelf. As regards boundaries, however, the main issue was not that of boundaries between States but of the seaward limit of the area, in which the coastal State could claim exclusive rights for exploitation.[51] Given the maritime delimitation provisions contained in the 1958 Continental Shelf Convention, it was somewhat embarrassing that the notion of equidistance was considered during the early discussion at the ILC. It was not until after the matter had been referred to a committee of hydrographical experts in 1953 that the equidistance principle began to take precedence over other possibilities.[52] Defining the continental shelf on the basis of dual criteria, 200-meter isobath, and exploitability, the Convention adopted the equidistance-special circumstances formula for maritime delimitation between neighbor States. Article 6 of the Convention provides:

> Where the same continental shelf is adjacent to the territories of two or more States whose coasts are opposite or adjacent, the boundary of the continental shelf shall be determined by agreement between them. In the absence of agreement, and unless another boundary line is justified by special circumstances, the boundary line is median line or equidistant line.

Professor Weil said, although the 1958 Convention on Continental Shelf did not mention the role of equity in Maritime delimitation, the idea of equity, which was logically underlying any international agreements, come to dominate subsequent maritime delimitation cases.[53]

4-2. North Sea Continental Shelf Cases and International Customary Law

In the North Sea Continental Shelf cases, Germany contended that the correct standard to be applied should be a "just and equitable share" of the continental shelf. However, the ICJ said that this doctrine appeared to be wholly at variance with the fundamental rules of law relating to the continental shelf. Denmark and the Netherlands stressed that the equidistance-special circumstances rule constituted a mandatory rule either on a conventional or on a customary international law basis. There is no doubt that this very convenient method had been widely used. As the Court aptly put it, this method has practical convenience and certainty of application, but these factors were not sufficient to convert a method into a rule of law.[54]

In the 1969 North Sea Continental Shelf cases, the Court recognized the equitable solution to be the purpose of maritime delimitation. In determining the customary international law on the delimitation of continental shelf boundaries, the Court was influenced by the Truman Proclamation, which stated that the continental shelf boundary should be determined in accordance with the equitable principles.[55] In its judgment on the North Sea cases, the Court said that delimitation is to be effected by agreement in accordance with the equitable principles, and taking account of all the relevant circumstances, in such a way as to leave as much as possible to each Party all those parts of the continental shelf that constitute a natural prolongation of its land territory into and under the sea, without encroachment on the natural prolongation of the land territory of the other.[56]

For the Court, the rights of a coastal State in respect of the area of the continental shelf that constitutes a natural prolongation of its land territory into and under the sea exist *ipso facto* and *ab initio*, by virtue of its sovereignty over the land, and as an extension of it in exercise of sovereign rights for the purpose of exploring the seabed and exploiting its natural resources. The ICJ said that from the beginning there were principles which reflected the *opinio juris* in the matter of delimitation. The principles were that delimitation must be the object of agreement between the States concerned, and that such agreement must be reached in accordance with the equitable principles.[57]

The ICJ made clear the principles and rules of international law applicable to maritime delimitation as between the Parties of the areas of the continental shelf in the North Sea. First, delimitation is to be effected by agreement in accordance with the equitable principles, and taking account of all the relevant circumstances, in such a way as to leave as much as possible to each Party all those parts of the continental shelf that constitute a natural prolongation of its land territory into and under the sea, without encroachment on the natural prolongation of the land territory of the other. Second, if the delimitation leaves to the Parties areas that overlap, these are to be divided between them in agreed proportions or, failing agreement, equally, unless they decide on a regime of joint jurisdiction, user, or exploitation for the zones of overlap or any part of them. Third, the factors to be taken into account in the course of the negotiations are (i) the general configuration of the coasts of the Parties, as well as the presence of any special or unusual features, (ii) so far as known or readily ascertainable, the physical and geological structure, and natural resources, of the continental shelf areas involved, (iii) the element of a reasonable degree of proportionality between the extent of the continental shelf area appertaining to the coastal State and the length of its coast measured in the general direction of the coastline.[58]

Subsequent Decisions on continental shelf delimitation cases by international courts and tribunals followed the points rendered by the ICJ in the North Sea Cases. Decisions in the Anglo-French

Continental Shelf case (1977), Tunisia/Libya Continental Shelf case (1982), and Gulf of Maine case (1984) stressed the equitable principles in maritime delimitation.

The ICJ, in the Continental Shelf case between Tunisia and Libya (Tunisia/Libya case), considered arguments and evidences based on geology, physiography, and the natural prolongation of its land territory. in its judgment of February 24, 1982, the Court ruled that, since the two countries abutted on a common continental shelf, it had to be guided by the "equitable principles" and by certain factors such as the necessity of ensuring a reasonable degree of proportionality between the areas allotted and the lengths of the coastlines concerned.[59] The Court made clear its result-oriented approach as follows:

> The result of the application of equitable principles must be equitable. This terminology, which is generally used, is not entirely satisfactory because it employs the term equitable to characterize both the result to be achieved and the means to be applied to reach this result. It is, however, the result which is predominant the principles are subordinate to the goal. The equitableness of a principle must be assessed in the light of its usefulness for the purpose of arriving at an equitable result.[60]

Canada and the United States notified to the ICJ a Special Agreement whereby they referred to a Chamber the question of maritime boundary making to divide the continental shelf and fisheries zones of the two Parties in the Gulf of Maine area. The Chamber delivered its judgment on October 12, 1984. It reviewed the origin and development of the dispute and laid down the principles and rules of international law governing the issue. It indicated that the delimitation was to be effected by the application of equitable criteria and by the use of practical methods capable of ensuring an equitable result. It defined the criteria and methods which it considered to be applicable to the single delimitation line which it was asked to draw. It applied criteria of a primarily geographical nature and used geometrical methods appropriate both for the delimitation of the seabed and for that of the superjacent waters.[61]

The Continental Shelf case between Libya and Malta, which was submitted to the Court by a Special Agreement, related to the delimitation of areas of the continental shelf appertaining to each of the States. In this case, Libya relied on the principle of natural prolongation and the concept of proportionality. Malta maintained that States' rights over areas of the continental shelf were now governed by the concept of distance from the coast, which was held to confer a primacy on the equidistance method of defining boundaries between areas of the continental shelf, particularly when these appertained to States lying directly opposite to each other, as in this case. The Court found that the delimitation is to be effected in accordance with the equitable principles and taking account of all relevant circumstances, so as to arrive at an equitable result. The Court also found that, in view of developments in the law relating to the rights of States over areas of the continental shelf, there was no reason to assign a role to geographical or geophysical factors when the distance between the two States was less than 400 miles. It took account of the main features of the coasts, the difference in their lengths, and the distance between them. It took care to avoid any excessive disproportion between the continental shelf appertaining to a State and the length of its coastline and adopted the solution of a median line transposed northwards over a certain distance.[62]

4-3. UNCLOS Convention and Recent Developments

The Convention on the Law of the Sea has articles dealing with maritime delimitation of the territorial sea (Art. 15), EEZ (Art. 74), and the continental shelf (Art. 83). Among these, Article 15 was adopted with comparative ease at the UNCLOS III. However, Articles 74 and 81 were subject to a lengthy discussion and debate between the Equidistance Principle Group and Equitable Principle Group. Tommy Koh, the president of the Conference, submitted a compromised proposal in August 1981, which was finally accepted by the Conference. Articles 74(1) and Article 81(1) provide that "The delimitation of the continental shelf (or EEZ) between States with opposite or adjacent coasts shall be effected by agreement on the basis of international law, as referred to in Article 38 of the Statute of the International Court of Justice, in order to achieve an equitable solution." This provision was welcomed by the Equitable Principle Group because it refers to an equitable solution without reference to equidistance or a median line. The Equidistance Group also welcomed this provision because there is a reference to "international law, as referred to in Article 38 of the Statute of the ICJ." However, the clauses of the UNCLOS Convention on delimitation of the continental shelf and EEZ lack precision and do not provide objective criteria. Therefore, in the long run, international courts and tribunals are expected to take an important role again to interpret and apply the provisions.

Tension between the need for particular justice arising from the uniqueness of specific cases and the demand for universalized justice caused a legal debate.[63] An excessive individualization of rule in the name of equity met the criticism that it lacked consistence and predictability essential to law. On the contrary, an excessive generalization of rules in the name of law frustrates equitable results. With regard to maritime delimitation, international courts and tribunals have been under criticism for decades. Their decisions have been swung between two positions. Since the ICJ judgment on the North Sea cases in 1969, the applicability of the equidistance rule has been demised. The equity doctrine which was introduced in the North Sea cases enjoyed its heyday at the Tunisia/Libya and Gulf of

Maine cases. However, the equidistance rule returned in full strength in the Libya/Malta Case with the support of the then emerging EEZ regime.[64] In this case, the ICJ ostensibly emphasized the principle of equity, but in actual delimitation, it used the median line method and said that natural prolongation of the land territory had no meaning within 200 nm of a coastal State.

In the Case concerning Territorial and Maritime Dispute between Nicaragua and Honduras in the Caribbean Sea, the ICJ commented on recent trend in maritime delimitation. In the judgment of 2012, the Court said, "The jurisprudence of the Court sets out the reasons why the equidistance method is widely used in the practice of maritime delimitation. It has a certain intrinsic value because of its scientific character and the relative ease with which it can be applied. However, the equidistance method does not automatically have priority over other methods of delimitation and, in particular circumstances, there may be factors which make the application of the equidistance method inappropriate."[65] To be sure, there are cases where it is impossible to achieve an equitable result with minor modifications of the provisional equidistance or median lines. Where adjacent States have only one or two base points each on long coasts, a perpendicular line to a line representing the general direction of the coast of the two adjacent States could be an alternative. In this case, ICJ recognized the equidistance to be the general rule in territorial sea delimitation, but presented its position that special circumstances required the use of a different method of delimitation in the EEZ and continental shelf, the bisector method.[66]

Nowadays, maritime delimitation usually proceeds step by step following three stages, which was explained by the ICJ in its judgments in the Libya/Malta case and Black Sea case between Romania and Ukraine. This three stage method has been entertained by those insisting delimitation by the equidistance line, but those favoring the equity principle do not refuse to use it. In the Black Sea case, the ICJ had another opportunity to restate its jurisprudence regarding the methodology for maritime delimitation.[67] At the first stage, provisional delimitation lines are established using methods that are geometrically objective and appropriate for the geography of the delimitation area. Equidistance or median lines will be drawn between adjacent or opposite coasts respectively, unless there are compelling reasons that make this unfeasible.[68] At the second stage, relevant factors calling for adjustment of the provisional lines are considered. The Court will consider whether there are factors calling for adjustment or shifting of the provisional lines for an equitable result.[69] As Roach noted, the relevant factors to be considered in the second step are disproportionate coastal length, geographic context such as concavity of coasts, and outlying islands of little significance. However, population, socioeconomic factors, conduct of parties in other negotiations, size of landmass, and lack of natural resources are not relevant.[70] At the third stage, equitableness of the boundary lines will be examined. Considering balance between the ratio of the respective coastal lengths and the ratio between the relevant maritime areas of the coastal States, the Court verifies whether the delimitation lines produce an equitable result.[71]

In the Nicaragua v. Colombia case, the Court followed the three-stage procedure. First, it selected the base points and constructed a provisional median line between the Nicaraguan coast and the western coasts of the Colombian islands. Second, the Court considered any relevant circumstances which might have called for an adjustment or shifting of the provisional median line so as to achieve an equitable result. The substantial disparity between the relevant Colombian coast and that of Nicaragua (approximately 1:8.2), and the need to avoid a situation whereby the line of delimitation cut off one of the Parties' ties from maritime areas were recognized to be relevant circumstances. In the relevant area between the Nicaraguan mainland and the western coasts of the Colombian islands, the relevant circumstances called for the provisional median line to be shifted eastwards. To that end, the Court determined that different weightings (3:1) should be given to the base points situated on Nicaraguan and Colombian islands. Third, the Court checked that, taking account of all the circumstances of the case, the delimitation thus obtained did not create a disproportionality that would render the result inequitable.[72]

Given the relevant customary law and the provisions of the UNCLOS Convention, equitable principles could be recognized as the main principle in maritime delimitation. However, in practice, only few maritime delimitations followed the equitable principle while most of the cases were determined by the equidistance or median line rule. This trend has been found not only in the decisions of international courts and tribunals, but also in relevant agreements between coastal States. According to Antunes, a comprehensive analysis on maritime delimitation practices by States showed that reference to equitable principles are found in 10% of the cases analyzed, which was later cut to 2%. In fact, the equitable principle has been rarely mentioned in the cases of EEZ delimitation. Two-thirds of unilateral declarations by States have regarded the equidistant line as a provisional boundary line.[73] Recently, a majority of maritime delimitation have been effected by application of the equidistance or median rule for equitable results, if there are no factors which make the application of the rules inappropriate. Today, however, the equitable principle and the equidistance principle are considered to be in a complementary relationship. In the Qatar v. Bahrain case, the ICJ noted that the equitable principle-relevant circumstances rule which was developed in case law and the equidistance-special circumstances rule were closely interrelated.

5. KOREA-JAPAN JDZ IN THE EAST CHINA SEA

In the late 1960s, as the Yellow Sea and East China Sea were expected to be an abundant oil fields, continental shelf issues among East Asian States were raised. In 1966, the Committee for Coordination of Joint Prospecting for Mineral Resources in East Asian Offshore Areas (CCOP) was organized for a geophysical survey in the Yellow Sea and East China Sea under the auspices of the United Nations Economic Commission for Asia and the Far East (ECAFE). The survey report released in 1969 indicated that the continental shelves of the East China Sea and Yellow Sea had a high probability to be one of the most prolific oil reservoirs in the world.[74] This report caused a competition for maritime jurisdiction among Northeast Asian countries. They hastily claimed jurisdiction over the continental shelf as wide as possible and established development zones. By late September 1970, seventeen zones were established by Korea, Japan, and Taiwan, resulting in overlapping maritime zones.[75]

By the way, the Seas in Northeast Asia such as the Yellow Sea, East China Sea, and East Sea (Sea of Japan in Japan) are land-locked and very complex from the perspectives of geography, geology, and geomorphology. The geographic situation in this area is complicated because of the deeply indented coasts, and scattered insular formations and peninsulas. The Yellow Sea and East China Sea have shallow waters and are connected by a single continental shelf, except for the Okinawa Trough. The complicated geography and topography of this area foresee the negotiations for maritime delimitation would be tricky. What makes the circumstances more complicated is the unresolved conflicts over the ownership of some islands and historical issues still left unsettled.

Regarding the continental shelves of the Yellow Sea and East China Sea, positions of the coastal States were different. Relying on the ICJ's logic in the North Sea cases decision, Taiwan (China) maintained that the continental shelf is the natural prolongation of the land territory and that maritime boundaries should be established by the equitable principle taking into account the relevant circumstances. Japan insisted maritime delimitation by the equidistant or median rule. Korea claimed the equidistant line toward China in the Yellow Sea, but it insisted the natural prolongation theory toward Japan on the ground that Okinawa Trough is a deep rift disconnecting the continental shelf between Korea and Japan. Regarding the Okinawa Trough, China views it as a disconnection of the continental shelf, while Japan views it as a minor and temporary sink of the seafloor.

In order to break the stalemate, Korea, Japan, and Taiwan agreed in 1970 to pursue joint development. When they agreed to undertake joint development, China raised a strong protest in December 1970. At the same time, China intensified its claims to the ownership of the Senkaku Islands. The United States government warned American oil companies involved that it would not intercede even if their vessels were seized by China. All exploration activities in the Yellow and East China Seas stopped.[76]

Then the ICJ delivered its judgment on the North Sea Continental Shelf cases in 1969. The ICJ, in its epoch-making judgment, declared that the continental shelf is a natural prolongation of the land territory into the sea and that continental shelf delimitation is to be effected by agreement in accordance with the equitable principles taking account of all the relevant circumstances in such a way as to leave as much as possible to each Party all those parts of the continental shelf that constitute a natural prolongation of its land territory. The natural prolongation theory and the equity principle stated by the World Court have had tremendous impacts on international jurisprudence, and laws and policies of national governments. The ICJ's ruling on the North Sea cases had an impact on the maritime policies of Northeast Asian States, too. The positions of Korea and China were strengthened in the East China Sea. Traditionally, Japan had argued delimitation by the equidistant or median line under the assumption that Okinawa Trough is only an incidental sinking. The 1958 Convention on Continental Shelf established the scope of the continental shelf based on 200 meters depth and exploitability, but in 1969, the ICJ rejected such a definition and declared that the continental shelf is basically a natural prolongation of the land territory. Japan was shocked by the Court's ruling on the North Sea cases and agreed on joint development with Korea in the East China Sea.

In January 1974, Korea and Japan concluded two agreements on the continental shelf between them. The Agreement Concerning Joint Development of the Southern Part of Continental Shelf Adjacent to the Two Countries (Joint Development Agreement) established a Joint Development Zone (JDZ) of the size of 82,000km² for joint development of resources in the East China Sea seabed and subsoil. The Agreement divides the JDZ into nine sub-zones, and Korea and Japan selected mining concessionaires for each sub-zone. Mining concessionaires receive equal shares of natural resources produced in the JDZ and cover the costs used for exploration and exploitation of natural resources. The Agreement established the Korea-Japan Joint Committee to discuss issues related to the implementation of the Agreement. Decisions of the Committee are made only by agreement between the two sides. On the other hand, the Agreement provides that either party may terminate the JDZ Agreement at any time after the expiration of the 50-year period by giving three years' prior written notice to the other party. Since the JDZ Agreement chose the Joint Commission System with weak authority, not the Joint Authority System with relatively strong authority, joint development of marine resources tended to be sluggish when the relationship between Korea and Japan was not smooth. In any case, for several years after the entry into force of the Agreement, Korea and Japan conducted joint exploration of seabed resources in the JDZ. But before long the exploration was stopped due to Japan's negative stance. Japan's change of attitude raised suspicions that it may be due to the perception that the median or equidistance line method is becoming more and more prevailing than the natural prolongation theory in continental shelf delimitation.

Korea and Japan have to decide the future of the Korea-Japan JDZ Agreement. Will they decide to terminate the Agreement and begin negotiations for a final maritime delimitation? Or will they opt to maintain the JDZ Agreement, which was once praised as a model JDZ Agreement, with minor alterations?

Once the bilateral negotiation for maritime delimitation begins, the States will reiterate their existing positions. Korea will insist an equitable solution considering the natural prolongation of the land territory as the basis of its sovereign rights over the continental shelf. As Korea has asserted that the Okinawa Trough is a fundamental discontinuity of the continental shelf, it could suggest a line connecting 85 fixed points located 60 nm from the foot of the continental slope (FOS), which was included in its official document submitted to the CLCS. Japan will insist that maritime delimitation should be effected by application of the equidistance or median line method. For Japan, natural prolongation of the land territory cannot be applied because the width between the two States are less than 400 nm. It will also emphasize that Okinawa Trough is not a discontinuity of the continental shelf.

Above all, Japan will want to take advantage of the recent trend in international society that puts more importance on distance than natural prolongation of the land territory in maritime delimitation. This trend was initiated by the judgment on the Libya/Malta case of the ICJ, which then considered the new trend appeared in the UNCLOS III. The Court said that the continental shelf appertaining to a State extends up to 200 nm from its coast, whatever the geological characteristics of the seabed and subsoil, there is no reason to ascribe any role to geological or geophysical factors within that distance either in verifying the legal title of the States concerned or in proceeding to a delimitation as between their claims. This is clear and shocking statement because, where verification of the validity of title is concerned, at least in so far as those areas are situated at a distance of under 200 nm from the coasts in question, title depends solely on the distance from the coasts of the coastal States. Subsequent decisions of international courts and tribunals did not take clear stances preferring the distance standard to natural prolongation. By the way, international courts and tribunals sometimes recognized the sovereign rights of States to the extended continental shelves. The ITLOS, in its 2012 judgment in the Bangladesh/Myanmar case, and the Annex VII Tribunal, in its 2014 Award in the Bangladesh v. India case, recognized the rights to the extended continental shelves from coastal States. Consequently, the international judicial organs decided to create wedge-shaped gray zones.

The ICJ considered this issue in depth in the Continental Shelf between Nicaragua and Colombia beyond 200 nm from the Nicaraguan Coast case (Nicaragua v. Colombia 2023). The World Court, in its judgment, ruled clearly that, under customary international law, a State's entitlement to the continental shelf beyond 200 nm from the territorial sea baselines may not extend within 200 nm from the baselines of another State. Therefore, even if a State is entitled to an extended continental shelf, the entitlement may not extend within 200 nm from the baselines of any State. Regardless of the criteria that determine the outer limit of the extended continental shelf, there is no overlapping entitlements over the same maritime areas within 200 nm from the baselines of another State. So, the Court concluded that there was no need to proceed with maritime delimitation in this case.[77]

The ICJ determined clearly that it is impossible for a State to assert rights over the continental shelf to areas beyond 200 nm from its baselines to areas which lie within 200 nm of the baselines of another State. In this context, this judgment could be said to be "overruling" the judgment by the ICJ in the North Sea cases in deciding the entitlement to the continental shelf.[78] However, various objections have been raised as to whether the decision of the ICJ to establish customary international law was appropriate. First, the Court presented the position that the distance standard (EEZ) is superior to natural prolongation (continental shelf), suggesting that the 1982 UNCLOS Convention system gives preference to EEZ (distance) over the continental shelf (natural prolongation) and that the extended continental shelf can only be expanded to the Area. However, if it is necessary to limit the scope of the extended continental shelf, the UNCLOS Convention must have introduced relevant provisions in the Convention. There are no such provisions suggesting this in the Convention. Second, as Judge Tomka said in his dissenting opinion, the Court had not taken its task of identifying customary international law seriously. The Court found that "the vast majority of parties" to the Convention which have made submissions to the CLCS have not extended its continental shelf within 200 nm from the baselines of another State. Thus, the Court recognized the establishment of relevant practices and *opinio juris*, which are components of customary international law. However, criticism has been raised that the submissions are only scientific documents and are inappropriate as data to determine the final policy of States. Furthermore, due to various reasons, there were not a few States that did not submit data related to the continental shelf beyond 200 nm from its baselines. The judgment in Nicaragua v. Colombia 2023 was a very clear answer to a poorly phrased question, but several questions were raised which now will need to be answered.[79]

Therefore, if Japan wants to take advantage of the Nicaragua v. Colombia case judgment during the negotiation process, Korea will be able to deal with the logic and find ways to limit its influence. In spite of the so-called general conception that distance is superior to natural prolongation, the presence of a rift zone on the ocean floor will be a strong proof implying the discontinuity of the continental shelf. Korea will argue that, in continental shelf demarcation, if there is a break in the seabed, even in waters within 200 nm from the baselines of Japan, this discontinuity must be respected. The natural prolongation of the land territory theory which was developed by the ICJ in the North Sea cases is still very important for Korea.

Given the conflict between the natural prolongation theory of Korea and the distance standard of Japan, and the necessity of unitization of mineral resources in the East China Sea, maintaining the existing JDZ system could be a good alternative. Korea could pursue final maritime delimitation insisting the natural prolongation theory and discontinuity of the continental shelf due to the presence Okinawa Trough, but maintaining the framework of the JDZ Agreement system would not be a bad option, either. Maintaining the existing JDZ system would be a reasonable choice, because the JDZ Agreement (1974) was the product of difficult negotiations for continental shelf delimitation that took place when the legal system of the continental shelf and claims of the parties were not significantly different compared to now. If Korea and Japan decide to maintain the existing JDZ Agreement system, that will also have the effect of preventing the intervention of China, which has consistently opposed the Agreement. If the Parties agree to maintain the JDZ Agreement, the Joint Committee System could be reformed to the Joint Authority System so that the joint management organization can promote exploration and development activities more autonomously and efficiently.

6. SOME OBSERVATIONS

The ICJ rendered its historical and landmark judgment in the North Sea Continental Shelf cases on February 20, 1969. Rejecting the principle stipulated in the 1958 Convention on Continental Shelf, the Court ruled that the continental shelf is the natural prolongation of the land territory into the sea and that delimitation is to be effected by agreement in accordance with the equitable principles, taking account of all the relevant circumstances. This ICJ judgment has had great influence on the international jurisprudence, subsequent decisions of international courts and tribunals, and the law and practices of national governments. However, in the Libya/Malta case, the Court said, whatever the geological characteristics of the corresponding seabed and subsoil, there is no reason to ascribe any role to geological or geophysical factors within 200 nm of another State either in verifying the legal title of the States concerned or in maritime delimitation. The Court also deliberated the rift-zone issue with a similar logic.

The UNCLOS Convention's provisions on the definition of the continental shelf recognized the natural prolongation of the land territory and the 200 nm distance to be the legal basis for sovereign rights over the continental shelf. So, there could be a conflict between the natural prolongation and 200 nm distance in deciding outer limits of the continental shelf of coastal States. The Convention does not have any provisions as to which of these titles would be granted a superior status in the event of a conflict. Against this backdrop, the issue whether the sovereign rights to an extended continental shelf based on the natural prolongation of the land territory can be recognized in waters within 200 nm from the coast of another State became the most sensitive issue in international law of the sea. This issue is very important and complex because it concerns the relationship between the continental shelf and EEZ and the competition between natural prolongation and distance standards.

Regarding this question, international courts and tribunals have showed a zigzag stance. However, the ICJ, in its recent judgment in the Nicaragua v. Colombia case, declared clearly that, under customary international law, a State's entitlement to a continental shelf beyond 200 nm from its baselines may not extend within 200 nm from the baselines of another State. Therefore, even if a State is entitled to an extended continental shelf, the entitlement may not extend within 200 nm from the baselines of another State. However, various objections have been raised as to the appropriateness of the Court's decision on the formation of international customary law, and representative character and authenticity in judging the States' practices based on submissions to the CLCS.

Regarding maritime delimitation, there have been competition between the equidistance principle and equity principle. Given the relevant customary law and the provisions of the UNCLOS Convention, the equitable principles could be recognized as the main principle in maritime delimitation. However, in practice, only a few maritime delimitations followed the equitable principle while most of the cases were determined by the equidistance or median line rule. Nowadays, maritime delimitation usually proceeds step by step following the three stages method which was suggested by the Equidistance Group.

The Korea-Japan JDZ Agreement, which was concluded in 1974, established a Joint Development Zone of the size of 82,000km^2 for the joint development of resources in the East China Sea seabed and subsoil. However, as the time the Parties can terminate the Agreement is approaching, Korea and Japan have to decide the future of the Agreement. If Korea or Japan choose to terminate the Agreement with prior notice, they will begin new negotiations for final maritime delimitation. Or they could agree to maintain the JDZ

Agreement. Once the bilateral negotiation begins, Korea and Japan will reiterate their existing positions. Korea will insist the natural prolongation of the land territory as the basis of its sovereign rights over the continental shelf. It will also assert that Okinawa Trough is a fundamental discontinuity of the continental shelf. Japan will insist that maritime delimitation should be effected by application of the median line method and that the natural prolongation of the land territory cannot be applied because the width between the two States in the East China Sea is less than 400 nm. It will also emphasize that Okinawa Trough is not discontinuity of the continental shelf. Japan will try to take advantage of the recent trend in international society that puts more importance on distance than natural prolongation of the land territory. If Japan's continental shelf policy is aggressive, Korea will have to assert the relevance of the 1974 JDZ Agreement as a previous Agreement.

Given the close conflict between the natural prolongation standard of Korea and distance standard of Japan, and the necessity of unitization of the fluid mineral resources in the East China Sea, maintaining the existing JDZ system could be the second-best choice. Maintaining the existing JDZ system would be a reasonable and amicable choice, because the JDZ Agreement was the product of hectic bilateral negotiations for continental shelf delimitation that took place when the legal system of the continental shelf and claims of the Parties were not significantly different compared to now. If the two States decide to maintain the JDZ Agreement system, that will also have the effect of preventing the intervention of China. Only this time the inefficient joint management system should be reformed to a more efficient system.

Notes

* This article is a revised and supplemented paper, which was presented at the KSIL-Kyushu University Seminar on the 40th Anniversary of the ICJ Judgment on the North Sea Continental Shelf cases held at Kyushu University (Japan) on August 21, 2009. The title of the article presented was "1969 North Sea Continental Shelf Cases, the Law of the Sea, and Korean Legislation and Policy."

** Emeritus Professor of Law, Hannam University.

1. North Sea Continental Shelf, Judgment, *ICJ Reports*, 1969. para.101.

2. Jose Maria Ruda, "Some of the Contributions of the International Court of Justice to the Development of International Law," *New York University Journal of International Law and Politics*, vol. 24, 1991, p.35.

3. North Sea cases, *op. cit.*, paras.2-3.

4. The Parties agreed on partial delimitation by concluding two agreements between Germany and the Netherlands (December 1964) and between Germany and Denmark (June 1965).

5. North Sea cases, *op. cit.*, pp.11~12.

6. *Ibid.*, p.12.

7. *Ibid.*, para.13.

8. *Ibid.*, paras.15~16.

9. *Ibid.*, para.101.

10. Robin Churchill, Vaughan Lowe, and Amy Sander, *The Law of the Sea*, 4th edition, Manchester University Press, 2022, p.221.

11. Policy of the United States with Respect to the Natural Resources of the Subsoil and Sea Bed of the Continental Shelf, United States Presidential Proclamation 2667, September 28, 1945; Donald R Rothwell and Tim Stephens, *The International law of the Sea*, 2nd edition, Hart Publishing, 2016, p.105.

12. Churchill Lowe, and Sander,, *op. cit.*, pp.224~225.

13. Nuzgar Dundua, *Delimitation of Maritime Boundaries between Adjacent States*, United Nations, 2007, pp.8~9.

14. Satya N. Nandan and Shabtai Rosenne, *United Nations Convention of the Law of the Sea 1982 : A Commentary*, Martinus Nijhoff Publishers, 1993, pp.828~829.

15. North Sea cases, *op. cit.*, para.43.

16. Ibid., para.44.

17 D. P. O'Connell, *The International Law of the Sea*, vol. 1, Clarendon Press, 1982, pp.490~491.

18. Continental Shelf (Tunisia/Libyan Arab Jamahiriya), Judgment, *ICJ Reports*, 1982, p.18.

19. Continental Shelf (Libyan Arab Jamahiriya/Malta), Judgment, *ICJ Reports*, 1985, para.26.

20. *Ibid.*, para.30.

21. *Ibid.*, paras.32~33.

22. *Ibid.*, para.34.

23. *Ibid.*, para.36.

24. *Ibid.*, para.39.

25. *Ibid.*, para.41.

26. Churchill, Lowe, and Sander, *op. cit.*, p.229.

27. Nandan and Rosenne, *op. cit.*, p.831.

28. Bernard B. Oxman, *Memorandum for Korea*, 2008, pp.6~7.

29. Churchill, Lowe, and Sander, *op. cit.*, p.301.

30. Malcolm D. Evans and Nicholas A. Ioannides, "A Commentary on the 2033 Nicaragua v. Colombia case," EJIL: Talk, p. 3 <https://www.ejiltalk.org/author/malcolmevans> (March 5, 2024).

31. *Ibid.*

32. Delimitation of the Maritime Boundary in the Bay of Bengal (Bangladesh/Myanmar), Judgment, *ITLOS Reports*, 2012, paras.460-463 and 472; Rothwell and Stephens, *op. cit.*, pp.429-431; David P. Riesenberg, "Recent Jurisprudence Addressing Maritime Delimitation beyond 200 nm from the Coast," *2024 ASIL Annual Meeting*, vol. 18, Issue 21. <https://www.asil.org/insights/volume/18/issue/21> (March 4, 2024).

33. Ibid; Question of the Delimitation of the Continental Shelf between Nicaragua and Columbia beyond 200 nm from the Nicaraguan Coast (Nicaragua v. Colombia 2023), Judgment, *ICJ Reports*, 2023, Overview of the Case.

34. Hilde Woker, "Preliminary reflections on the ICJ Judgment in Question of the Delimitation of the Continental Shelf between Nicaragua and Colombia beyond 200 nm from the Nicaraguan Coast (Nicaragua v. Colombia) of July 13, 2023," EJIL: Talk,< https://www.ejiltalk.org/preliminary-reflections-on-the-icj-judgment-in-question-of-the-delimitation-of-the-continental-shelf-between-nicaragua-and-colombia-beyond-200-nautical-miles-from-the-nicaraguan-coast-nicaragua-v-co/> (Feruary 25, 2024).

35. Nicaragua v. Colombia 2023, *op. cit.*, para.79.

36. Delimitation of the Maritime Boundary in the Bay of Bengal (Bangladesh/Myanmar), Judgment, *ITLOS Reports*, 2012, paras.460~463 and 472.

37. Matei Alexianu,"The Nicaragua v. Colombia Continental Shelf Judgment: Short but Significant," *2024 ASIL Annual Meeting*, vol. 27, Issue 9. <https://www.asil.org/insights/volume/27/issue/9> (March 4, 2024).

38. Nicaragua v. Colombia 2023, *op. cit.*, para.76.

39. *Ibid.*, para. 70; Libya/Malta case, *op. cit.*, para.34.

40. *Ibid.*, Separate Opinion of Judge Xue.

41. Woker, *op. cit.*, p.4.

42. Nicaragua v. Colombia 2023, *op. cit.*, para.77.

43. Woker, *op. cit.*, p.5; *Ibid.*, para.57.

44. *Ibid.* (Woker), p.5.

45. *Alexianu, op. cit.*

46. Nicaragua v. Colombia 2023, *op. cit.*, Dissenting Opinion of Judge Robinson.

47. *Ibid.*, para.79.

48. *Ibid.*, paras.81~82.

49. Evans and Ioannides, *op. cit.*

50. S. Whittemore Boggs, *International Boundaries: A Study of Boundary Functions and Problems*, Columbia University Press, 1940, pp.178-183; Rothwell and Stephens, *op. cit.*, pp.414~415.

51. North Sea cases, *op. cit.*, para.48.

52. *Ibid.*, para.50.

53. P. Weil, *The Law of Maritime Delimitation: Reflections(trans. by M. Macglashan)*, Grotius Publications, 1989, p.162.

54. North Sea case, *op. cit.*, paras.19~23.

55. Churchill, Lowe, and Sander, *op. cit.*, p.319.

56. North Sea cases, *op. cit.*, para.101.

57. *Ibid.*, para.19.

58. *Ibid.*, para.101.

59. In Tunisia/Libya case, ICJ decided on the proposition that each boundary is a *unicum*, that is to say, it is unique or monotypic. L. D. M. Nelson, "The Roles of Equity in the Delimitation of Maritime Boundaries," *AJIL*, vol. 84, 1990, pp.837~838.

60. Continental Shelf (Tunisia/Libyan Arab Jamahiriya), Judgment, *ICJ Reports*, 1982, para.70.

61. Delimitation of the Maritime Boundary in the Gulf of Maine Area (Canada/United States of America), *ICJ Reports*, 1985, Overview of the Case.

62. *Libya/Malta case*, op. cit., para.79, Overview of the Case.

63. Nelson, *op. cit.*, p.842.

64. Weil, *op. cit.*, pp.169~177.

65. Case Concerning Territorial and Maritime Dispute between Nicaragua and Honduras in the Caribbean Sea, *ICJ reports*, 2007, para.271.

66. David H. Anderson, "Maritime Delimitation in the Black Sea Case (Romania v. Ukraine)," *The Law and Practice of International Courts and Tribunals*, vol. 8, 2009, p. 326; Shi Jiuyong, "Maritime Delimitation in the Jurisprudence of the International Court of Justice," *Chinese Journal of International Law*, Vol. 9, 2010, p.281.

67. *Ibid.* (Anderson), p.306.

68. Maritime Delimitation in the Black Sea (Romania v. Ukraine), Judgment, *ICJ Reports*, 2009, para.116.

69. *Ibid.*, para.120.

70. J. Ashley Roach, "Maritime Boundary Delimitation: United States Practice," *Ocean Development and International Law*, vol. 44, p.2.

71. Black Sea case, *op. cit.*, para.122.

72. Nicaragua v. Colombia case 2012, *op. cit.*, Overview of the Case.

73. Nuno Marques Antunes, *Towards the Conceptualization of Maritime Delimitation: Legal and Technical Aspects of a Political Process*, Martinus Nijhoff Publishers, 2003, pp.96~97.

74. CCOP/ ECAFE, "Geological Structure and Some Water Characteristics of the East China Sea and the Yellow Sea," *Technical Bulletin*, No.2, 1969, pp.39~40.

75. Choon-Ho Park, *East Asia and The Law of the Sea*, Seoul National University Press, 1985, pp.6-13. South Korea established 7 development zones by the Submarine Mineral Resources Development Act which was enacted in January 1970 and the Presidential Decree which was proclaimed in May 1970.

76. *Ibid.* (Park), pp.128-130.

77. Nicaragua v. Colombia 2023, *op. cit.*, paras.81~82.

78. Evans and Ionnides, *op. cit.*

79. *Ibid.*

KYIL

A Case about the Avalokiteshvara Statue of Buseoksa Temple (Seoju, Goryeo) and the International Cultural Heritage Law
— After the Final Decision

Jaehyun RYU
Public Prosecutor
Gwangju District Prosecutor's Office (Gwangju, Korea)
Ph.D. Candidate
Seoul National University (Seoul, Korea)

Sungjae HWANG
In-house Counsel
Hyundai Motor Company (Seoul, Korea)
Ph.D. Candidate
Seoul National University (Seoul, Korea)

Key Words

International Cultural Heritage Law, Cultural Heritage Protection Act of Korea, UNESCO 1970 Convention, UNIDROIT 1995 Convention, lex originis, adverse possession

1. INTRODUCTION

The case of the Avalokiteshvara Statue (hereinafter, the "Object of Dispute") of Buseoksa Temple, stemming from events in 2012 when the statue was stolen from Kannon temple on Tsushima Island, Japan, and smuggled into the Republic of Korea (hereinafter "Korea"), represents a pivotal intersection of cultural heritage law and private international law. This incident catalyzed a series of legal challenges involving Buseoksa Temple (hereinafter, the "Plaintiff") in Seosan, Korea, which claims descent from the "Buseoksa Temple of Seoju,[1] Goryeo"[2] and asserts ownership over the Object of Dispute. In 2013, the Plaintiff secured a preliminary injunction to halt the transfer of the Object of Dispute to Japan, leading to a protracted legal dispute that culminated in a definitive Supreme Court decision in 2023.

This paper delves into the broader implications of this case about the Object of Dispute within the realm of international cultural heritage law, focusing particularly on the issues about private international law, the UNESCO Convention on the Means of Prohibiting and Preventing the Illicit Import, Export and Transfer of Ownership of Cultural Property of 1970 (hereinafter, the "UNESCO 1970 Convention")[3] and the Cultural Heritage Protection Act of Korea. While previous studies have often emphasized the theoretical aspects of international norms and legislative frameworks, this discussion aims to anchor these abstract elements within the tangible context of specific legal disputes. By exploring this landmark case, the paper seeks to shed light on the operational challenges and successes of international cultural heritage law, offering insights into the ongoing evolution of seeking restorative justice.

2. BACKGROUND AND JUDGMENTS OF THE KOREAN COURTS

2-1. Summary of Facts

This section briefly outlines the facts surrounding the theft and proceedings about the Object of Dispute in chronological order.

- **October 8, 2012**: Two Buddhist statues, including the Object of Dispute, were stolen from temples on Tsushima Island, Japan, and illegally smuggled into Korea via Busan port.
- **December 17, 2012**: The Japanese police, through the Interpol, requested assistance from the Korean police to investigate the theft.
- **January 24, 2013**: The Cultural Heritage Administration of Korea, in coordination with the police, successfully recovered the two stolen statues.
- **February 15, 2013**: The Japanese government requested Korea to return the stolen artifacts.
- **February 18, 2013**: The Plaintiff, asserting ownership of the Object of Dispute, applied for an injunction from the Daejeon District Court to prevent the transfer of the Object of Dispute to Japan.
- **February 25, 2013**: The Daejeon District Court approved the injunction, effectively halting any transfer of the Object of Dispute.
- **April 20, 2016**: The Plaintiff initiated a civil lawsuit against Korea (hereinafter, the "Defendant") in the Daejeon District Court.
- **January 26, 2017**: The Daejeon District Court ruled in favor of the Plaintiff, ordering the Object of Dispute's return to the Plaintiff. Simultaneously, the Defendant appealed against the decision.
- **2017 – 2023**: During the appeal process in the Daejeon High Court, the case was notified[4] to the Kannon Temple (hereinafter, the "Defendant's Auxiliary Participant") in Japan, under the international judicial mutual assistance procedure, and it then participated in the lawsuit.[5]
- **February 1, 2023**: The Daejeon High Court overturned the initial decision and dismissed the Plaintiff's claim.

- **February 10, 2023**: The Plaintiff filed a final appeal to the Supreme Court of Korea.
- **October 26, 2023**: The Supreme Court dismissed the final appeal, concluding the legal dispute over the Object of Dispute's ownership.

2-2. The Decision of the First Instance: Daejeon District Court Decision 2016Ga-Hap102119, Rendered on January 26, 2017[6]

On January 26, 2017, the Daejeon District Court rendered its decision, siding with the Plaintiff. The decision was based on a detailed assessment of historical evidence regarding the origins and subsequent movements of the Object of Dispute, although there was no consideration of private international law matters.

The court first established foundational details about the Plaintiff, an institution of the Jogye order of Korean Buddhism with historical roots dating back to 677 ACE. It is situated in Seosan, Korea. The court reviewed the Plaintiff's historical claims to the Object of Dispute, supported by documents and experts, which suggested that the Object of Dispute was originally dedicated to the "Buseoksa Temple of Seoju, Goryeo" and might have been taken to Japan under contentious circumstances. The absence of traditional records, which would normally accompany the legitimate transfer of a religious artifact, was significant in evaluating the legitimacy of the Object of Dispute's removal and subsequent possession. Finally, the court concluded that the evidence presented by the Plaintiff substantiated its claim to the Object of Dispute, leading to a ruling in the Plaintiff's favor.

2-3. The Decision of the Second Instance: Daejeon High Court Decision 2017Na10570, Rendered on February 1, 2023

On February 1, 2023, the Daejeon High Court overturned the first instance decision and dismissed the Plaintiff's claim. The rationale behind the appellate court's decisions regarding each issue is detailed as follows:

2-3-1. Main Issue: Is the Plaintiff Original Acquirer of the Object of Dispute?

The appellate court first addressed the primary issue of original acquisition by determining that the governing law should be that of Goryeo. However, due to the inability of both parties to provide sufficient evidence regarding the Goryeo Civil Act, and lacking its own findings, the court decided to apply the current Civil Act of Korea. Under this governing law of original acquisition, the court recognized "Buseoksa Temple of Seoju, Goryeo" as the original acquirer of the Object of Dispute. However, due to insufficient evidence to establish that the Plaintiff is identical to the "Buseoksa Temple of Seoju, Goryeo," the appellate court concluded that the plaintiff was not indeed the original acquirer.

Accordingly, the plaintiff's claim was dismissed, but the court of second instance also decided the supplementary issues as follows.

2-3-2. Supplementary Issue 1: Legality of the Adverse Possession by the Defendant's Auxiliary Participant

Regarding the legality of the acquisition by the Defendant's Auxiliary Participant, the court applied the Japanese Civil Code as the governing law under the 1962 Conflict of Laws Act of Korea, rejecting the Plaintiff's request to apply the Civil Act of Korea as an overriding mandatory rule or to not apply the Civil Code of Japan for the public policy. The court found no legal basis to support that the founder of the Defendant's Auxiliary Participant had lawfully acquired the Object of Dispute. However, it recognized the acquisition by adverse possession, noting that more than 20 years had passed since the Defendant's Auxiliary Participant began occupying the Object of Dispute, effectively satisfying the requirements for adverse possession under not only the Civil Code of Japan, but also the Civil Act of Korea.

2-3-3. Supplementary Issue 2: Applicability of Adverse Possession Exclusion under the Cultural Heritage Protection Act of Korea or the UNESCO 1970 Convention

The appellate court dismissed the argument of the Plaintiff that adverse possession was precluded under the Cultural Heritage Protection Act of Korea, due to ambiguities over its application to the case. Similarly, the court rejected the application of the UNESCO 1970 Convention on the grounds that the first alleged illegal removal of the Object of Dispute predates the Convention's enforcement, thus rendering it inapplicable in this case.

2-3-4. Mention of the Unidroit 1995 Convention and Its Purpose

Lastly, the court added some discussions related to the UNIDROIT Convention on Stolen or Illegally Exported Cultural Objects of 1995 (hereinafter, the "UNIDROIT 1995 Convention"), emphasizing that while the Convention advocates for the return of illegally removed cultural objects to their countries of origin, overriding civil law notions of *bona fide* or adverse possession, its provisions were not directly applicable to this civil dispute. However, the court noted that the ideals of cultural property protection endorsed by the Convention should influence the Defendant - Korea - despite not being a signatory to the Convention. The precise intent of the obiter dictum mentioning the Convention of the court remains somewhat unverified.

2-4. The Supreme Court Decision 2023da215500, Rendered on October 26, 2023[7]

On October 26, 2023, the Supreme Court of Korea delivered its final judgment in the prolonged legal dispute over the Object of Dispute, regarding the case among the Plaintiff, the Defendant and the Defendant's Auxiliary Participant. The court recognized that the Plaintiff and the "Buseoksa Temple of Seoju, Goryeo," where the Object of Dispute was originally made and consecrated, are indeed the same legal entity. However, despite acknowledging this error relating to the identity and continuity of the Plaintiff over centuries, the court concluded that is did not influence the ultimate outcome of the case because of adverse possession of the Defendant's Auxiliary Participant under the governing law, Japanese Civil Code. Consequently, the court upheld the second instance's decision, agreeing that the dismissal of the Plaintiff's claim was justified.

3. REVIEW OF JUDGMENT OF THIS CASE FROM THE PERSPECTIVE OF PRIVATE INTERNATIONAL LAW

3-1. Scope of the Review

This analysis will focus exclusively on the legal determinations made under private international law, deliberately excluding evaluations related to factual findings or conclusions drawn from the facts.[8]

3-2. Governing Law of Original Acquisition

Regarding the governing law of original acquisition, the judgment of the second instance court chose the perspective of the intertemporal law (or "temporal conflict of laws") although it omitted the approach on private international law.[9] The Supreme Court upheld this approach, affirming the application of the law of Goryeo, historically relevant at the time of the original acquisition. This recognition was pivotal as it aligns with the intertemporal perspective that governing laws should reflect the temporal (or "historical") contexts of the matters.[10]

On the other hand, after once selecting the historical governing law, when the law of Goryeo is unclear, the alternative choice to apply the current Civil Act of Korea — based on Article 2 of the Addenda to the Act enacted in 1958[11] — was deemed appropriate given the practical necessities.

3-3. Governing Law of Adverse Possession and Related Issues - *lex originis*, Public Policy, and Overriding Mandatory Rules

The complexities of Private International Law were thoroughly addressed in the judgments concerning adverse possession and related issues. Generally, the conclusions of both the second instance and the Supreme Court are commendable for their direct engagement with challenging questions of Private International Law.

3-3-1. *Lex originis* as an Alternative to *lex rei sitae*

In addressing the governing law of adverse possession, it is essential to first establish the governing law of ownership for chattels. Although this has been determined by the *lex rei sitae* principle, recent discussions in international cultural heritage disputes have introduced the *lex originis*, the law of country of origin as a potential alternative. This approach suggests determining the origin country based on a combination of several factors such as (1) religious values, (2) national identity of the creator, (3) where the cultural property was created, (4) where it exists as a cultural property, (5) where it was located, (6) where it was found, (7) where it was succeeded - the so-called *"rezeptionstheorie,"* (8) where it has historical relevance, and (9) where it has been designated as *res extra commercium.*[12]

The authors find many aspects of *lex originis* appealing, but also acknowledge ambiguities in application of the country of origin, such as the determination of *rezeptionstheorie* and resolving conflicts among different factors.[13] These issues likely require resolution through explicit legislative measures. Furthermore, considering its scope, *lex originis* might be more applied not as a governing law for whole property rights but as an international mandatory rule focused on cultural heritage.[14]

It is somewhat disappointing from the perspective of International Cultural Heritage Law that the courts have applied the *lex rei sitae* directly without considering *lex originis* in their decisions. However, the conclusions reached are generally acceptable within the current legal framework.

3-3-2. Public Policy

In Private International Law, the public policy doctrine is invoked based on the consequences of applying foreign law, rather than the content of the law itself.[15] Therefore, the judgments of both the second instance and the Supreme Court were appropriately grounded in principle when they rejected the Plaintiff's public policy argument. This rejection was justified by the minimal differences between the civil laws of Korea and Japan, and the identical outcomes that their application would produce.

3-3-3. Overriding Mandatory Rule

As previously discussed, *lex originis* may be applied as an international mandatory rule,[16] and the Cultural Heritage Protection Act of Korea could potentially be applied to this case as an international mandatory rule of the forum State.[17] At the very least, there is a considerable need for closer examination, and it is therefore somewhat disappointing that the courts simply stated that it is unclear whether the Cultural Heritage Protection Act of Korea is applicable in this case.

However, there is broad agreement that while the Act prohibits *bona fide* acquisition, it does not restrict adverse possession.[18] Thus, (despite some reservations about the current stance of the Act) the courts' final rulings of acknowledging adverse possession are seen as justified.

4. REMAINING ISSUES IN INTERNATIONAL CULTURAL HERIGAGE LAW AFTER THE JUDGMENT

4-1. Background

While the Supreme Court's final ruling has resolved the dispute over private ownership between the Plaintiff and the Defendant's Auxiliary Participant regarding the Object of Dispute, in principle, the broader issue of public law obligations remains unresolved.[19] Specifically, the obligations of the Defendant as a state under public international law (the UNESCO 1970 CONVENTION) and domestic administrative law (the Cultural Heritage Protection Act) require further scrutiny.

4-2. Issues Related to the UNESCO 1970 Convention

This section examines the applicability of the UNESCO 1970 Convention to the case, revealing complexities and requiring a closer analysis:

4-2-1. Article 4(b) of the Convention - "Found" within the Territory

The applicability of the UNESCO 1970 Convention hinges on whether the Object of Dispute fits within the categories defined in paragraphs (a) to (e) of Article 4, notably in paragraph (b), which provides, "cultural property found within the national territory." At first glance, one might argue that the Object of Dispute was "found" in Japan. However, the term "found" should be interpreted strictly. Historically, Article 4(f) of the Draft Convention — more fit to this case — would have covered "cultural property acquired by a State or its nationals before the entry into force of the Convention in that State" but was eventually removed.[20] In the regard, the Commentary to the UNESCO 1970 Convention indicates that "found" can be viewed as a limited term, such as when a forgotten or buried cultural property is archaeologically excavated.[21] Thus, applying Article 4(b) to this case is problematic and requires further scrutiny.

4-2-2. Article 7(b)(i) of the Convention - "Religious or Secular Public Monument or Similar Institution"

The Commentary also cautions that the scope of Article 7(b)(i) is extremely limited and questions whether "religious public monument" can be applied to small churches or temples that are objects of private worship in rural or regional areas and explains that it is unclear whether small churches and temples are even "similar institutions," although they are often targeted by thieves.[22]

The Defendant's Auxiliary Participant, Japanese Kannon temple, is known as an "unattended temple" without resident staff. Given the Commentary's limitations for Article 7(b)(i) of the UNESCO 1970 Convention, it is difficult to definitively classify the temple as a "religious 'public' monument" or a "similar institution." This situation calls for further careful review to determine if this case falls under the scope of the Convention according to the Article 7(b)(i).

4-2-3. Other Issues - Local Cultural Property and Self-Enforceability

In addition, it is necessary to examine the issues regarding the Object of Dispute as local cultural property of Japan[23] and self-enforceability of the UNESCO 1970 Convention,[24] but this paper will just introduce these issues and leave a detailed examination of them as a future task.

4-2-4. Comments

In the end, many issues or questions remain regarding the applicability of the UNESCO 1970 Convention to this case, and the authors believe that further careful review is necessary in the future. However, even if the Convention does not apply, Article 20 of the Cultural Heritage Protection Act of Korea,[25] which has a broader scope of application, may still be applicable.[26] Hence, in the next chapter, we will examine the issues that arise when Article 20 of the Cultural Heritage Protection Act of Korea is applied.

4-3. Issues Related to Article 20 of the Cultural Heritage Protection Act of Korea

4-3-1. Required Actions, or "Necessary Measures" of the Cultural Heritage Administration of Korea

If the case falls under the scope of Article 20 of the Cultural

Heritage Protection Act of Korea, it raises the question of what specific actions the Cultural Heritage Administration (hereinafter, the "CHA") is required to take. According to Article 20(2), the CHA "may" seize a cultural heritage believed to be illegally expatriated from the foreign country. Meanwhile, Article 20(5) mandates that the CHA "shall" take only "necessary measures" for returning such heritage to the relevant foreign country. Consequently, the CHA, or more broadly, Korea, has no obligation to take any specific type of action but retains wide discretion to decide which measures are necessary, guided by general principles of administrative law, such as proportionality.

In this context, to further clarity the meaning of the "necessary measures," it may be beneficial referring to the interpretation of the "appropriate steps" in Article 7(b)(2) of the UNESCO 1970 Convention, which parallels Article 20. According to the Commentary, the concept of the "appropriate steps" is quite flexible. For instance, in disputes over ownership, merely advising or guiding about necessary legal proceedings may suffice.[27] Therefore, actions taken by the Defendant in above case, such as notifying the Defendant's Auxiliary Participant through international judicial mutual assistance procedure, can be considered as fulfilling not only the "appropriate steps" of the Convention, but also the "necessary measures" stipulated by Article 20. Thus, the obligations of the Defendant derived from Article 20, are deemed to have been adequately met.

4-3-2. Relationship with "Return to Victims" in Criminal Proceedings

There have been discussions regarding the relationship between the return procedure under Article 20 of the Cultural Heritage Protection Act of Korea and the return to victims in criminal proceedings. While criminal procedures require that stolen goods be returned to victims by prosecutors, Article 20 stipulates that stolen cultural properties should be returned by the CHA. It is proposed that a special rule is needed to be legislatively created for criminally seized or confiscated cultural properties.[28]

4-3-3. Need for Further Research and Legislative Action

Apart from the State's obligations under public law to return cultural heritage, Article 20 of the Cultural Heritage Protection Act of Korea does not address how to provide just compensation to individuals in Korea with judicial rights over such properties. This lack of provision is widely regarded as a significant legislative omission or gap that needs to be corrected.[29]

Considering the limited scope of the UNESCO 1970 Convention as shown above, it is crucial to evaluate whether the scope of application of Article 20 of the Cultural Heritage Protection Act of Korea should align with the Convention. Given the discrepancies in the scope between the two, further assessment is needed to determine if legislative adjustments are warranted, especially if Korea decides to participate in the UNIDROIT 1995 Convention, which defines a broader range of return.

5. CONCLUSION

Based on the foregoing, it can be concluded that: (1) the decisions of the court of second instance and the Supreme Court in this case are highly appreciated for their thorough examination and judgment of the relevant issues on private international law; (2) the applicability of the UNESCO 1970 Convention to the subject matter of this case appears to be in need of further examination; and (3) Korea has, to date, generally adequately fulfilled its obligations and responsibilities under Article 20 of the Cultural Heritage Protection Act and has taken "necessary measures."

However, it is also true that the current norms have certain limitations, so in the short term, efforts for continuous conversation and negotiation should be pursued in addition to judicial means, and in the long term, the international community should work to develop a uniform substantive law governing the issue of pre-modern looted cultural property that predates the UNESCO 1970 Convention. Such uniform substantive law should include: (1) clear and predictable rules for determining the country of origin; (2) whether and to what extent defenses to return, such as adverse possession, should be admitted; and (3) a system for reconciling the responsibility and sovereignty of States as subjects of public (international) law.

This case raises all these issues and is highly worthy of further study. We hope that further research and efforts will lead to the realization of true restorative justice in the field of international cultural heritage law.

References

* This paper is based on the authors' Article, "A Case about the Avalokiteshvara
  Statue of Buseoksa Temple (Seoju, Goryeo) and the International Cultural
  Heritage Law" in Korean, 29(1), *Korea Private International Law Journal* (2023), and
  updates, such as the Supreme Court Decision rendered after the publication of the
  above original Korean Article, were reflected. It is important to note that the
  contents of this Article solely represent the personal and scholarly opinions of the
  authors.

Ju, Jinyul, "Analysis of International Law Issues concerning the Return of a
  14th Century Korean Buddhist Statue Stolen from a Japanese Temple," 65(2),
  The Korean Journal Of International Law (2020).

Kim, Cheonsoo, "Requirements and Procedure for Restitution of Stolen Cultural
  Objects," 15, *Korea Private International Law Journal* (2009).

Lee, Gyooho, "Current Developments in and Practices of the Korean Law
  Implementing the 1970 Convention on the Means of Prohibiting and
  Preventing the Illicit Import, Export and Transfer of Ownership of Cultural
  Property," 26(2), *Korea Private International Law Journal* (2020).

Lee, Jong Hyeok, "Private International Law Issues of the Implementation
  Legislations for the 1970 UNESCO Convention," 26(2), *Korea Private International
  Law Journal* (2020).

Lee, Keun-Gwan, "An Inquiry into the Drafting History of the 1970 UNESCO
  Convention – With Particular Reference to the Impact of the Draft
  Conventions Prepared under the Auspieces of the League of Nations in the
  1930s –," 26(2), *Korea Private International Law Journal* (2020).

Lee, Phil-Bok, "International Transaction of Cultural Heritage and Overriding
  Mandatory Provisions- Focused on the Overriding Mandatory Provisions of
  lex originis -," 27(1), *Korea Private International Law Journal* (2021).

Lee, Soon-Ok, "A Study on the Criminal Seizure and Confiscation related to
  Restitution of Cultural Properties," 24(2), *Korea Private International Law Journal*
  (2018).

Lee Won-jo, "Regrets Over the Decision to Return the Buseoksa Temple Statue
  to Japan," *Law Times*, November 2, 2023.

Lee Won-o, "Regarding the Rebuttal to 'Regrets Over the Decision to Return
  the Buseoksa Temple Statue to Japan,'" *Law Times*, December 3, 2023.

O'Keefe, Patrick J., *COMMENTARY ON THE UNESCO 1970 CONVENTION ON ILLICIT TRAFFIC,*
  2nd ed. (UK: Institute of Art and Law, 2007).

Park, Sun Ah, "A Study on Restitution of Looted Cultural Properties and Principle of Return to Original Owners," 34(3), *Hanyang Law Review* (2020).

Song, Ho Young, "A Study on the Rule of lex originis for the Cultural Properties in the International Private Law," 30(1), *The Journal of Property Law* (2013).

Song, Ho Young, "Who owns the Goryeo Buddhist Statue?," 36(1), *Hanyang Law Review* (2019).

Suk, Kwang-Hyun, *Private International Law* (Seoul: Pakyoungsa, 2013).

Suk, Kwang-Hyun, "The Role of the Private International Law Act and the Cultural Property Protection Act of Korea as Means of Protecting Cultural Property from International Illicit Transactions and the Proposal for Improvement," 56(3), Seoul Law Journal (2015).

Suk, Kwang-Hyun, "Korea's Efforts and Role in Preventing Illicit Trafficking of Cultural Properties: Including Discussions on the Concept of Cultural Properties and Cultural Heritage," 26(2), *Korea Private International Law Journal* (2020).

Suk, Kwang-Hyun, "Reading 'Regrets Over the Decision to Return the Buseoksa Temple Statue to Japan,'" *Law Times*, November 19, 2023.

Suk, Kwang-Hyun, "Reading 'Regarding the Rebuttal to 'Regrets Over the Decision to Return the Buseoksa Temple Statue to Japan,''" *Law Times*, February 7, 2024.

Notes

1. "Seoju" is a historical name of Seosan, where the Plaintiff is now situated in.
2. "Goryeo" is a medieval kingdom that existed in Korea from 918 ACE to 1392 ACE.
3. For a first discussion on the relationship between this case and the Convention, see Suk, Kwang-Hyun, "Korea's Efforts and Role in Preventing Illicit Trafficking of Cultural Properties: Including Discussions on the Concept of Cultural Properties and Cultural Heritage," 26(2), *Korea Private International Law Journal* (2020), p.256 et seq.
4. It was pursuant to Article 84 of the Civil Procedure Act of Korea.
5. For the legal basis and effect, see Articles 71, 76 and 77 of the Civil Procedure Act of Korea.
6. For the assessment of this judgment, see Ju, Jinyul, "Analysis of International Law Issues concerning the Return of a 14th Century Korean Buddhist Statue Stolen from a Japanese Temple," 65(2), *The Korean Journal Of International Law* (2020), pp.351~379; Park, Sun Ah, "A Study on Restitution of Looted Cultural Properties and Principle of Return to Original Owners," 34(3), *Hanyang Law Review* (2020), pp.325~342; and Song, Ho Young, "Who owns the Goryeo Buddhist Statue?," 36(1), *Hanyang Law Review* (2019), pp.279~313.
7. For the assessment of this judgment, particularly there are series of op-eds: see Lee Won-jo, "Regrets Over the Decision to Return the Buseoksa Temple Statue to Japan," *Law Times*, November 2, 2023; Suk, Kwang-Hyun, "Reading 'Regrets Over the Decision to Return the Buseoksa Temple Statue to Japan,'" Law Times, November 19, 2023; Lee Won-jo, "Regarding the Rebuttal to 'Regrets Over the Decision to Return the Buseoksa Temple Statue to Japan,'" Law Times, December 3, 2023; and Suk, Kwang-Hyun, "Reading 'Regarding the Rebuttal to 'Regrets Over the Decision to Return the Buseoksa Temple Statue to Japan''", Law Times, February 7, 2024.
8. In civil trials, finding of fact primarily depend on the parties' statements and evidence, hence it's challenging to validate these without accessing complete litigation records.
9. For a view that private international law is equally applicable to domestic matters, but that domestic law is designated as a result of its application, see Suk, Kwang-Hyun, *Private International Law* (Seoul: Pakyoungsa, 2013), p. 51 et seq.
10. See Suk, Kwang-Hyun (2020), op.cit., p.18.
11. This is because if a right has already arisen under the law of Goryeo prior to the enactment of the Civil Act of Korea, the right will be recognized regardless of enactment of the Act, and if a right has arisen under the enacted Civil Act, the result will be retroactive by addendum, so if the result of the right arising under the latter is recognized, as in the present case, the conclusion will be the same.

12. See Song, Ho-Young, "A Study on the Rule of *lex originis* for the Cultural Properties in the International Private Law," 30(1), *The Journal of Property Law* (2013), pp.79~109; It was the first introdunction of *lex originis* and the criteria in Korea.

13. The uncertainty of the concept of the country of origin has been pointed out as a difficult point in the application of *lex originis*, see Suk, Kwang-Hyun, "The Role of the Private International Law Act and the Cultural Property Protection Act of Korea as Means of Protecting Cultural Property from International Illicit Transactions and the Proposal for Improvement," 56(3), *Seoul Law Journal* (2015), p.136 et seq.

14. See Lee, Phil-Bok, "International Transaction of Cultural Heritage and Overriding Mandatory Provisions - Focused on the Overriding Mandatory Provisions of lex originis -," 27(1), *Korea Private International Law Journal* (2021), p.125 et seq.

15. See Suk, Kwang-Hyun, *Private International Law* (2013), op.cit., p.175 et seq.

16. See Lee, Phil-Bok (2021), op.cit.

17. See Article 20 of the Act on Private International Law of Korea.

18. See Kim, Cheonsoo, "Requirements and Procedure for Restitution of Stolen Cultural Objects," 15, *Korea Private International Law Journal* (2009), pp.230~262; and Lee, Phil-Bok (2021) op.cit., p.162.

19. For example, even if the Plaintiff is determined to be the owner of the Object of Dispute, there may still be cases where the Defendant, as a State, is obligated to return it under public law. See Ju, Jinyul (2020), op.cit.

20. See O'Keefe, Patrick J., *COMMENTARY ON THE UNESCO 1970 CONVENTION ON ILLICIT TRAFFIC, 2nd ed.* (UK: Institute of Art and Law, 2007), p.46; and Lee, Keun-Gwan, "An Inquiry into the Drafting History of the 1970 UNESCO Convention – With Particular Reference to the Impact of the Draft Conventions Prepared under the Auspieces of the League of Nations in the 1930s –," 26(2), *Korea Private International Law Journal* (2020), pp.293~342.

21. See O'Keefe (2007), op.cit., p.45 et seq.

22. See O'Keefe (2007), op.cit., p.59 et seq.

23. See contrasting views: Lee, Gyooho, "Current Developments in and Practices of the Korean Law Implementing the 1970 Convention on the Means of Prohibiting and Preventing the Illicit Import, Export and Transfer of Ownership of Cultural Property," 26(2), *Korea Private International Law Journal* (2020), pp.377~404; and Suk, Kwang-Hyun (2020), op.cit.

24. See Lee, Jong Hyeok, "Private International Law Issues of the Implementation Legislations for the 1970 UNESCO Convention," 26(2), *Korea Private International Law Journal* (2020), pp.343~376.

25. It provides the obligations or responsibilities of the State, or its organs, for returning a cultural heritage believed to be illegally expatriated from the foreign country.

26. See contrasting views: (pros) Suk, Kwang-Hyun (2020), op.cit.; and (cons) Lee, Gyooho (2020), op.cit.

27. See O'Keefe (2007), op.cit., p.60 et seq.
28. Lee, Soon-Ok, "A Study on the Criminal Seizure and Confiscation related to Restitution of Cultural Properties," 24(2), *Korea Private International Law Journal* (2018), pp.397~430.
29. For the same view, see Suk, Kwang-Hyun (2020), op.cit.

SPECIAL REPORTS

Recovering of Space Objects and Legal Status of Drop Area between Korea and Japan

Chang Wee LEE
University of Seoul

Key Words

space launch vehicle, Outer Space Treaty, Rescue Agreement, Registration Convention, Liability Convention, EEZ, JDZ

1. INTRODUCTION

On May 25, 2023, the Republic of Korea (hereinafter, "Korea") successfully launched Nuri, a Korean Space Launch Vehicle (KSLV-II), from the Naro Space Center in Goheung, South Jeolla Province. With the successful launch of Nuri, Korea became one of the world's seven major space powers. The launch of space objects requires a number of issues to be examined under international law, including the recovery of the propellant, the legal status of the drop area, issues of ownership and jurisdiction over the vehicle, and the concentration of State responsibility for space activities.

Korean space launch vehicle debris typically falls in the intermediate zone of the East China Sea or around areas considered to be part of Japan's exclusive economic zone (EEZ). The phrase "areas considered to be EEZ" is defined in the 1998 Korea-Japan Fisheries Agreement.[1] The areas where the maritime boundaries have not been delimited are referred to as the intermediate zones, and the other areas outside the intermediate zones stipulated in the fisheries agreement are called the "areas considered to be EEZ."

In this context, this paper will review and analyze the relevant international law issues that accompany the launch of space vehicles. In particular, it will focus on several issues that are jointly related to space law and the law of the sea. Specifically, it will analyze the law of the sea issues on the drop area of space objects, and the integration of space law and municipal law issues of registration, and management and regulation of space launch vehicles. The allocation of national jurisdiction is significant because the ocean and space are areas where international law and municipal law intersect.

2. DROP AREA OF SPACE OBJECTS

2-1. Legal Status of the EEZ

The legal status of the EEZ and Japan's position on the matter are of significant importance when Korean space launch vehicle debris falls into the intermediate zone or areas considered to be part of Japan's EEZ. First, we need to look at the EEZ issue under the provisions of the United Nations Convention on the Law of the Sea (LOSC). The provisions of the LOSC regarding the legal status of the EEZ are not clear.[2] The Convention states that th EEZ is an area beyond and adjacent to the territorial sea, subject to the specific legal regime set forth in the Convention, under which the rights and jurisdiction of the coastal State, and the rights and freedom of other States are governed by the relevant provisions of the Convention.[3]

Specifically, in the EEZ, coastal States exercise a wide range of rights, including sovereign rights to explore, exploit, conserve, and manage the natural resources of the waters superjacent to the seabed, and of the seabed and its subsoil; sovereign rights to engage in other activities for the economic exploitation and exploration of the zone, such as the production of energy from the water, currents, and winds; and jurisdiction over the establishment and use of artificial islands, installations, and structures, marine scientific research, and the protection and preservation of the marine environment.[4] However, the rights exercised by a coastal State in the EEZ are of a limited nature, unlike sovereignty in the territorial sea.

The launching State of a space launch vehicle is not subject to restrictions on flights over the EEZ. All States shall enjoy freedom of navigation and overflight as well as freedom of the laying of submarine cables and pipelines in the EEZs. They also shall enjoy and other internationally lawful uses of the sea related to these freedoms, such as those associated with the operation of ships, aircraft, and submarine cables and pipelines, and compatible with the other provisions of this Convention.[5] The freedom of the use of the sea provided for herein refers to the freedom of the high seas as set forth in Article 87 and has been recognized since the 1958 Convention on the High Seas.

Among the traditional freedom of the high seas, fisheries and marine scientific research were excluded because they fell under the jurisdiction of the coastal state of the EEZ. However, the freedom of navigation and overflight were bound to survive in the EEZ because they relate to the vital use of the oceans by all States. Of course, unlike the freedom of the high seas, the freedom of navigation and overflight in the EEZ of other States may be limited to a certain extent by the relevant provisions of the Convention. Thus, issues may arise where the freedom of overflight of a space launching State may conflict with the jurisdiction or sovereign rights of a coastal State.

2-2. Competing Rights and Jurisdictions

If a Korean space launch vehicle were to fall into areas considered to be part of Japan's EEZ, it would raise the issue of competing rights between Japan and other States or third parties in the EEZ. The LOSC provides guidance for such cases, namely, that when rights and jurisdiction are not clearly allocated or attributed to both the coastal State and the other State by the relevant provisions, equity, and consideration of relevant circumstances shall be the standard for resolving the dispute, as follows:

"Basis for the resolution of conflicts regarding the attribution of rights and jurisdiction in the exclusive economic zone."

In cases where this Convention does not attribute rights or jurisdiction to the coastal State or to other States within the exclusive economic zone, and a conflict arises between the interests of the coastal State and any other State or States, the conflict should be resolved on the basis of equity and in the light of all the relevant circumstances, taking into account the respective importance of the interests involved to the parties as well as to the international community as a whole."[6]

The settlement of disputes under this article was proposed at the Third United Nations Conference on the Law of the Sea (UNCLOS III) as the Castaneda formula. The original proponent, Ambassador Castaneda, proposed it as a basis for resolving controversial attributions of rights, such as military activities in the EEZ. When maritime powers and coastal States were unable to reach an agreement on the legal nature of the EEZ and the corresponding rights, the formula was adopted to resolve the conflict.[7]

Whether it is certain military activities or the overflight of space vehicles, conduct that is difficult to attribute to a coastal State or to a third State and that involves disputes can, in principle, be resolved through the dispute settlement procedures provided for in Part XV of the LOSC. However, the compulsory settlement procedure, which entails binding decisions under the Convention, is subject to limitations and exceptions to its application, allowing for the exclusion of the procedure by a Party.[8]

In such cases, the Convention provides for the peaceful settlement of disputes between the Parties, and such vaguely existing rights are referred to as residual rights. It is envisioned that this provision will apply not only to military uses, but also to new uses of the ocean, such as navigation and overflight, resulting from advances in science and technology.[9]

Although the EEZ was introduced in the 1982 United Nations Convention on the Law of the Sea, the legal status of the air space over those areas remained largely unchanged. While the EEZ included vast areas outside the territorial sea, it did not impose any new restrictions on the traditional freedom of overflight recognized above it. There is no exclusion of military activities or military use of the air space. Space launch vehicles may also fall into this category, as their purpose may be of a military nature. In exercising their rights and performing their duties under the Convention in the EEZ, States shall have due regard to the rights and duties of the coastal State and shall comply with the laws and regulations adopted by the coastal State in accordance with the provisions of the Convention and other rules of international law.[10]

In any case, the most difficult question that arises today regarding the EEZ regime is that of residual rights. The lack of consensus at the UNCLOS III was due to the differing positions of the maritime powers and the coastal States group on the issue. The coastal States generally believed that such residual rights belonged to the coastal States, while the maritime powers took the position that such rights belonged to the international community as a whole. In particular, developing countries have expressed their position on the attribution of residual rights to coastal States through declarations when signing or acceding to the LOSC.[11]

It is worth noting that the LOSC provides that the conflicts should be resolved in accordance with equity and in the light of all relevant circumstances, taking into account the respective importance of the interests involved to the parties as well as to the international community as a whole.[12] Korea should argue that the issue of the passage and overflight of space launch vehicle, and drop of space objects should be approached in the light of the interests of the international community as a whole, rather than the interests of coastal States.

2-3. Japan's EEZ and Maritime Boundary Delimitation

Japan has long been a leading maritime power in support of freedom of the seas. Of the 1958 Law of the Sea Conventions, Japan acceded to the Convention on the Territorial Sea and the Contiguous Zone (CTS) and the Convention on the High Seas (CHS), but the Convention on Fishing and Conservation of the Living Resources of the High Seas (CFCLR) or the Convention on the Continental Shelf (CCS).[13] At the UNCLOS III, Japan was dubbed "Mr. Except One" for its steadfast opposition to the EEZ proposal.[14]

However, as the extension of maritime jurisdiction became a trend in the late 1970s, Japan responded with the "Law on the Territorial Sea" and the "Law on the Provisional Measures in the Fishing Areas," which extended the breadth of the territorial sea and fishing areas to 12 nautical miles and 200 nautical miles, respectively. Following the entry into force of the LOSC in 1994, Japan introduced the EEZ with the enactment of the "EEZ and Continental Shelf Law" in 1996. Japan further institutionalized the exercise of its jurisdiction in the EEZ by enacting the "Act on the Exercise of Sovereign Rights in Fisheries in the EEZ" and the "Act on the Conservation and Management of Marine Living Resources."

The "Fisheries Resources Protection Act," the "Nuclear Materials and Reactors Regulation Act," and the "Coast Guard Act" have also been amended.[15]

Regarding the management and operation of the EEZ, Japan regulates the preservation of the marine environment and marine scientific research through separate laws and systems. For the former, there is the "Law Relating to the Prevention of Marine Pollution and Maritime Disaster," and for the latter, there is the "Guidelines for Conducting Marine Scientific Research." Japan has not defined the concept of marine scientific research in the guidelines. As an advanced maritime nation, it views marine scientific research as an important part of the freedom of the seas.[16]

Japan's detailed definition of its jurisdiction in the EEZ indicates that it intends to exercise the jurisdiction thoroughly. When other countries exercise residual rights in Japan's EEZ, it is important to fully understand Japan's policy and respond accordingly. In this context, it is also necessary to understand the issue of maritime boundary delimitation, which is the agreement between countries on the scope of Japan's EEZ or the areas considered to be part of Japan's EEZ.

Japan insists on the application of the equidistance principle to its maritime boundary delimitation. Japan's domestic law recognizes that its EEZ includes the continental shelf and states that the equidistance principle should be applied to both. Japan's position has been publicly stated since the early days of the UNCLOS III.[17] Japan insisted on the equidistance principle because the seabed topography off its coast is unfavorable to maritime boundary delimitation if the theory of "natural prolongation" is applied.[18]

Japan is currently advocating for the equidistance principle in maritime boundary delimitation between States with opposite coasts, Korea and China. Korea does not oppose the use of the equidistance principle in the East Sea but opposes the application of the equidistance principle in the East China Sea. Japan and Korea have not been able to agree on the delimitation of the continental shelf and have shelved the maritime boundary delimitation in the 1978 Joint Development Agreement on the Continental Shelf.[19] Japan can give notice of termination of the Agreement in 2025, three years before it ends, so a potential conflict could erupt between Korea and Japan at any time. Therefore, it is important to approach the issue of space objects drops carefully and without affecting such issues.

2-4. Legal Status of the Intermediate Zone in the East China Sea

The two States were also unable to agree on the delimitation of the EEZ in the East Sea and East China Sea (South Sea), and the 1998 New Korea-Japan Fisheries Agreement established two intermediate zones. In the East Sea, Dokdo was a stumbling block, but in the East China Sea, disagreement over the principle of maritime boundary delimitation was a serious impediment. In the East China Sea, the intermediate zone agreed upon by Korea and Japan is included in the drop area for Korean space objects.

It is likely that the drop area of space objects separated from a space launch vehicle will be the intermediate zone or areas considered to be part of Japan's EEZ to the right of it, as described above. This raises several issues that need to be examined closely. For example, the legal status and nature of such areas and the impact on maritime boundary delimitation with Japan would need to be fully analyzed to address the issues involved in dropping of space objects.

In their Fisheries Agreement, Korea and Japan did not describe the name of the intermediate zone, but only its coordinates. Korea refers to it as an intermediate zone and Japan, as a provisional zone.[20] Japan refers to the intermediate zone of the East Sea as the Northern provisional zone and the intermediate zone of the East China Sea, as the Southern provisional zone.[21]

Japan views the intermediate zone as an area in which both countries jointly manage their fisheries resources.[22] Although the authority of the Joint Fisheries Commission is not the same in the two intermediate zones, Japan said that it is considered to have joint conservation management measures for fishery resources.[23] The Japanese government also officially recognizes the two zones as jointly managed areas.[24] Some experts have not taken the same position as the Japanese government and have reserved judgment.[25]

Unlike Japan, Korea does not think that the joint conservation management measures apply to the intermediate zone of the East Sea. However, it considers that the joint conservation management measures apply to the intermediate zone of the East China Sea. Of course, such joint management is limited to the exploitation and conservation of fishery resources and should be approached separately from the issue of space launch vehicles.[26] Therefore, even if space objects were to fall, Korea's preferential rights would be recognized. However, there may be some problems if the drop area is part of those areas considered to be Japan's EEZ.

Although Korea and Japan jointly fish in the intermediate zone of the East China Sea, both countries exercise enforcement jurisdiction over fishing vessels under their respective flag State jurisdiction. However, since neither country has any influence on international legal issues other than fisheries under the Fisheries Agreement, the issue of the fall of space objects needs to be approached separately.[27] In other words, this issue should be analyzed by examining the manner and structure of the exercise of rights and the fulfillment of obligations by coastal States and other States in the EEZ.

3. JURISDICTION OVER SPACE LAUNCH VEHICLES

3-1. Freedom of Space Activities and Prohibition of Territorial Claims to Space

The Space Treaty stipulates that the exploration and use of outer space, including the moon and other celestial bodies, shall be carried out for the benefit and in the interests of all countries, irrespective of their degree of economic or scientific development, and shall be the province of all mankind.[28] This means that every State has the right to conduct space activities without the permission or consent of any other State and without any interference. This is interpreted to mean that no State may exercise jurisdiction or take any other action in such a way as to interfere with or deny the space activities of space objects carried out by other States, including brief transits through their airspace. Thus, all States enjoy the freedom of unimpeded space activities.

No state can claim sovereignty over outer space, including celestial bodies. The fact that space is not subject to sovereignty has been established by state practice from the earliest days of space activities. For example, no State has ever protested the passage of satellites, rockets, or other space vehicles over its territory on the grounds of airspace sovereignty.[29]

With this rapid creation of customary international law, the Outer Space Treaty articulated the principle of non-possession, stating that "the outer space, including the moon and other celestial bodies, is not subject to national appropriation by claim of sovereignty, by means of use or occupation, or by any other means."[30] This is one of the most important principles of the Outer Space Treaty, stating that States cannot claim sovereignty over outer space and other celestial bodies.

3-2. Registration, Control, and Jurisdiction over Space Objects

The Outer Space Treaty provides that a State party to the treaty on whose registry an object launched into outer space is carried shall retain jurisdiction and control over such object, and over any personnel thereof, while in outer space or on a celestial body.[31] The term "jurisdiction" in the treaty refers to the power under international law of a State to apply and exercise its domestic law specifically to a particular class of persons, property or facts. The term "control" shall be construed to refer to the actions of a registered State in supervising and managing the technical condition of a space object.[32]

In practice, the activities of States for the purpose of exploring and utilizing outer space and celestial bodies are carried out through satellites and other "space objects." No State can claim control of outer space or celestial bodies as its territory due to the prohibition of territorial claims to space set forth in the Outer Space Treaty.[33] Therefore, the country of origin of an individual space object should exercise control and jurisdiction over it. In this sense and context, the principle of exclusive State supervision, control, and jurisdiction over certain space objects is crucial to the order of space law. In any case, the launching State has absolute and permanent ownership of a particular space object.

However, the Outer Space Treaty does not apply the concept of "nationality" to space objects. This was done to avoid the exclusive attribution of space objects to a particular State. The exclusion of the concept of nationality is reasonable and justified, even when considering cases such as the joint launch of space objects. Therefore, the treaty does not directly address the registration process or requirements for space objects. States can handle these issues at their discretion.

In this regard, the Convention on Registration of Objects

Launched into Outer Space (Registration Convention) requires that States Parties to the Convention register detailed specifications for space objects and inform the Secretary-General of the United Nations of the establishment of such a registry.[34] However, this does not establish the nationality of the space object, so the issue of the "genuine link" between the State of registration and the space object does not arise as it does for ships.[35]

The active application of jurisdiction, management, and control over such space objects is ultimately intended to strongly recognize and protect the exclusive rights of a particular State to the space objects. It means that the absolute ownership and jurisdiction of the launching or registering State is recognized, regardless of whether the space object exists in the outer space, celestial bodies, airspace, high seas, or the territory of another State. Therefore, no matter where a Korean space object falls or exists, it is owned by Korea under international space law.

3-3. The Rescue Agreement

The Rescue Agreement of 1968 supplements the Outer Space Treaty on international cooperation in space activities. The full name of the treaty is the Agreement on the Rescue of Astronauts, the Return of Astronauts and the Return of Objects Launched into Outer Space. The preamble emphasizes the assistance and international cooperation for astronauts provided for in Article 5 of the Outer Space Treaty. The Agreement requires contracting parties to provide the launching authority and the Secretary-General of the United Nations with information on astronauts in accidents or distress in their territory, on the high seas or in other international areas.[36] Contracting parties are obliged to safely and expeditiously return any personnel of a spacecraft found in such places. They are also obliged to take measures to rescue and provide necessary assistance to any personnel in an accident, distress, emergency or unintended landing.[37] It stipulates the cooperation and allocation of powers between the contracting parties and launching States.[38]

The Rescue Agreement stipulates that contracting parties have the same obligations with respect to space objects as they do with respect to astronauts in accidents or distress. With regard to the recovery or return of space objects such as launch vehicle or its component parts, the following provisions should be noted. These provisions are of utmost importance in the event of the recovery of fallen Korean space objects.

Firstly, each contracting party which receives information or discovers that a space object or its component parts has returned to Earth in territory under its jurisdiction or on the high seas or in any other place not under the jurisdiction of any State, shall notify the launching authority and the secretary general of the United Nations.[39]

Next, each contracting party having jurisdiction over the territory on which a space object or its component parts has been discovered shall, upon the request of the launching authority and with assistance from that authority if requested, take such steps as it finds practicable to recover the object or component parts.[40] This means that the State in whose territory the space object is found is obliged to recover and deliver it to the launching State upon request of the State. The costs of recovery and delivery are borne by the launching State.

And then, upon request of the launching authority, objects launched into outer space, or their component parts found beyond the territorial limits of the launching authority shall be returned to or held at the disposal of representatives of the launching authority, which shall, upon request, furnish identifying data prior to their return.[41]

For the purposes of this agreement, the term "launching authority" shall refer to the State responsible for launching, or where an international organization is responsible for launching, that organization, provided that that organization declares its acceptance of the rights and obligations provided for in this agreement and a majority of the States members of that organization are contracting parties to this agreement and to the Outer Space Treaty.[42]

Since the contracting parties are responsible for the return of space objects under the provisions of the Rescue Agreement as described above, the issue of the return of Korea's space object should be viewed in that context. Korea and Japan ratified the agreement in April 1969 and June 1983, respectively, and are currently contracting parties. As such, both countries are obligated to comply with the agreement with respect to the issue of return of space objects. Korea's domestic law, the Space Development Promotion Act, also stipulates this.[43]

4. CONCLUSION

The successful launch of Nuri raises several legal issues that span the law of the sea and space law, including the recovery of the space objects separated from the vehicle, the legal status of the drop area, and issues of ownership and jurisdiction over the vehicle. The issue of space objects or components falling in or around the intermediate zone of the East China Sea can be approached from three perspectives.

First, the issue can be analyzed in terms of the competing rights or jurisdiction between coastal States and other States in the EEZ under the law of the sea. The question is how the recovery of a space object or its components can be assessed in light of the legal nature of the EEZ or continental shelf. This issue can be understood as an extension of the flight of space objects over the EEZ. While issues may arise over the recognition of residual rights of coastal

States and other States, it is unlikely that space objects are subject to sovereign rights or jurisdiction in a coastal State's EEZ. However, the possibility of damage to the marine environment from space objects cannot be ruled out. The legal status of space objects should be understood in the context of freedom of overflight and space activities in the EEZ.

Next, it is necessary to review the legal nature of the space object and possibility of conflicts between its jurisdiction and ownership. The principles of space law on this issue are relatively clear, and there are a number of State practices that prove this. A space object is subject to the exclusive jurisdiction and control of a State once it has completed the domestic registration process and notified and registered with the relevant international organizations.[44] As a result, all State responsibilities associated with the launch of space objects and space activities are concentrated on that nation.[45] To paraphrase, the registration or launch country hold jurisdiction and control over space objects, regardless of whether they are in the territory or areas of any other country.[46] Therefore, if a Korean space object or its components fall into areas considered to be part of Japan's EEZ, there would be no legal problem in recovering them. A coastal State cannot claim jurisdiction or ownership over another country's space object or its components in its EEZ.

In addition, the legal status of the intermediate zone of the East China Sea and the impact of the space object issue will need to be examined. This is an area where neither Korea nor Japan have agreed on maritime delimitation of their EEZs or continental shelves. Therefore, both countries should approach the issue of space launch vehicles carefully. It is important to make every effort to enter provisional arrangements of a practical nature and not to jeopardize or hamper the reaching of the final agreement.[47]

The issue of space objects should be approached with a comprehensive understanding of the law of the sea and space law.

The principles of the law of the sea and aviation law, which allocate jurisdiction to ships and aircrafts according to their registration and nationality, can be applied by analogy to space law. In this context, it is important for Korea and Japan to coordinate and resolve competing jurisdictions over space objects through international law and negotiation.

Notes

1. Korea-Japan Fisheries Agreement of 1998 Article 7, Annex Ⅱ Article 1.

2. F. Orrego Vicuña, *The Exclusive Economic Zone*, Cambridge Studies in International and Comparative Law - New Series, Cambridge University Press, Cambridge, 1989, pp.16~48.

3. LOSC Article 55.

4. LOSC Article 56.

5. LOSC Article 58.

6. LOSC Article 59.

7. David Joseph Attard, *The Exclusive Economic Zone in International Law*, Oxford: Clarendon Press; New York: Oxford University Press, 1987, pp.63~65.

8. LOSC Article 297, Article 298.

9. Barbara Kwiatkowska, *The 200 Mile Exclusive Economic Zone in the New Law of the Sea*, Dordrecht, Boston, London: Martinus Nijhoff Publishers, 1989, pp.227~228.

10. LOSC Article 58, paragraph 3.

11. Barbara Kwiatkowska, *op. cit.*, pp.228~229.

12. LOSC Article 59.

13. Ko Nakamura, "UN Convention on the Law of the Sea and Basic Law of the Sea," *Jurist* No.1096, pp.34~35.

14. Tadao Kuribayashi, *Modern International Law*, Keio University Press, 1999, pp.291~292.

15. Tadao Kuribayashi, "The Development of the Law of the Sea and Japan," *Japan and 100 Years of International Law*, Vol 3 2001, p.13.

16. Atsuko Kanehara, "MSR in the Areas Where Claims of the EEZ Overlap between Japan and Korea in 2006-, *JAIL* No.49 (2006), pp.104~105.

17. Chiyuki Mizukami, *Japan and the Law of the Sea*, Yushindo, 1995, p.121.

18. Kyoko Hamakawa, "Boundary Delimitation between Japan and China in the East China Sea," National Diet Library ISSUE BRIEF NUMBER 547 (JUN 16, 2006), pp.3~7.

19. Sookyon Heo, "Joint Development of the Continental Shelf in the Areas near Boundary," *Jurist* No.1365 (October 15, 2008).

20. Jong Wha Choi, *Modern History of Fisheries Relation between Korea and Japan*, Sejong Publishing Company 2000, p.367.

21. Shigeki Sakamoto, "New Japan-Korea Fisheries Agreement," *Seoul International Law Review*, Vol. 6, No. 1, 1999, pp.61~63.

22. Tadao Kuribayashi, *Modern International Law*, Keio University Press, 1999, pp.291~292.

23. Kiminobu Fukamachi, "*Fisheries Relation between Korea and Japan*," *Modern Law of the Sea*, Yushindo, 2003, p.21.

24. Chosunilbo September 26, 1998.

25. Kentaro Serita, *Territoriality of Islands and Boundary Delimitation of the EEZ*, Yushindo, 1999, pp.246~248.
26. Korea-Japan Fisheries Agreement of 1998 Article 7, Annex I , Article 3.
27. Korea-Japan Fisheries Agreement of 1998 Article 15.
28. Outer Space Treaty Article 1.
29. Tadao Kuribayashi, *Modern International Law*, Keio University Press, 1999, pp.366~367.
30. Outer Space Treaty Article 2.
31. Outer Space Treaty Article 8.
32. Tadao Kuribayashi, *Modern International Law*, Keio University Press, 1999, pp.368~369.
33. Outer Space Treaty Article 2.
34. Registration Convention Article 2, paragraph 1.
35. Tadao Kuribayashi, *Documents of Space Law*, Keio University Press, 1995, pp.34~35.
36. Rescue Agreement Article 1.
37. Rescue Agreement Articles 2 and 4.
38. Rescue Agreement Article 2.
39. Rescue Agreement Article 5, paragraph 1.
40. Rescue Agreement Article 5, paragraph 2.
41. Rescue Agreement Article 5, paragraph 3.
42. Rescue Agreement Article 6.
43. Space Development Promotion Act Article 23.
44. Registration Convention Article 3, Article 4.
45. Outer Space Treaty Article 6.
46. Outer Space Treaty Article 8.
47. LOSC Article 74.

International Legal Review of Japan's Invasion of Dokdo and History of Japanese Colonialism

See-Hwan DOH
Director General of Office of Dokdo Research and Public Relations
Northeast Asian History Foundation, Seoul, Korea

Key Words

International Law, Korea's sovereignty over Dokdo, invasion of Dokdo, 1905 Korea-Japan Protective Treaty, the Daijokan directive, International Law Journal, Japanese colonialism, occupation of *terra nullius,* inherent territory, Japanese Society of International Law, The Temporary Investigation Committee of the Ministry of Foreign Affairs

1. INTRODUCTION

This year marks the 120th anniversary of the Russo-Japanese War and the 130th anniversary of the Sino-Japanese War, both provoked by Japan. Furthermore, we are just around the corner for 2025, the 120th anniversary of Japan's invasion of Dokdo, a symbol of the territorial sovereignty of the Republic of Korea (hereinafter, "Korea"), and the forced signing of the 1905 Japan-Korea Protective

Treaty.[1]

Against this background, it is necessary to pay attention to two recent studies reported in relation to the Japanese Society of International Law. First, the Takeshima documents study group, which has claimed Japan's sovereignty over Korea's Dokdo, is openly researching the Daijokan directive, which can be said to be the Achilles' heel of its sovereignty claim over Dokdo.[2] Second, the issue of the theory of protectorate related to the Korea-Japan Treaty of 1905, which has been debated several times and remains controversial, is being discussed again.

The former seeks to advance the theory of occupation of *terra nullius* on Dokdo in 1905 by denying and discrediting the legal validity of the 1877 Daijokan directive, while the latter is notable in that the protectorate debates between Nagano Ariga and Sakutaro Tachi share a common denominator of support for Japanese expansionism, but are critical of Sakutaro Tachi's harsh arguments for Korean colonization, which moved toward Japanese-style legal realism.[3] Ultimately, the key themes of both are not only oriented towards 2025, but also led by the Japanese Society of International Law.

On this premise, when I examine the state practice of Japan, a late-imperialist country, before and after the invasion of Dokdo in 1905, I can see that it was building a legal foundation for international law in foreign policy by mobilizing the Japanese Society of International Law, established in March 1897. The Japanese Society of International Law was established mainly by international law faculty from Tokyo Imperial University and the Army and Naval Universities, and working-level officials from the Ministry of Foreign Affairs also participated.

On the surface, the Japanese Society of International Law presented its purpose as academic research into international law, but in reality, its true purpose was to utilize international law as a tool to adjust interests between imperialist countries.

Moreover, seriously, the Japanese Society of International Law is problematic in that it has taken the lead in presenting a paper that seeks not to simply justify or legalize Japan's foreign policy, specifically the policy of aggression against Korea, after the fact, but to proactively develop a policy and logic of invasion and urge its realization.

The "International Law Journal," published since February 1902, contains many discussions about the Japanese government's policy of invading Korea, especially before the Korean Empire's declaration of neutrality on January 21, 1904, and the forced annexation on August 22, 1910. Even taking into account the time it takes to publish in academic journals, the distortion of international legal principles through treaty coercion related to Korea's protectorate status and forced annexation were presented several years in advance and insisted on their realization.

However, ultimately, even though international law before and after 1905 was at a point where Japanese-style legal positivism as an extreme form of nationalism associated with aggressive state practices was in decline and the normativity of universal international norms was being enhanced, it went directly against this and was used as an argument for invasion. We cannot help but point out that the mobilization of international law itself is an illegal act that is invalid under international law.

At this point, it is urgent to identify the distortion of international law principles based on Japanese colonialism of the Temporary Investigation Committee of the Ministry of Foreign Affairs linked to the Japanese Society of International Law, which provided the international legal basis for the aggression policy against Korea. The Japanese government concealed the Temporary Investigation Committee of the Ministry of Foreign Affairs, which existed from March 1904 to February 1906, and referred to it as an institution established solely to investigate the theory of protectorate.

However, it is worth noting that its duration not only coincides with the period of Dokdo's invasion and treaty coercion in 1905 but also its members were international law scholars who led the theory of subsequent forced annexation after the denial of the Korean Empire's neutrality declaration.

2. INTERNATIONAL LEGAL PROBLEMS IN THE GENEALOGY OF THE CLAIMS TO DOKDO BY THE JAPANESE SOCIETY OF INTERNATIONAL LAW

The Japanese territorial sovereignty exhibition hall, which was reopened in 2020, the 120th anniversary of Korea's declaration of sovereignty over Dokdo, asserts Japan's legal domination of Dokdo under international law and Korea's illegal occupation of Dokdo since 1905, and openly reopens the attempt to make original title under international law on the theory of occupation of terra nullius on Dokdo in 1905.

Prior to that, the Japanese government resumed the theory of occupation of terra nullius by mobilizing the 1951 Rusk Letter, which was only released to Japan in 1978 by the publication of the U.S. foreign documents, including the note verbales filed with the Korean government, to neutralize the peace line declaration on January 18, 1952, issued by the Korean government to protect the sovereignty over Dokdo. On such premises, I have reviewed the legal problems and traced the genealogy of the study on the legal principle of titles of the Japanese Society of International Law, which is establishing the policy basis for Japan's claim to Dokdo based on Japanese colonialism.

Through this, I confirmed the genealogy of the study of the title to Dokdo in the Japanese Society of International Law leads to

"Theory of historical title" by Takeshi Minagawa, "Theory of original title" by Toshio Ueda, "Theory of substitutional title" by Kanae Daijudo, and "Theory of commonable title" by Gentaro Serita. And I reviewed "Theory of effective title" by Yoshio Hirose based on the View of History on International Law, the epitome of the lineage of research on titles to Dokdo's sovereignty.

After the "the theory of effective title" by Yoshio Hirose, international legal scholar such as Takashi Tsukamoto[4] and Tetsuya Nakano,[5] who appear as mainstream researchers, are all classified as genealogy of "the theory of original title on terra nullis" and are in line with the claims of the Territorial Sovereignty Exhibition Hall.

At this point, the Japanese government, which had been claiming the theory of occupation of terra nullius as an international legal principle for the invasion of Dokdo since 1905, submitted a note verbale to the Korean government in 1962 to replace the flaws in international law as its original title. However, since the Ulleungdo dispute began in 1693 with the abduction of Yong-bok Ahn, it was impossible to establish a historical title based on the 17th century inherent territory theory,[6] given the Edo Shogunate's prohibition of crossing the sea in 1696 and the Dajokan Directive of 1877. In this regard, I identified the problem of resuming the San Francisco Peace Treaty and the theory of occupation of *terra nullius,* which is being mobilized by the Japanese government and the Japanese Society of International Law.

First, the territorial provisions of the San Francisco Peace Treaty, which specified Dokdo as Korean territory until the fifth draft, were changed from the Seabald Opinion dated November 19, 1949, to Japanese territory in the sixth draft, and Dokdo was not only omitted from the final draft after the seven draft, but the Japanese Territorial Reference Map prepared by the Japanese Maritime Security Agency in August 1951 in the process of requesting the Japanese Parliament's consent to ratify the treaty, also indicated Dokdo as

Korean territory.

Second, the Rusk Letter of August 10, 1951, which claims that the Japanese government has had jurisdiction over the Dokdo since 1905, is based on a false document provided by Japan, but was not disclosed to the Japanese government as a secret document that was later published in the April 28, 1978, U.S. Foreign Relations file, which is a typical distortion of not only historical facts but also international law principles.

Moreover, in the research of title by the Japanese Society of International Law, the advocates on the theory of occupation of *terra nullius* such as Toshio Ueda, Kanae Taijudo, Yoshio Hirose, and Takashi Tsukamoto argue that, with regard to the time of Korea's independence in Article 2(a) of the San Francisco Peace Treaty, Dokdo became Japanese territory prior to the forced annexation of Korea in 1910, and is Japanese territory acquired on the basis of the doctrine of *terra nullius* in 1905.

Therefore, in addition to the temporal categories of World War I and the Sino-Japanese War in the Cairo Declaration, it is a question of whether Dokdo is included in the Korean territory before 1910 as the essence of territorial aggression of "violence and greed," and it boils down to the question of the legality and legitimacy of Japan's invasion of Dokdo in 1905.[7]

After all, this is a matter of legal distortion of historical facts, which Japan claims to be legitimate because Japan's 1905 invasion of Dokdo took place before Japan's forced annexation of Korea in 1910, which Japan arbitrarily set up. But it should be noted that not only is Japan's invasion of Dokdo itself illegal, but also that the Japanese invasion of Korea began on February 6, 1904, just before the outbreak of the Russo-Japanese War on February 8, 1904.[8]

3. THE AGGRESSION POLICY AGAINST KOREA OF THE TEMPORARY INVESTIGATION COMMITTEE OF THE MINISTRY OF FOREIGN AFFAIRS LINKED TO THE JAPANESE SOCIETY OF INTERNATIONAL LAW

3-1. The Aggression Policy against Korea's Sovereignty of the Japanese Society of International Law

Before and after the 1905 Japan's invasion of Korea's sovereignty over Dokdo, Japan, a late-imperialist country, mobilized the Japanese Society of International Law, founded on March 4, 1897, to establish the legal basis of international law in its aggressive foreign policy. The Japanese Society of International Law was the first to organize and implement interconnection between Japanese Ministry of Foreign Affairs and international law scholars on the premise of the close relation between Japan's foreign policy and international law.

Regarding the purpose of the establishment of the Japanese Society of International Law, it is suggested that "In order to meet the demands of a new era in which Japan became a great power in the East as a result of the Sino-Japanese War and joined the Family of Nations as a complete independent country with the revision of the treaty, it is intended to (1) study international law, (2) disseminate international knowledge, and (3) study the revised treaty."

Although the Japanese Society of International Law ostensibly aims to advance the academic study of international law and promote the principles of justice and humanitarianism in human society based on the premise of international law, its true purpose was to utilize international law as a tool to reconcile the interests of imperialist countries in the colonial struggle, starting with the invasion of

Dokdo, which was confirmed in the process of invading Korea's sovereignty and invading the continent.

Moreover, the Japanese Society of International Law has taken the position of not merely justifying or legalizing Japan's policy of aggression against Korea as part of Japan's foreign policy after the fact, but rather proactively developing the policy and logic of invasion and urging its realization. This is confirmed in a number of papers published in the International Law Journal since February 1902. These are international legal discussions that lead the Japanese government's policy of aggression against Korea.[9]

The list of members of the Japanese Society of International Law was published in the first issue of the "International Law Journal," published in February 1902, and is as follows.[10]

〈Members of the Journal〉
Tomizu Hirondo, Professor of Roman Law, Faculty of Law, Tokyo University
Sakuye Takahashi, Professor of Public International Law, Faculty of Law, Tokyo University
Shingo Nakamura, Professor, Kakushuin University
Tetsukichi Kurachi, Ministry of Foreign Affairs
Saburo Yamada, Professor of Private International Law, Faculty of Law, Tokyo University
Tadao Yamakawa, Counselor, Navy
Matsunami Niichiro, Professor of Commercial Law, Faculty of Law, Tokyo University
Hidei Fukuoka, Professor of International Law, Tokyo University of Foreign Studies
Toru Terao, Professor of International Law, Faculty of Law, Tokyo University of Economics
Nagao Ariga, Professor of International Law, Army·Navy University

Toyoji Kafuku, Staff Attorney, Judicial Affairs Office
Harukazu Nagaoka, Counselor, the Ministry of Foreign Affairs,
Bachelor of Laws, Executive Secretary

⟨Councilors⟩
Nobushige Hozumi, Professor, Faculty of Law, Tokyo University
of Economics
Yatsuka Hozumi, Professor, Faculty of Law, Tokyo University
Toru Terao, Professor, Faculty of Law, Tokyo University
Tomizu Hirondo, Professor, Tokyo University
Nagao Ariga, Professor of International Law, Army·Navy
University

3-2. Identification on the Substance of the Temporary Investigation Committee of the Ministry of Foreign Affairs, a Confidential Organization

It is an urgent task to investigate the distortion of international
law based on Japanese colonialism by the Temporary Investigation
Committee of the Ministry of Foreign Affairs, which was concealed
by Japan in connection with the Japanese Society of International
Law, which provided the international legal basis for its aggression
against Korea.

The Temporary Investigation Committee of the Ministry of
Foreign Affairs, which existed in secret from March 1904 to
February 1906, was referred to as an organization established for the
purpose of investigating the theory of protection, but it is an
organization that legally established the aggression policy against
Korea based on Japanese colonialism.

Moreover, it is worth noting that its period of existence not only
coincides with the exact time of the invasion of Dokdo and the
coercion of treaty in 1905, but its members are also leading the

subsequent forced annexation theory, so a legal review is necessary.

If so, it is necessary to examine the designers and members of the Temporary Investigation Committee of the Ministry of Foreign Affairs, which was designed by Enjiro Yamaza, the director general of the Ministry of Political Affairs, who established a plan to invade the continent starting with Dokdo. The fact that the Committee was composed of all international law scholars, not the "Seven Doctors of Tokyo University,"[11] who declared the theory of opening of war against Russia on June 10, 1903, suggests that Enjiro Yamaza intended to mobilize international law to legally enhance Japanese colonialism and to establish the foundation for the Japanese invasion policy.

The Temporary Investigation Committee of the Ministry of Foreign Affairs, which was linked to the Japanese Society of International Law, was established through the Command of the Ministry of Foreign Affairs on March 5, 1904, under the leadership of Enjiro Yamaza, consisted of senior officials of the Foreign Ministry and international law scholars.

The members of the Temporary Investigation Committee, who were all international law scholars from Tokyo Imperial University, Kakushuin University, and the Ministry of Foreign Affairs, to materialize the plan to conquer Korea as the basis for Enjiro Yamaza's plan to invade the continent.[12] The list of investigators was as follows.

<The Temporary Investigation Committee of the Ministry of Foreign Affairs>
• Chairman of the Temporary Investigation Committee
  Sutemi Chinda, Vice Minister of Foreign Affairs
• Members of the Temporary Investigation Committee
  Enjiro Yamaza, Director General of the Political Affairs, Ministry of Foreign Affairs

Toru Terao, Professor of International Law, Faculty of Law, Tokyo University

Tetsukichi Kurachi, Counselor, Ministry of Foreign Affairs

Sakuye Takahashi, Professor of Public International Law, Faculty of Law, Tokyo University

Shingo Nakamura, Professor of International Law, Kakushuin University

Sakutaro Tachi, Professor of International Law, Faculty of Law, Tokyo University

3-2. Identification of the Concealed Establishment Purpose of the Temporary Investigation Committee of the Ministry of Foreign Affairs

Japan has concealed the purpose of the Temporary Investigation Committee of the Ministry of Foreign Affairs, but it can be seen in an article written in the Tokyo Nichinichi Shimbun in 1904 by Sakuye Takahashi, a founding member of the Japanese Society of International Law.[13]

Sakuye Takahashi explains that the study of international law in Japan was further developed after the Sino-Japanese War and the Russo-Japanese War, and that the Japanese government's emphasis on international law issues, especially in the face of the Russo-Japanese War, led the Ministry of Foreign Affairs to establish an "Investigation Committee" that included international law scholars.

It is noteworthy that on the premise of the development of international law research, the Ministry of Foreign Affairs and international law scholars need to be linked under the premise of "solving international law problems in favor of Japan in the Russo-Japanese War," and the Ministry of Foreign Affairs' systematic close relationship with international law scholars is highly appreciated. In the end, it was confirmed that the purpose of the

establishment of the concealed Temporary Investigation Committee
was to seek a solution in favor of Japan in the Russo-Japanese War
through the distorted mobilization of international laws.

Most of the members of the Temporary Investigation Committee
resigned mid-term during their term, but it was Sakutaro Tachi who
fulfilled his responsibilities until the end of the deadline, including a
thorough research investigation into various issues, including
protectorates countries under international law.

Unlike scholars who resigned in June 1905, the assessment[14]
that Sakutaro Tachi fulfilled his responsibilities at the Temporary
Investigation Committee until the end of the deadline is paradoxically
that he took the lead in establishing the foundation for an invasion
policy against Korea. Therefore, we must examine the problem of
Tachi's distortion of international legal principles.[15]

4. A REVIEW ON THE DISTORTION OF INTERNATIONAL LAW PRINCIPLE BY THE JAPANESE SOCIETY OF INTERNATIONAL LAW BEFORE AND AFTER JAPAN'S INVASION OF DOKDO IN 1905

Regarding Japan's policy of invading Korea, starting with the
Korean Empire's declaration of neutrality in 1904, to the invasion of
Dokdo and the coercion of the Korea-Japan Treaty in 1905, the
prelude to Japan's invasion of Korea before the establishment of the
Japanese Society of International Law was the fabricated Unyo
incident and Japan-Korea Treaty of 1876, a typical example of an
unequal treaty under the threat of gunboats, which was the beginning
of Japan's claim to legitimize its invasion of Korea by mobilizing
international law.[16]

The seriousness of the problem exists in that at least months to
years ago, through the Japanese International Law Journal, the

distorted legal principles of Korea's aggression policy were developed in advance and international law arguments urging its realization were presented.

Under such premise, it is an urgent task to examine the preemptive denial of Korea's declaration of neutrality prior to the Russo-Japanese War as well as the legal problems of Japanese invasion based on Japanese colonialism inherent in the thesis including the changes in the basis of the argument for preoccupying the territories related to the invasion of Dokdo and the protectorate debate, by focusing on the members of the Foreign Ministry's Temporary Investigation Committee that existed during the invasion of Dokdo and forced the Korea-Japan Treaty of 1905.

4-1. The Russo-Japanese War and the Effect of Korea's Declaration of Neutrality

It is worth paying attention to the presentation of a preliminary review paper by the Japanese Society of International Law to block the Korean government's declaration of neutrality in the face of the expected outbreak of the Russo-Japanese War.

Regarding the value of Korea's declaration of neutrality, Sakuye Takahashi, who served as a member of the Temporary Investigation Committee of the Ministry of Foreign Affairs, mentioned the case of Denmark in the early 19th century. At that time, Denmark had a substantial naval force, but it was severely lacking an army to defend against the French army. France had acquired the right to use the Danish navy against Britain through a secret treaty, which was extremely dangerous for Britain. When the British realized this, they sent troops to Denmark to capture the Danish navy. In concluding that the British government's actions were justified in such an emergency, he said, "If we apply this precedent to the current situation in Korea, it is all valid. There is no doubt that Japan can occupy Korea even if Korea declares neutrality," disparaging the value of declarations of neutrality in international law.[17]

It was nothing more than an extension of the illegal act of using international law as a means of foreign aggression based on Japanese colonialism, which thoroughly denied and disparaged the system and effect of neutrality[18] under international law.

4-2. Dokdo Invasion and Changes to the Requirements for Occupation of *Terra Nillius*

Sakutaro Tachi, who published the paper on the requirements for occupation, can also be evaluated as not different from the general theory of the time. Sakutaro Tachi also presents *terra nullius*, indication of the intention of territorial possession, and effective control as requirements for occupation.

Sakutaro Tachi refers to the Berlin Protocol of 1885 in relation to preoccupation. He notes that the Protocol establishes notification of preoccupation as a requirement for preoccupation.[19] However, he does not specify whether this requirement is a general international law requirement for preoccupation or a special requirement that applies only to parties to the Berlin Protocol. Sakutaro Tachi merely states that after the Berlin Protocol, "notification became enforceable in the case of preoccupation." This is in sharp contrast to Masanosuke Akiyama's account.[20]

However, in the end, just as Masanosuke Akiyama is denying the obligation to notify, unlike before, Sakutaro Tachi also states that notification of preoccupation to a foreign country has not yet been established as a requirement that must be carried out as one of the requirements for preoccupation under actual international law.[21] At the same time, unless effective preoccupation is completed, foreign countries do not need to acknowledge territorial acquisition even if they are notified of preoccupation, denying the obligation to notify, which is ultimately analyzed as an attempt to legalize Japan's invasion of Dokdo.

4-3. The Protectorate Debate over Korea

The core of the debate between Sakutaro Tachi[22] and Nagao Ariga regarding Japan's foreign policy toward Korea after the protected country is Sakutaro Tachi's criticism of Ariga Nagao's typology of protection.[23] Sakutaro Tachi criticizes the fact that Japan's policy toward Korea is bound and restricted in the case of Nagao Ariga's typology, which is said to be Japan's role in helping Korea become a full member of the international community.[24] In response, when Nagao Ariga responded that the type of protection country for Korea was not fixed,[25] Sakutaro Tachi criticizes again that if new political facts are required to change the type of protection country in Korea, they will be a limiting factor in Japan's free policy choices and practices.[26]

There is no fundamental difference between the two in that Japan's policy toward Korea should not be bound by the law on protective relations, but there are differences of opinion on how to legally understand the change in protective relations due to changes in policy toward Korea. However, in that it tries to avoid the question of whether the Korea-Japan Treaty of 1905 constitutes a violation of the previous treaty that guaranteed Korea's independence in 1905, this seems to be nothing more than a clever logic and difficult to justify from a legal point of view. This is because the term "independence" defined in the treaty cannot be deprived of its legal meaning by simply calling it a "diplomatic slang." It can be assessed that Nagao Ariga's perception is superior to Sakutaro Tachi in that he recognized at least the fact that the Japan-Korea Treaty of 1905 was inconsistent with the previous treaty and had a problematic consciousness to explain it in a harmonious legal theory.[27]

Sakutaro Tachi's argument that "not only does our present or future policy toward Korea not have to aim at bringing Korea into the ranks of the nations, but if Japan's interests require it, we must adopt a policy that will take Korea further away from the nations than it is at present,[28] so that the current doctrine of protective relations does not bind Japan" has been criticised as Tachi's harsh colonization of Korea, a step toward Japanese-style legal realism.[29]

5. CONCLUSION

In this article, I examined the problems of Japanese colonialism inherent in the Japanese Society of International Law and the resulting distortion of international law principles in the process leading to Japan's invasion of Dokdo in 1905 and forced protection and annexation.

As noted, Japan, as a late-imperialist country, in its state practice before and after the invasion of Korea's Dokdo sovereignty in 1905, not only mobilized the Japanese Society of International Law, which was established in March 1897, but also established a confidential organization, the Temporary Investigation Committee of the Foreign Ministry, which was linked to the Japanese Society of International Law. Thus, it was confirmed that the foundation of international law that justifies and legalizes aggression in foreign policy was being established.

On the surface, the Japanese Society of International Law presents for the purpose of academic research on international law, but in practice, it uses international law as a tool to reconcile the interests of imperialist countries, and specifically, the seriousness of the problem exists in that it leads Japan's foreign policy to raise policies and logic for invading Korea and calls for realization.

Furthermore, as Sakuye Takahashi, who was a member of the

Committee, mentioned, the Temporary Investigation Committee of the Ministry of Foreign Affairs, which was linked to the Japanese Society of International Law, presupposes the development of nominal international law research but emphasizes the linkage between the Ministry of Foreign Affairs and international law scholars in order to solve international law problems in the Russo-Japanese War in favor of Japan. In this premise, I cannot help but point out the essential problem of the legal distortion of Japanese colonialism under the guise of international law.

More importantly, by identifying the reality of the Temporary Investigation Committee of the Ministry of Foreign Affairs, which had been concealed, it proved the distortion of the non-connection theory[30] that the Japanese Society of International Law had argued that it had nothing to do with the invasion of Dokdo in 1905 and the forced protection and annexation process.

It is an organization that the Temporary Investigation Committee of the Ministry of Foreign Affairs has established policies of Japanese colonial rule of Korea and continental aggression, and its duration is exactly the same as that of the invasion of Dokdo and the enforcement of the treaty in 1905, after that the members of the Committee were leading up to the subsequent forced annexation.

Thus, a series of invasions by Japan leading to Jinhae Bay, Masan Port, and Dokdo before the outbreak of the Russo-Japanese War after the denial of the Korean Empire's declaration of neutrality, and the enforcement of treaties for legalization under international law is nothing more than a distortion of typical international law principle.

In short, through a review of the legal principles of Japanese colonialism before and after the invasion of Dokdo in 1905, the Japanese government declared sovereignty over Dokdo four times since 1953 in order to neutralize the "Peace Line Declaration" announced by our government on January 18, 1952. It can be clearly confirmed that the 17th century inherent territory theory, first raised by the Japanese government in the 4th note verbale in 1962, among the note verbale arguing for it, did not exist at the time of Japan's invasion of Dokdo in 1905.

Ahead of 2025, the 120th anniversary of Japan's invasion of Korea's Dokdo sovereignty, I traced and reviewed the distortions of international law principles by the Japanese Society of International Law, which has been building the policy basis for the Japanese government's claim to Dokdo sovereignty. It is necessary to clearly recognize that the deep-rooted violence and greed inherent in the Japanese government's claim to Dokdo is Japanese colonialism, as declared in the Cairo Declaration.

Therefore, as Dokdo is a symbol of Korea's true territorial sovereignty and the cornerstone of an East Asian peace community, I would like to once again urge Japan to fulfill its true historical and international legal responsibilities in relation to Korea's sovereignty over Dokdo.

Notes

1. See-Hwan DOH, "History of Dokdo invasion and Japanese colonialism," *Korea Times*, Nov. 29, 2023, p.13.
2. Report of the Takeshima Document Study Group, *Verification of the Daijokan Directive of 1877*, Japan Institute of International Affairs, 2022.
3. Nishi Taira, Toyoda Tetsuya, Kawazoe Rei, Kwon Namhee, Wakatsuki Tsuyoshi, "Controversy on protectorate: A case study on the practical meaning of European international law doctrines in East Asia," *Nomos*, Institute of Law of Kansai University, 2022, pp.1~11.
4. Takashi Tsukamoto, "Protection and annexation of Korea and the territorial recognition of Japan - over Takeshima," *Modern East Asian History*, No. 14, 2011, pp.52~67.
5. Tetsuya Nakano, "Legal Nature of Japan's Territorial Incorporation of Takeshima in 1905," *Kansai University Law Review*, Vol. 61, No. 5, 2012, pp.113~166.
6. The 17C inherent territory theory is criticized by many scholars, including Haruki Wada. Haruki Wada, *How to solve Northeast Asia's territorial issues-from confrontation to reconciliation*, Four Seasons, 2013, p.41; Norio Naka, *From Territorial Issues to Border Demarcation Issues: Senkaku, Takeshima, and the Four Northern Islands from the Perspective of Conflict Resolution*, Akashi Shoten, 2013, p.34; Taruhiko Toyoshita, *What is Senkaku issue*, Iwanami Shoten, 2012, p.142; Kumiko Haba, "The Danger of the National Territory Theory Regarding Senkaku Takeshima: From European International Politics," *Sekai*, No. 839, Iwanami Shoten, 2013, p.43.
7. See-Hwan DOH, "The Cairo Declaration and the Korean Independence Issue from the Perspective of International Law," *The Monthly Soongook*, December 2023, pp.42~47.
8. Haruki Wada, "The Russo-Japanese War and the Annexation of Korea-Considering the Factor of Russia," *One Hundred Years after Japan's Forced Annexation of Korea: History and Tasks*, Peter Lang Pub Inc, 2015, pp.67~82.
9. Choong-hyun Paik and Tae-jin Yi, "Role of the Japanese Society of International Law in Formulating Policy on Deprivation of Korean Sovereignty," *Seoul International Law Journal*, Vol. 6, No. 2, 1999, p.598.
10. Japanese Society of International Law, *International Law Journal*, Vol. 1, No. 1, February 1902, pp.84~85.
11. "Seven Doctors of Tokyo University" are Tomizu Hirondo, Tomii Masaaki, Kiheiji Onozuka, Noburu Kanai, Toru Terao, Sakuye Takahashi, and Shingo Nakamura. Among them Toru Terao, Sakuye Takahashi, and Shingo Nakamura are international law scholars.
12. Shinichi Tanaka, "The Global Position of Land Survey Projects in Korea - Special Japan for Imperialist and Colonial Land Policy = Korean Characteristics (1)," *Social Sciences Studies*, the Institute of Social Sciences of Tokyo University, 1977, Vol. 29, No. 3, p.61.

13. Sakuye Takahashi, "The Evolution of International Law Studies in Japan," *Tokyo Nichi Nichi Shimbun*, November 10, 1904.

14. Shinichi Tanaka, *op. cit.*, pp.62~63.

15. The period of existence of the Temporary Investigation Committee of the Ministry of Foreign Affairs, which was established by the Director General of the Political Affairs Bureau of the Ministry of Foreign Affairs, Enjiro Yamaza, to carry out the plan to invade the continent starting from the invasion of Dokdo, coincides with the period of the invasion of Dokdo and the forced Korea-Japan Treaty of 1905. However, the reason why it is not easy to find related materials is that Enjiro Yamaza mentioned to a disciple from the same hometown, Koki Hirotai, "Diplomats emphasized the prohibition of records, including diaries, as a taboo." Regarding the invasion of Dokdo, it is analyzed that there is an intention to legalize Japan's invasion of Dokdo, as in the argument of Sakutaro Tachi, who is evaluated to have fulfilled his duty until the end of the term of the Temporary Investigation Committee, regarding the duty of notification, as he denies the duty of notification, unlike in the beginning. Ryuzo Hattori, *Koki Hirota - The Real Image of "The Prime Minister of Tragedy,"* Chuokoron Shinsha, 2008, p.28.

16. Suzuki Jun, "Report on the Ganghwa Island Incident by Captain Inoue Ryokei of the Unyo, dated September 29, 1875," *Shigaku Zasshi*, 2002, pp.111~112.

17. Sakuye Takahashi, "The Value of Korean Neutrality," *Journal of International Law*, Vol. 2, No. 5, 1904, pp.28~32.

18. Han-ki Lee, *Lectures on International Law*, new edition, 2000, pp.805~806.

19. Sakutaro Tachi, *International Public Law in Peacetime*, Lectures of Tokyo Imperial University in 1913, mimeographed edition, Vol. 1, 1913, pp.186~187.

20. Pae-keun Park, Theories of International Law concerning Occupation of Terra Nullius around the Year 1905, *Territory and Sea*, No. 6, 2013, p.53.

21. Sakutaro Tachi, "Legal Principles and Precedents of the Occupation of Islands of Terra Nullius," *Journal of International Law and Diplomacy*, Vol. 32, No. 8, 1933, pp.1~48.

22. Sakutaro Tachi, "The Theory of Classification of Protectorates," *International Law Journal*, Vol. 5, No. 4. p.23.

23. Nagao Ariga, "The Theory of the Protectorate," Waseda University Press. 1906, p.2.

24. Sakutaro Tachi, "Independence and Protection Relation of states," *Journal of National Studies*, Vol. 20, No. 11, 1906, p.28.

25. Nagao Ariga, "The Theory of Classification of Protectorates," *Diplomacy Times*, No. 110, 1907, p.57.

26. Sakutaro Tachi, "Reply to Dr. Nagao Ariga on the Theory of the Protectorate," *International Law Journal*, Vol. 5, No. 6, 1907, pp.36~37.

27. Pae-keun Park , "Tendency and Contents of Studies Related with Japanese Aggression of Korea Appearing in the Japanese Journal of International Law : Debate concerning Protectorate under International Law," *New Perspective on*

Historical Issues in Korean -Japanese Relations - from the Point of International Law, Northeast Asian History Foundation, 2009, pp.247.

28. Sakutaro Tachi (1907), *op. cit.,* pp.36~37.
29. Nishi Taira, Toyoda Tetsuya, Kawazoe Rei, Kwon Namhee, Wakatsuki Tsuyoshi (2022), *op. cit.,* pp.1~11.
30. Takashi Tsukamoto (2011), *op. cit.,* pp.52~67.

Loss and Damage under the UN Climate Change Regime

JunHa KANG
Professor, Hongik University

Key Words

COP 28, Loss and Damage Fund

1. INTRODUCTION

At the recent 28th Conference of the Parties to the United Nations Framework Convention on Climate Change (COP 28), the official launch of the Loss and Damage Fund was announced. The idea of developed countries, responsible for greenhouse gas emissions, compensating developing countries for damage has been under discussion since the 1990s. However, over the past three decades, reaching an agreement on this topic has proven to be challenging work. Therefore, the launch of this fund can be seen as a victory for developing countries in their 30-year struggle to receive financial assistance for climate-related damage, although issues remain around the operation of the fund, such as fund management, the allocation of contributions, the selection of beneficiary countries, and other pertinent considerations. The discussion on Loss and Damage initiated at COP in 2007 has now culminated in the formal establishment of the Loss and Damage Fund at COP 28 in 2023.

This article aims to examine the evolution of discussions on Loss and Damage, and review its current development, highlighting its implications for the Republic of Korea (hereinafter, "Korea").

2. LOSS AND DAMAGE UNDER THE UNFCCC

2-1. Concept of Loss and Damage

Loss and Damage refers to the adverse consequences resulting from the inevitable risks of climate change. There is no unified definition of loss and damage in the international community. "Loss" generally refers to the irreversible disappearance of flora, fauna, cultural heritage, or civilizations due to climate change, while "damage" denotes harm that is potentially recoverable to some extent.[1] Loss and damage arise as a consequence of inadequate responses to climate change[2]. In other words, inadequate efforts to mitigate and adapt to climate change result in Loss and Damage.[3] Mitigation involves reducing greenhouse gas emissions, while adaptation addresses the impacts of climate change, such as constructing barriers to prevent flooding. Mitigation and Adaptation are two main elements identified by the United Nations Framework Convention on Climate Change (UNFCCC) for dealing with climate change.

The concept of Loss and Damage can also be categorized into two types: Economic Loss and Damage, and Non-Economic Loss and Damage. Economic Loss and Damage includes quantifiable negative impacts, while Non-Economic Loss and Damage encompasses adverse effects that cannot be measured in monetary terms. Non-Economic Loss and Damage is often more profound and irreversible.

2-2. Discussions at the UNFCCC COP

The concept of Loss and Damage can be traced back to a proposal made by the Alliance of Small Island States (AOSIS) in 1991. Although Loss and Damage was not directly included in the UNFCCC, discussions on the topic have continued at subsequent COPs.

The Bali Action Plan, adopted at COP 13 (2007), firstly introduced Loss and Damage as part of enhanced action on adaptation.[4] At COP 16 (2010), a work program on Loss and Damage was established under the Subsidiary Body for Implementation (SBI).[5] The SBI undertook technical work in assessing the risk of Loss and Damage and a range of approaches to address Loss and Damage.[6]

COP 19 hosted by Poland in 2013 established the Warsaw International Mechanism for Loss and Damage (WIM), which would be a main vehicle for Loss and Damage in the UNFCCC process.[7] The WIM addresses Loss and Damage associated with climate change impacts in developing countries that are particularly vulnerable to the adverse effects of climate change. The WIM promotes the implementation of approaches to address Loss and Damage in a comprehensive, integrated, and coherent manner by undertaking functions such as enhancing action and support, including finance, technology, and capacity-building.[8]

The Executive Committee of the WIM, established at COP 19, guides the functions of the WIM. COP 20 (2014) decided on the composition and governance of the Executive Committee and approved the initial two-year work plan of the Committee.[9]

The Paris Agreement, adopted at COP 21, provides a specific provision on Loss and Damage. Article 8 of the Paris Agreement sets out areas of cooperation and facilitation to enhance understanding, action, and support, stating that the WIM shall be subject to the authority and guidance of the Conference of the Parties serving as the meeting of the Parties to the Paris Agreement (CMA). The areas of cooperation and facilitation include events that may involve irreversible and permanent loss and damage, non-economic losses, and resilience of communities, livelihoods, and ecosystems.

COP 22 (2016) conducted the first review of the WIM and recommended a periodic review process, with the next review to be held in 2019.

At COP 25 (2019), the second review of the WIM outlined steps to strengthen its effectiveness, emphasizing increased collaboration and coordination to enhance resource mobilization, action, and support for developing countries. In line with these efforts, the CMA established the Santiago Network to provide technical assistance to the most vulnerable countries.[10]

3. LOSS AND DAMAGE FUND

3-1. Creation of the Fund

The Loss and Damage Fund was created at COP 27 (2022). COP 27 recognized that a collective response is imperative and that this requires countries to respond individually "in accordance with their common but differentiated responsibilities and respective capabilities." However, the parties deferred decisions on the details of the operationalization of the fund until COP 28.

The Loss and Damage Fund needs to address the gaps that current climate finance institutions, such as the Green Climate Fund, fail to cover. In 2020, the combined adaptation and mitigation funding fell short by at least USD 17 billion of the promised USD 100 billion allocated to developing countries. To ensure the successful establishment of the Loss and Damage Fund, a transitional committee consisting of 24 country representatives was formed in early 2023. This committee is tasked with providing recommendations on operationalizing the fund, including decisions on eligible countries for funding and contributors to the fund.

3-2. Discussions at COP 28

At COP 28[11], all parties showed solidarity by agreeing to operationalize the Loss and Damage Fund and funding arrangements. This financial support initiative aims to assist developing countries vulnerable to climate change. According to the preliminary terms of the agreement, this marks the establishment of the first-ever UN body at a global level dedicated to addressing climate-related damage. The newly established organization will function under the authority of the United Nations, with the World Bank, managing the funds for the first four years. The agreement includes provisions encouraging the participation of not only developed countries but also affluent developing countries. The United States has consistently pressed for the involvement of emerging economies such as China, Saudi Arabia, and the UAE. The agreement explicitly mentions that contributions to the fund are "voluntary." However, the exact target amount for fund collection is not specified in the agreement.

The Loss and Damage Fund at COP 28, aimed at addressing the irreversible economic and non-economic losses suffered by developing countries due to the climate crisis, constitutes only 0.2% of the total estimated losses.[12] According to news media, the accumulated funds currently stand at approximately USD 700 million.[13] The UAE, as the presiding nation for COP 28, and Germany have each pledged USD 100 million. The European Union (EU), representing 27 member countries, has pledged USD 245 million. The United States, the second-largest greenhouse gas emitter this year, has committed USD 17.5 million, while Japan, the third-largest economy following the United States and China, has pledged USD 10 million.[14]

4. LOOKING FORWARD: REMAINING ISSUES

While the Loss and Damage Fund has been launched, several issues regarding its operation remain unresolved. In particular, clear criteria for determining the status of countries have not yet been established, and there is ambiguity about who should contribute to the fund and who should benefit from it. Advanced countries, including the United States, argue that countries with significant greenhouse gas emissions, such as China and India, should not only take responsibility for emissions reduction but also contribute to the fund. Conversely, China and India oppose such claims, emphasizing the historical responsibility of already industrialized countries. They argue that, as developing countries, they should qualify to receive funds rather than contribute to them.

As the ongoing confrontation between developed and developing countries persists, the future of the Loss and Damage Fund remains uncertain. Korea is under increasing international pressure to contribute to the fund due to its status as a G20 member, its classification as a high-income country by World Bank standards, and its position as the 9th largest emitter globally. Given Korea's standing and its responsibilities regarding greenhouse gas emissions, it is essential for the country to contribute to the Loss and Damage Fund in some capacity. As a significant global player, Korea must develop a comprehensive response strategy that aligns with its national policies.

Notes

1. https://www.lawfaremedia.org/article/what-comes-after-loss-and-damage-fund-respo nsibility-and-repair-climate-disrupted-world
2. *Ibid.*
3. https://www.ipcc.ch/site/assets/uploads/2018/02/ar4-wg2-chapter18-1.pdf
4. The Bali Action Plan calls for "disaster reduction strategies and means to address Loss and Damage associated with climate change impacts in developing countries that are particularly vulnerable to the adverse effects of climate change." Decision 1/CP.13.
5. The purpose of this work program is to consider approaches to address Loss and Damage, including impacts of extreme weather events and slow onset events in developing countries that are particularly vulnerable. It also aims to strengthen international cooperation and expertise in order to understand and to reduce Loss and Damage. Decision 1/CP.16.
6. Decision 1/CP.16.
7. Decision 2/CP.19, para.1.
8. Decision 2/CP.19, para.5.
9. Decision 2/CP.20.
10. Decision 2/CMA.2.
11. COP 28 was held in Dubai, UAE during Nov 30 - Dec 12, 2023.
12. https://www.theguardian.com/environment/2023/dec/06/700m-pledged-to-loss-and-damage-fund-cop28-covers-less-than-02-percent-needed
13. *Ibid.*
14. https://www.reuters.com/business/environment/cop28-summit-opens-with-hopes-ear ly-deal-climate-damage-fund-2023-11-30/

Recent Discussions on the Hague Jurisdiction Project

Soo-Jin CHO
Presiding Judge Eastern Branch of Busan District Court (Busan, Korea)

Key Words

HCCH, jurisdiction project, parallel proceedings, concurrent proceedings, related matters

1. INTRODUCTION

The Hague Conference on Private International Law successfully delivered the "Convention of 2 July 2019 on the Recognition and Enforcement of Foreign Judgments in Civil or Commercial Matters (Judgments Convention)," establishing a global framework facilitating the cross-border movement of judgments. This marks the second achievement of the Judgments Project, following the Choice of Courts Convention in 2005. Both conventions originated from a broader project initiated in 1996, focusing on specific topics due to the consensus that a comprehensive convention was nearly unattainable.

Currently, the Permanent Bureau (PB) of the HCCH, along with several experts, is endeavoring to draft a third convention on "parallel proceedings and related matters." If accomplished, this new convention "would close gaps left by the other two conventions and complete the goal of the original Judgments Project."[1] The Working Group has convened six meetings thus far, with two additional meetings scheduled in accordance with the mandate of the CGAP in 2024.[2] In this report, I aim to highlight some aspects of the recent discussions concerning the Jurisdiction Project of the HCCH.

2. BACKGROUND OF THE NEW CONVENTION

2-1. Mandate of the CGAP

In March 2021, CGAP mandated the establishment of a Working Group on matters related to jurisdiction in transnational civil or commercial litigation to work based on the Experts' Group's work. The CGAP specifically tasked the Working Group with the following:

(i) to develop draft provisions on matters related to jurisdiction in civil or commercial matters, including rules for concurrent proceedings, to further inform policy considerations and decisions about the scope and type of any new instrument.

(ii) to proceed inclusively and holistically, with an initial focus on developing binding rules for concurrent proceedings (parallel proceedings and related actions or claims), and acknowledging the primary role of both jurisdictional rules and the doctrine of *forum non conveniens*, notwithstanding other possible factors, in developing such rules.

(iii) to explore how flexible mechanisms for judicial coordination and cooperation can support the operation of any future instrument on concurrent proceedings and jurisdiction in transnational civil or commercial litigation.[3]

2-2. Importance of the New Convention

As cross-border litigation becomes increasingly common, the need for a new convention addressing parallel proceedings grows more pressing. It is not difficult to anticipate that some parties might seek a more favorable outcome by initiating duplicate proceedings in a forum they perceive as advantageous.

As it is crucial to establish a standard for resolving concurrent proceedings, the Brussels I Regulation (recast) addresses this issue in Articles 29 to 34. However, while the Brussels I Regulation (recast) governs disputes among EU member States with similar legal backgrounds, the new convention is expected to encounter challenges, primarily due to conflicts between civil law and common law traditions.

The disparity between civil law and common law jurisdictions poses a profound and challenging obstacle to reconciling issues related to concurrent proceedings. Civil law jurisdictions typically prioritize the first-seized court, dismissing subsequently filed ones. On the other hand, common law jurisdictions display significant reluctance toward such criteria as they believe it inevitably leads to a "race to judgments."

In common law jurisdictions, litigations in multiple countries can proceed, with the matter being resolved during the stage of recognizing and enforcing the first judgment issued by the various courts involved.[4] If a court in one country deems the exercise of international jurisdiction inappropriate, it may refuse to exercise it. From the perspective of civil law jurisdictions, this approach in common law jurisdictions presents unpredictable challenges.

With this context in mind, the next chapter will explore three issues highlighted in the discussions of the Working Group meetings thus far.

3. ISSUES OF THE NEW CONVENTION

3-1. Scope of the New Convention: Inclusion of "Related Matters"

The discussions in the Working Group up to the 4th meeting were focused on pure parallel proceedings, where the same parties (and the same subject matter) are involved. However, before the 5th meeting, some experts criticized that the Working Group had been neglecting the mandate of the CGAP. In the 5th meeting, a proposal was made to expand the scope of concurrent proceedings and to add a definition on "concurrent proceedings."[5]

However, no consensus was reached on the definition of concurrent proceedings. Thus, the Working Group discussed adding "and the related actions" to Article 1 of the draft concerning the scope of the convention and decided to consider using the word "concurrent proceeding" and its definition in a later stage.

The proposers argued that merely regulating pure parallel proceedings in the convention would make it too limited and not very useful. They added that applying different principles within the scope of the convention is not advisable and it would be overly complex and unnecessary.[6]

I understand and sympathize with the proposers' argument. However, it's also meaningful to focus on pure parallel proceedings while keeping in mind the need for discussions on related matters. Currently, even discussions on pure parallel proceedings have not reached a consensus, and whether related matters can be regulated by the same criteria as pure parallel proceedings is another issue. Even within the civil courts of the Republic of Korea (hereinafter, "Korea"), there are often cases where lawyers lack understanding when dealing with issues of concurrent proceedings, and both subject and objective extent of *res judicata* in domestic cases. Despite the existence of clear legal principles and precedents within a single country, confusion arises. It raises questions about how feasible it is to regulate matters when different legal systems are involved in different countries. Once an agreement on principles dealing with pure parallel proceedings is reached, the next step would be to define "related matters" in the new convention and to assess whether those principles can be directly applied to "related matters," too.

Up to this point, the Working Group of the HCCH has faced challenges in defining core concepts such as "parallel proceedings," "concurrent proceedings," and "related matters." It is neither feasible nor desirable to encompass all possible scenarios regarding related matters within the convention. Given that litigation can take on various forms even based on the same facts and contracts, it is questionable whether it is possible to clearly define the scope of related proceedings and regulate them in the same manner as pure parallel proceedings. Thus, it might be more practical to establish some fundamental principles, mainly on pure parallel proceedings, and anticipate resolution of other issues through communication and cooperation mechanisms among courts in different jurisdictions.

3-2. Approaches

Regarding the pressing challenge of resolving parallel proceedings, many experts have submitted working documents and tried to propose solutions that might be accepted in both civil law and common law jurisdictions.

The Working Group discussed a possible determination of a better forum. Some experts proposed an article trying to balance the necessary flexibility and discretion with the need for legal certainty, by combining elements of different legal traditions.[7] In this proposal, where parallel proceedings are pending in the courts of two or more Contracting States, a party may, no later than the first defense on the merits, make an application to the court first seized to determine whether any other seized court in a Contracting State that has jurisdiction/connection under this convention is clearly more appropriate to resolve the dispute. Then, any other court seized must suspend its proceedings. The proposal also included a timeframe and stipulated that courts seized in Contracting States may exchange information at any stage of the determination through the communication mechanism.

However, some experts of the Working Group worried that the proposed article could hinder the promotion of the future convention, as the obligation to analyze the more appropriate forum is performed by only one court. Some experts were concerned that the provision favored the first-in-time court performing the analysis. Questions about the length of time permitted for the determination were also raised. For these reasons, this proposed article was not reflected in the draft, but the chair acknowledged that this proposal stimulated further work on the issue.[8]

Addressing the problem, another expert suggested an alternative article, attempting to balance the interests of the two or more courts by giving the appropriate forum decision to the second court seized, too.[9] However other experts worried that this option may negatively incentivize parties to commence a second set of proceedings in a second court.

In any case, a procedure for resolving parallel proceedings is necessary, and setting a timeframe for it is also essential. I believe it is desirable to declare that the jurisdiction issue should be discussed before the first defense on the merits. It is unlikely that common law jurisdictions would accept prioritizing the first-seized court once parallel proceedings have arisen in two or more courts. However, unless there is an exclusive connection, it is preferable to anticipate a reasonable conclusion through a communication mechanism between the courts. Considering a scenario where, in country A, a considerable lawsuit is already underway, all evidence has been presented, and there has been no objection of international jurisdiction, and then a lawsuit is refiled in country B afterward, I believe most judges would find that country A should proceed with the case. It is because the new lawsuit in country B can be seen as a clear attempt by a party feeling disadvantaged in the litigation to delay the proceedings and seek a second chance.

3-3. Judicial Cooperation and Communication

Due to the diverse nature of "parallel proceedings and related matters," communication between courts is of utmost importance. The communication mechanism is particularly crucial as the new convention deals with the resolution of "ongoing" concurrent proceedings. This issue also falls within the explicit scope of the CGAP's mandate.

In the context of the new convention, when establishing the communication framework between courts, there are options, similar to other conventions, regarding whether to establish a central authority or to adopt direct communication as the default. The Working Group previously decided to adopt direct communication as the default while allowing for the possibility of opting out. In the 5th meeting, some experts proposed alternatives, such as an option for States to choose between direct communication and indirect communication (working documents 27 and 27rev), and an option establishing a central authority as a default (working document 28).

In my opinion, communication among courts can undoubtedly be helpful. While there may be concerns about direct communication involving elements of sovereignty infringement, I support the new convention that allows both direct and indirect communication but primarily adopts direct communication. Using a central authority can be time-consuming. The information required for communication between the courts will likely relate to ongoing cases, making the use of a central authority inappropriate in some aspects, such as privacy issues.

Language barriers may pose challenges, but I don't believe a central authority is necessary solely for this reason. If needed, countries can establish institutions to provide interpretation or translation support. Direct communication between the courts can be viewed in the context of exchanging information for the resolution of concurrent proceedings. Despite differences in legal systems, the foundation for determining a better forum in most cases is similar. Therefore, one can expect problem-solving through communication.

The challenge with the new convention, compared to the Judgments Convention, arises from its closer connection with direct jurisdiction rules and the evident divergence in positions between common law countries and civil law countries concerning the first-seized rule. Consequently, it is not easy to anticipate a compromise between them. While experts continue to formulate compromise proposals, it appears challenging to create a proposal that garners overwhelming support without encountering explicit opposition.

I believe that establishing core rules within a minimum scope, along with communication mechanisms between courts, could be beneficial enough. In areas where States cannot reach a consensus, it should generally be left to the communication mechanisms, and experts should focus on establishing the fundamental principles. While predictability is a key issue and benefit of the Judgments Convention, problem-solving itself would be more important than predictability in the new convention. Regardless of their legal background, most judges possess the capability to find the best and most reasonable solution in a specific case.

4. CONCLUSION

The Supreme Court of Korea is moving towards respecting foreign judgments,[10] and courts in other countries are increasingly inclined to respect judgments from Korea's courts.[11] Within this trend, there is an increased possibility of international parallel proceedings in Korea. However, there is not yet a precedent accumulated for the resolution of international parallel proceedings.

Korea should adopt a more proactive stance in these discussions, as it stands to benefit from the potential establishment of the new convention. Many steps are yet to be taken before the new convention is finalized. Regrettably, apart from Singapore, most other Asian countries have not been able to present working documents proposing possible articles at the Working Group meetings. I hope that Korean experts can participate more actively in the remaining Working Group meetings, and to achieve this, they need to engage in communication with neighboring States.

Notes

1. Matthias Lehmann, "Incremental international law-making: The Hague Jurisdiction Project in context," Journal of Private International Law (2023), p.27.
2. Conclusions and Decisions adopted by the CGAP, March 2024 (paras, 4-7).
3. Conclusion & Decisions of the Council on General Affairs and Policy (CGAP), March 2021.
4. Paul Herrup & Ronald A. Brand, "A Hague Convention on Parallel Proceedings," Harvard Int'l Law Journal Online Volume 63 (2022), p.9.
5. Work.Doc. No. 19 rev, PROPOSAL OF THE MEMBERS OF THE DELEGATIONS OF BRAZIL, MEXICO, THE UNITED STATES, AND URUGUAY (IN THEIR PERSONAL CAPACITIES), September 13, 2023.
6. *Ibid.*
7. Working Document No. 24, Proposal of the delegations of Australia and the European Union, Sep. 2023.
8. Chair's Report of the 5th Working Group Meeting (draft).
9. Working Document No. 29, Proposal of the delegations of the United Kingdom, Sep. 2023.
10. e.g. December 23, 2021, 2017da257746 en banc decision and March 11, 2022, 2018da231550 decision: In the above decisions, the Supreme Court of Korea declared that "the stability and predictability of the international transaction order should be considered" and acknowledged the importance of "international trust in legal procedures (of Korea).
11. e.g., China once refused to recognize a Korean judgment (Shenzhen Intermediate People's Court, September 30, 2011). However, on March 25, 2019, the Qingdao Intermediate People's Court recognized the judgment of the Suwon District Court in Korea, citing the fact that a Korean court had recognized a Chinese judgment.

KYIL

Private International Law Issues in Recent Korean Court Rulings from 2020 to 2023 on Criminal Cases

Jung-Hwa YOU
Judge
Seoul Eastern District Court, Seoul, Korea
Ph.D. Candidate in International Business Transactions Law, College of Law, Seoul National University, Seoul, Korea

Key Words

private international law issues, Korean criminal cases involving foreign elements, Korean court precedent, governing law, Korean Act on Private International Law

1. INTRODUCTION

In determining the factual background where a criminal case arises, not the criminal punishment itself, such civil law issues as who owns the property that was stolen or embezzled (i.e., the attribution of ownership), it is not always right that Korean Civil Act is automatically applied to the case. Instead, by the analysis of the applicable law through the conflict-of-laws rule in the Republic of Korea (hereinafter, "Korea"), the foreign civil law determined as the governing law according to the rule is deemed to be applied to the case.[1]

2. LEADING CRIMINAL CASE-SUPREME COURT DECISION 2010Do15350

Supreme Court Decision 2010Do15350 rendered on April 28, 2011, is a leading case ruling that "If a foreign factor defined under Article 1 of the Korean Act on Private International Law ("KPILA") exists in a legal relationship regarding property of other persons because it involves nationality of parties, address, location of property, or location of act that is closely connected to a foreign nation, absent special circumstances, the applicable law under the KPILA shall be the primary standard in the determination of issues such as the ownership of a property in question." It was clearly confirmed in the Decision 2010Do1530 above that private international law applies to the underlying facts that form the premise of a criminal case.

3. RECENT CRIMINAL CASES FROM 2020 TO 2023

During the period from 2020 to 2023, eighteen decisions were rendered where the private international law issues were addressed, reviewed and ruled on. These decisions can be categorized in five groups of crimes: (i) property crimes (i.e., fraud, embezzlement), (ii) violation of the Korean Labor Standards Act, (iii) violation of the Korean Copyright Act and Korean Trademark Act, (iv) untrue entry in electronic records identical to officially authenticated original deed, and (v) offer of bribe, etc. The above crimes are necessarily based on the factual grounds which contain legal issues that should be determined under the civil law before they go through the legal analysis under the criminal law to reach a final conclusion of whether the defendant is guilty or not guilty.

The following paragraphs are focused on the court rulings

highlighted in italics in the table below.

Category	Court Decision No.
Property Crimes (i.e., Fraud, Embezzlement)	- *Seoul High Court Decision 2020No2255* - *Seoul High Court Decision 2020No629* - Seoul High Court Decision 2012No4144 - *Seoul Central District Court Decision 2020Gohap621* - Seoul Central District Court Decision 2017Gohap1270 - Seoul Eastern District Court Decision 2016Gohap18 - Suwon District Court Decision 2017No4743 - Uijeongbu District Court Decision 2011Gohap266
Violation of the Korean Labor Standards Act	- *Seongnam Branch Court of Suwon District Court Decision 2019Gojeong654* - Seoul Central District Court Decision 2017Gojeong367
Violation of the Korean Copyright Act and Korean Trademark Act	- Seoul Central District Court Decision 2017Godan4808 - Daejeon District Court Decision 2014No2441 - Daegu District Court Decision 2014No816 - Uijeongbu District Court Decision 2013No1554
Untrue Entry in Electronic Records Identical to Officially Authenticated Original Deed	- Uijeongbu District Court Decision 2015No2310 - Daejeon District Court Decision 2010Gojeong936 - Changwon District Court Decision 2005No72
Offer of Bribe, etc.	- Seoul Central District Court 2017Gohap194

3-1. Seoul High Court Decision 2020No2255 Rendered on October 14, 2021 [Finalized on October 22, 2021; neither parties appealed]

3-1-1. Factual Background

Defendant J served as the CEO of the Victim Company, C. LTD. (hereinafter, "the Victim Company"), located in P Building in Singapore from January 2007 to February 2016, overseeing the overall operations of the Victim Company. Defendant Y, the spouse of J, was responsible for the accounting duties as a director and secretary of the Victim Company from August 2007 to February 2016. The Victim Company, an affiliate of S Group, was engaged in

sales and post-delivery ship management for ship owners in
Southeast Asia and Europe on behalf of S Shipbuilding Co. Ltd.
(hereinafter, "S Shipbuilding"). Around December 2009, the
management of S Group became the subject of law enforcement
investigation, and S Shipbuilding entered into workout proceedings.
Taking advantage of this disarray of S Group, the Defendants
conspired to embezzle funds from the Victim Company.

Accordingly, on August 29, 2011, in the Victim Company's
office, the defendants withdrew 32,794 Singapore dollars (SGD) (J
20,271 SGD + Y 12,523 SGD, hereinafter, "dollars" unless
specifically distinguished) from a DBS bank account held in the name
of the Victim Company, purportedly as salaries. They arbitrarily used
it for operating expenses and living expenses for "G. LTD." ("this
private company"), established by the defendants, among other
things. By October 2012, as addressed in Crime Detail Tables 1 and
2, they freely used a total of 622,246,052 KRW under the guise of
salaries and expenses. Thus, the defendants conspired to embezzle
the property of the Victim Company.

3-1-2. Ruling on the Private International Law Issue

Legal Status of the Defendants and the Legal Effect of the
Directions Issued by Mr. Lee

Legal Basis for Determining Ownership and Custodial Status as
Conditions for the Establishment of the Crime of Embezzlement

To establish the crime of embezzlement, the perpetrator must be
someone "who keeps another person's property," and whether it is
another person's property or whether it is being kept is determined
by substantive laws such as civil and commercial laws (e.g., Korean
Civil Act, Korean Commercial Act). Therefore, if the legal
relationship related to whether it is another person's property
involves foreign elements such as the nationality or residence of the

parties, the location of the property, or the location where a certain type of activities took place, and is closely related to a foreign country, the governing law, which is primarily determined by the provisions of Article 1 of the KPILA (amended before Law No. 18670 of January 5, 2022, hereinafter referred to as the same),[2] should be used as the primary standard in determining the ownership of the property, and the possession and entrustment relationships, absent special circumstances (Supreme Court Decision 2010Da15350 rendered on April 28, 2011). However, according to Article 16 of the KPILA, unless a corporation established abroad has its main office or conducts its principal business in Korea, it shall be governed by the law of the place of its incorporation, and there are no provisions restricting the application of this clause, so its scope should be considered to include all matters related to the corporation including its establishment, dissolution, organization, internal relations, rights and duties of its organs and members, and its capacity to act (Supreme Court Decision 2017Da246739 rendered on August 1, 2018).

Thus, in determining whether the crime of embezzlement by business exists regarding the actions of the defendants, who were either the CEO or directors of the victim company, which was established under Singaporean corporate law in Singapore and conducts business activities such as information gathering or sales support for foreign ship owners from affiliated companies of the S Group, one must first examine the rules concerning the relationship between the shareholders and the company regarding the ownership of company assets, the delegation or entrustment relationship between the company and the directors, and the duties and responsibilities of the directors under the Singaporean corporate law and related regulations, and if these differ from the civil and commercial laws (e.g., Korean Civil Act, Korean Commercial Act) of Korea, they should be judged according to the law of its incorporation.

3-2. Seoul High Court Decision 2020No629 Rendered on January 21, 2021 [Finalized on January 29, 2021; neither parties appealed]

3-2-1. Factual Background

The defendant, related by marriage to the deceased Mr. M (hereinafter, "the Deceased"), began managing the domestic assets (deposits and real estate) owned by the deceased, a U.S. citizen, in 2009 under the Deceased's authorization. On March 31, 2016, the defendant was given a delegation of authority from the Deceased to sell a total of 5,906.92 *pyeong* of agricultural and field land located in Gwangju, along with 81 other plots. The defendant then sold this land to Ms. H for approximately 8.2 billion KRW. After paying expenses such as capital gains tax, the defendant deposited the remaining approximately 4.3 billion KRW into an account in the name of the Deceased at S Bank (hereinafter, "the Account in Question") and managed it.

3-2-2. Ruling on the Private International Law Issue

Meanwhile, the defendant, following the death of the deceased, claims that they were authorized to withdraw the funds in question from the Deceased's account based on a will (hereinafter, "the Will in Question") prepared by the Deceased during their lifetime. The defendant was designated as the executor of the Deceased's will by their daughter, Ms. Y, and therefore argues that they had the authority to prepare withdrawal slips in the name of the Deceased, or at least that they had no criminal intent regarding the alleged crime.

According to various pieces of evidence legally adopted and examined at the first instance and appellate trials, the Deceased was a U.S. citizen residing in the State of New York, and thus the execution of the will concerning the deposit should be governed by the laws of

New York State, where the Deceased was domiciled at the time of making the will (Article 50, paragraph 1 of the KPILA). New York State law specifies that "an executor has no authority to dispose of the decedent's estate prior to the appointment of the executor or preliminary executor, except for reasonable funeral expenses." Given that the probate process for the Will in Question had not been completed at the time of the incident, and it appears that the probate is still ongoing, it can be recognized that Ms. Y had very limited authority to dispose of the Deceased's property other than that.

Therefore, any claims by the defendant based on a different premise cannot be accepted.

3-3. Seoul Central District Court Decision 2020Gohap621 Rendered on February 15, 2023 [Pending in the Supreme Court upon both parties' appeal, Case no. 2023Do17596][3]

3-3-1. Ruling on the Private International Law Issue

Determination of Shareholder Status of LBO According to Cambodian Company Law

Article 16 of the previous KPILA states that "A corporation or organization shall be governed by the law of its place of establishment." This clause, which has no provisions limiting its applicability, is understood to encompass all issues relating to a corporation, including its establishment, dissolution, organization, internal relationships, rights and duties of organs and members, and capacity to act (Supreme Court Decision 2017Da246739 rendered on August 1, 2018).

Meanwhile, the proviso of the same Article 16 states, "However, if a corporation or organization established abroad has its main office or conducts its principal business in Korea, then it shall be governed by the laws of Korea," recognizing the exceptional application of the domicile law principle.

Although LBO is a company established under the laws of Cambodia, ① LBO is a subsidiary of LMW Co., Ltd., which is established under domestic law and has its main office in Korea, ② LBO is a Special Purpose Company (SPC) established locally in Cambodia by LMW Co., Ltd. for the resort project, with most tasks such as project planning, financing, accounting, and settlements conducted in Korea by employees of LMW Co., Ltd., including Mr. G and Ms. H, without a separate independent local office or staff, ③ the resort project did not undergo significant business progress for over ten years after land acquisition, and ④ the stakeholders of LBO, including the defendant, individual investors, and employees of LMW Co., Ltd. who performed LBO's operations, are all Korean nationals residing in Korea. Given these points, it is reasonable to consider LMW Co., Ltd.'s office in Korea as LBO's "*de facto* main office," so it is appropriate to regard the governing law in this case as the laws of Korea, according to the proviso of Article 16.

Furthermore, as reviewed above, Ms. Y was only a nominal shareholder registered in the articles of association without actual capital contribution, merely for accounting purposes, to comply with the land law regulations in Cambodia during the promotion and establishment of the local corporation for LMW Co., Ltd.'s resort project. The perception of the defendant as well as the associates of LMW Co., Ltd. and LBO was the same, indicating that Ms. Y cannot be recognized as an actual shareholder of LBO. Therefore, the arguments made by the defendant and their counsel based on a different premise are not accepted.

3-4. Seongnam Branch Court of Suwon District Court Decision 2019Gojeong654 Rendered on February 18, 2020 [The defendant's appeal denied by Suwon District Court Decision rendered on August 21, 2020, and finalized on August 29, 2020]

3-4-1. Factual Background

The defendant is the manager of YM Co., Ltd., located in Gwangju employing about 12 regular workers and operating a manufacturing business.

1. An employer must pay wages, compensation, and all other payments to workers who have died or retired within 14 days from the occurrence of the event that triggers the payment. However, if there are special circumstances, the payment date can be extended by agreement between the parties. Despite this, the defendant failed to pay a total of 24,968,374 KRW in wages to two workers, including 2,000,000 KRW for September 2018 wages of Mr. S, within 14 days of their resignation, without any agreement to extend the payment date, as listed in the attached crime summary table.

2. An employer must pay severance payments to workers who have retired within 14 days from the retirement date. However, if there are special circumstances, the payment date can be extended by agreement between the parties.

Nonetheless, the defendant failed to pay 4,147,550 KRW in severance to Mr. H, who worked at the said workplace from February 2, 2017, to October 13, 2018, within 14 days of the retirement date, without any agreement to extend the payment date.

3-4-2. Ruling on the Private International Law Issue

Judgment on the Claims of the Defendant and the Defense Counsel
A. Claims of the Defendant and the Defense Counsel
The defendant claims that the labor-related laws of Korea do not apply because the workers were employed in Vietnam and worked there.

B. Judgment
According to the evidence, the defendant employed the workers in Vietnam, designating "YV Co., Ltd." in Ho Chi Minh City, Vietnam, as their workplace. Consequently, it is recognized that these workers worked and retired in Vietnam.

The charge against the defendant assumes the obligation to pay wages and severance payments within 14 days from the occurrence of such payment reasons due to the workers' retirement. However, since the employment contract was concluded in Vietnam between Korean nationals and the workers provided labor in Vietnam, which involves foreign elements, the application of domestic labor laws, such as the Labor Standards Act to the defendant, should be determined primarily based on the governing law as defined by the rules of private international law (Supreme Court decision 2010Do15350 rendered on April 28, 2011, on the "property of another" in embezzlement).

Article 28(2) of the KPILA states, "If the parties have not chosen the governing law, the employment contract shall be governed by the law of the country where the worker habitually provides labor, notwithstanding the provisions of Article 26. If the worker does not habitually provide labor within any one country, the law of the country where the business that employed the worker is located shall apply." On the other hand, Article 8(1) of the same Act specifies, "If the designated governing law has only a minor relevance to the legal relationship, and another country's law, which is clearly more closely related to the legal relationship, exists, then the law of that other country shall apply."

Based on the evidence, it can be acknowledged that the employment contract was concluded in Korean between YM Co., Ltd., a domestic company, and the Korean national workers. The defendant, who operates businesses traveling between Korea and Vietnam, paid part of the wages to the workers into Korean bank accounts, such as Mr. S's SG Bank account or Mr. H's KB Bank account, in KRW, and enrolled the workers in domestic health and employment insurance. Given that the employment contract was concluded in Korean between a domestic company and Korean nationals, parts of the wages were paid into domestic accounts in KRW, and the workplace was a domestic corporation enrolled in domestic health and employment insurance, it might appear that the labor-related laws of Vietnam should initially apply as the governing law under Article 28(2) of the KPILA. However, since the employment relationship has only minor relevance to this, and the domestic Labor Standards Act and other related laws are most closely related, it should be recognized that the domestic labor laws apply according to Article 8(1) of the KPILA. Therefore, the claim that the Labor Standards Act does not apply is not accepted.

4. CONCLUSION

It has been observed that if a criminal case involves foreign elements, private international law must be applied, and various complex case issues exist. Considering the increasing frequency of recent incidents and the growing proportion of foreigners in the Korean society, along with the corresponding rise in related crimes, it is likely that a broader array of issues will arise in the future.

Notes

1. RYU Jaehyun, "Private International Law in Criminal Cases: Focusing on Korean Precedents," Korea Private International Law Journal Vol. 25, No. 2., p.69.

2. The relevant provisions of the KPILA referred to in the Supreme Court Cases introduced above are those of the previous KPILA before it was almost entirely revised on January 4, 2022, and entered into force on July 5, 2022.

3. Upon both parties' appeal, the second instance court rendered the partially revised decision on November 17, 2023 (Seoul High Court Decision 2023No852), but it did not revise the judgment in the first instance court's decision on the private international law issue.

Recent Developments

North and South Korean Satellite Launch, Space Security, and Space Law

Han Taek KIM
Emeritus Professor
School of Law, Kangwon National University

Key Words

space security, Outer Space Treaty, PPWT, ASAT

On November 22, 2023, North Korea launched a rocket carrying what it called a reconnaissance satellite, prompting South Korea to suspend a key part of the military agreement[1] it signed in 2018 with Pyongyang to ease tensions on the Korean peninsula. This launch attempt of North Korea, its third attempt after two failures in 2023, came two months after its leader, Kim Jong Un, met Russian President Vladimir Putin, who offered to help North Korea build a satellite.[2]

On December 2, 2023, South Korea's first homegrown spy satellite was launched from the U.S. Vandenberg Space Force Base in California on SpaceX Falcon 9 rocket. According to the defense ministry, it successfully entered orbit and communicated with the ground station a little over an hour after launch. Beginning with the electro-optical and infrared satellites, South Korea plans to launch four more synthetic aperture radar satellites by 2025 under a 1.2 trillion won (USD 918.2 million) project.[3] Additionally, two days

later, on December 4, South Korea's first solid fuel-propelled space
launch vehicle (SLV) developed by the state-run Agency for Defense
Development (ADD) was successfully launched from a barge 4
kilometers (2.4 miles) south of Jeju Island. The rocket is designed to
put a small satellite into a low-Earth orbit at about 650 kilometers
above the planet's surface for surveillance operations. Compared with
liquid-fuel space vehicles, solid-fuel ones are known to be simpler
and more cost-effective to launch. The 100-kilogram (220-pound)
synthetic aperture radar (SAR) satellite was made by Hanwha
Systems, which is the representative company of South Korea,
ranging with world-class companies in various business areas based
on avionics and space, security and safety, and information systems
service. The launch is the third test of a multi-stage South Korean
SLV, the development of which is being led by the ADD.[4]

Unlike South Korea, North Korea's satellite launch is considered
a violation of international law under paragraph 5 of the UN Security
Council Resolution 2270 of March 2, 2016,[5] which prohibits satellite
launches using ballistic missile technology. The Security Council
condemned in the strongest terms the nuclear test conducted by
North Korea on January 6, 2016, "in violation and blatant disregard"
of the relevant resolutions, stating that the act constituted a challenge
to the Treaty on the Non-Proliferation of Nuclear Weapons (NPT) of
1968[6] and to peace and stability in the region and beyond.

The 15-member Security Council unanimously adopted
Resolution 2270 (2016), condemning North Korea's rocket launch on
February 7, 2016, using ballistic missile technology and demanding
immediate compliance with its international obligations. Unlike the
advisory nature of the UN General Assembly resolutions, the UN
Security Council resolutions are legally binding.[7] Russia and China,
permanent members of the Security Council, also voted in favor of
the resolution, indicating that they agreed that North Korea's satellite
launches using ballistic missile technology were a threat to the

international community.

The renewed military cooperation between North Korea and Russia in 2023 could increase threats to global security in the coming years. As the Russia-Ukraine war approaches the second anniversary of the February 2022 invasion, Moscow has turned to North Korea for help in replenishing its depleted stockpile of arms. In exchange, Russia has suggested that it will help develop weapons that Pyongyang wants, including a spy satellite. China has not condemned Pyongyang's satellite launch or arms dealings between North Korea and Russia and has not used its leverage to curb North Korea's threatening behavior despite multiple requests from Washington and Seoul.[8]

The Soviet Union's launch of Sputnik 1[9] on October 4, 1957, served to intensify the arms race and increase tensions in the Cold War. In the 1950s, the United States and the Soviet Union worked hard to develop new technologies. In the meantime, outer space gradually became a place for warfare between countries, not much different from the existing land, sea, or upper atmosphere. As more and more nations rely on space assets for surveillance, reconnaissance and intelligence gathering, strategic and tactical communications, and missile early warning and tracking to support a wide range of military operations, the potential for conflicts in outer space is increasing.

The concept of "space security" has emerged for space, but each country has different interpretations of what "space security" means depending on its national interests. Based on the U.S. National Space Policy and other presidential directives, and our obligations under the 1967 Outer Space Treaty,[10] now called the *Magna Carta* of space law, and other international law, space-related "security" is associated with the pursuit of activities that ensure sustainability and stability, free access to, and use of, outer space to support vital national interests. This is reinforced by several other related principles of the new U.S.

national space policy - All nations have the right to explore and use space for peaceful purposes and for the benefit of all humanity under international law. This principle allows outer space to be used for "peaceful purposes" and for national security activities.[11]

Regarding the peaceful use of space, Article 4 of the 1967 Outer Space Treaty provides that the use of military personnel for scientific research or any other peaceful purposes shall not be prohibited. The use of any equipment or facility necessary for peaceful exploration of the moon and other celestial bodies shall also not be prohibited. The moon and other celestial bodies shall be used by all States Parties to the Treaty exclusively for peaceful purposes. As far as the term "peaceful purposes" is concerned, there was a difference in the interpretation of the Soviet Union as non-military and the United States as non-aggressive.[12] In fact, during the Cold War, which began immediately after World War II and continued until the collapse of the Soviet Union in 1991, approximately 75% of artificial satellites launched into space were military satellites.[13] Considering that situation, I think that interpreting the meaning of "peaceful" as "non-military" is not a very persuasive theory. Space launch vehicle engine technology is treated as a top secret by advanced space countries such as the United States, Russia, and China, and because this is linked to security issues, technology transfer between countries is virtually impossible. This is because commercial rocket development can also be used for military purposes.

According to Article 1(1) of the 1979 Moon Agreement,[14] references to celestial bodies stipulated in the treaty apply to "other celestial bodies in the solar system other than the Earth." If the OST does not mention the solar system, it can be broadly interpreted to apply to the entire universe, including the solar system and galaxy. As far as Article 3 of the MA is concerned, there has never been a ban on military use of outer space. Article 3 of the MA went further than Article 4 of the OST but was limited to partial demilitarization.

Therefore, other than prohibiting the deployment of weapons of mass destruction in the Earth's orbit, it is interpreted that all other military uses are permitted.[15]

In introducing the prohibition in Article 3(2) of the MA prohibiting the use of any threat, force, or any other hostile act, or threat of any hostile action, on the Moon, the MA enshrined Article 2(4) of the Charter of the United Nations that prohibits the threat or use of force, and calls on all Members to respect the sovereignty, territorial integrity, and political independence of other States. It is a repetition of the basic principles of international law and, at the same time, the "peaceful purpose" of the OST.[16] The MA is a treaty with very little influence compared to the OST in that it has been accepted only by a small number of countries, of which space-faring states such as the United States, Russia, and China are not members. As of January 2024, there are only 18 countries that have joined the MA.

Due to the development of space weapons, the discussion on militarization of space has changed to the weaponization of space. The Prevention of the Arms Race in Outer Space (PAROS) is a United Nations resolution that reaffirms the basic principles of the OST and advocates a ban on the weaponization of space. The PAROS resolution acknowledges the limitations of existing laws related to outer space and recognizes that the Outer Space Treaty "by itself does not guarantee the prevention of an arms race in outer space." The resolution advocates further measure to prevent an arms race in outer space by, among other things, calling on countries, particularly those with space capabilities, to comply with the objectives of the PAROS. In addition, it calls on the Conference on Disarmament (CD) — the UN disarmament negotiating forum — to establish an *ad hoc* committee on the issue of the PAROS resolution.

Russia and China found that the OST had too many loopholes to respond to this space weaponization matter, so they jointly submitted to the Conference on Disarmament (CD) the 2008 Draft Treaty on Prevention of the Deployment of Weapons in Outer Space, the Threat of Force against Outer Space Objects (PPWT), and the 2014 revised PPWT.[17] The two countries proposed signing a new international legal document through negotiations to prevent weaponization and the arms race in space, and to preserve peaceful outer space. However, the United States says that no problem can be solved through arms control because an arms race has not yet occurred in outer space and criticizes the PPWT as nothing more than a "diplomatic ploy by Russia and China to gain a military advantage."[18]

The United States concludes that the draft PPWT of 2014, like the earlier 2008 version, remains fundamentally flawed. These include a lack of verification mechanisms and no restrictions on the development and stockpiling of ground-based anti-satellite (ASAT) weapons. China has tested direct-ascent ASATs on several occasions, including one in January 2007 that destroyed a Chinese weather satellite, creating a significant amount of space debris, with 3,000 pieces of debris in orbit.[19]

Meanwhile, regarding space security, there are soft laws that are not legally binding, such as the "Hague Code of Conduct against Ballistic Missiles Proliferation (HCoC)"[20] and the "International Code of Conduct for Outer Space Activities (ICoC),"[21] which aim to establish voluntary "rules of the road"[22] for the increasingly important space domain - a domain intended for peaceful use and accessible to all nations. They play an important role in space law because they are norms promising that member States' space and rocket development will be used only peacefully.

The opinion of supporters of hard law that a legally binding treaty should be adopted to regulate the weaponization of outer space is correct, but, at present, when the establishment of treaties has become difficult after the 1979 Moon Agreement, it would be a good idea to encourage the participation of countries by developing soft law guidelines as an interim measure to ultimately create an integrated and binding legal instrument for all aspects related to the use of outer space. In this respect, I think the resolution (A/RES/77/41)[23] adopted by the United Nations General Assembly on December 7, 2022, to encourage not performing "destructive direct ascension (DA) ASAT testing" is a good model.[24] For example, the 1986 UN General Assembly resolution "Principles Relating to Remote Sensing of the Earth from Outer Space" played an equally important role as hard law.[25] Although this resolution is non-binding, the principles are widely accepted and have been incorporated into many countries' binding domestic licensing regulations. Therefore, it is largely recognized as an international obligation of the U.S. space regulatory regime, which requires licensees to operate any private remote sensing space system to comply with the key principles outlined in the resolution.[26] Regarding the legal effect of this soft law, on November 12, 1974, the United Nations adopted the General Assembly Resolution 3232 (XXIX) under the title, "Review of the Role of the International Court of Justice." It is worth recalling that it was recommended that "declarations" and "resolutions" be considered by the International Court of Justice (ICJ) in a way that can be reflected in the development of international law.[27]

To date, no armed conflict has occurred due to military operations by countries in outer space. Nevertheless, military manuals containing content on space operations can be reviewed from the perspective of national practice.[28] For example, the 2016 U.S. Department of Defense's "Law of War Manual" states that general international law is related to space operations. In its Advisory Opinion on the Legality of the Threat or Use of nuclear weapons in 1996, the ICJ stated that the legal principles of international humanitarian law apply to all forms of warfare and all kinds of

weapons, past, present, and future.[29] Thus, it could be interpreted
that the principles and norms of international humanitarian law can
also be applied to armed conflicts occurring in outer space. Important
norms in international humanitarian law that must be considered
include the principle of distinction[30] between civilians and
combatants, the principle of distinction between civilian objects and
military targets, the principle of proportionality of attacks,[31] and the
principles of attack. These include the principle of obligation to take
feasible precautions[32] and the principle of prohibition of
indiscriminate attacks.[33]

   Non-governmental efforts can help clarify the application of laws
on the use of force and the law of armed conflict to new areas,
means, and methods of armed conflicts. The success of the San
Remo Manual on International Law Applicable to Maritime Armed
Conflicts, the Harvard Manual on International Law Applicable to
Air and Missile Warfare, and the Tallinn Manual on International
Law Applicable to Cyber Operations (versions 1.0 and 2.0) shows
how international experts and associated engagement with
governments can offer an authoritative and clear articulation of
international law in new domains for government legal advisers,
decision-makers, and operators.[34]

   The Woomera Manual on the International Law of Military
Space Activities and Operations[35] aims to be a widely recognized
and accepted objective statement of existing international law (*lex lata*)
applicable to military space operations. Government lawyers
(especially military lawyers), policymakers, decision makers, and
military space operators comprise the manual's key target audience.
However, it is also expected to spark interest and debates among a
wide range of international institutions and the public, as well as to
serve as a platform for academic discourse and research, particularly
as legal principles and policies are further developed in response to
change.[36]

The space race between countries, which has recently entered the New Space era, is creating anxiety around the world as it is likely to unfold not only as a civilian-led space development but also as part of an arms race. The space environment is becoming increasingly congested, contested, and competitive. That means more equipment in orbit, more advanced threat capabilities that can disrupt or destroy space-based services, and greater economic demand for space access.[37]

The Korea National Intelligence Service announced that it understood that Russian Defense Minister Sergei Shoigu officially proposed joint training between North Korea, China, and Russia to Chairman Kim Jong Un during his visit to North Korea in July 2023. As South Korea, the United States, and Japan are strengthening military cooperationby including such agreeing to regularize joint exercises at the Camp David Summit in August 2023, North Korea, China, and Russia also appear to be trying to counter with joint exercises. China and Russia have been conducting joint training, but there has yet to be any occasion in which North Korea has participated. Amid tensions surrounding the Korean Peninsula, the launch of military satellites by North and South Korea is once again highlighting the importance of space security and space law.

Notes

1. The 9/19 South-North Korea's Military Agreement calls for the removal of landmines, guard posts, weapons, and personnel in the JSA (Joint Security Area) from both sides of the South-North Korean border. The agreement also called for the creation of joint military buffer zones, *available at* https://world.kbs.co.kr/service/news_view.htm?lang=e&Seq_Code=139465(last visited on Jan. 24, 2024).

2. North Korea's space launch program and long-range missile projects, Reuters, November 22, 2023.

3. (News Focus) Koreas' spy satellite launches heat up arms race in space, Yonhap News Agency, December 02, 2023.

4. South Korea successfully launches solid-fuel space rocket with satellite, Korea JoonAng Daily, December 4, 2023.

5. S/RES/2270 (2016), *available at*   https://www.un.org/securitycouncil/s/res/2270-%282016%29 (last visited on Jan. 8, 2024).

6. *Available at* https://treaties.unoda.org/t/npt (last visited on Jan. 8, 2024).

7. *Available at* https://unrcca.unmissions.org/sites/default/files/6-unrcca_handout_unsc_resolutions_eng_2020_1_2.pdf (last visited on Jan. 8, 2024).

8. North Korean-Russian Military Cooperation Could Threaten Global Security, VOA, January 01, 2024,   *available at* https://www.voanews.com/a/north-korean-russian-military-cooperation-could-threaten-global-security/7404703.html (last visited on Jan. 20, 2024).

9. Sputnik and the Space Race: 1957 and Beyond, *available at* https://guides.loc.gov/sputnik-and-the-space-race (last visited on Jan. 8, 2024).

10. Treaty on Principles Governing the Activities of States in the Exploration and Use of Outer Space, including the Moon and Other Celestial Bodies, *available at* https://www.unoosa.org/oosa/en/ourwork/spacelaw/treaties/outerspacetreaty.html (last visited on Jan. 8, 2024).

11. Defining Space Security, SPACENEWS, July 20, 2011, *available at* https://spacenews.com/defining-space-security/ (last visited on Jan. 23, 2024).

12. Bin Cheng, *Studies in International Space Law*, Clarendon Press, (1997), pp.513~522.

13. Setsuko Aoki, Law and Military Uses of Outer Space in Routledge Handbook of Space Law (edited by Ram S. Jakhu and Paul Stephen Dempsey), Routledge, (2017), p.197.

14. Agreement Governing the Activities of States on the Moon and Other Celestial Bodies, G.A. Res. 34/68, U.N. Doc. A/34/68 (Dec. 5, 1979).

15. Sylvia Maureen Williams, International Law and the Military Uses of Outer Space, 9 *International Relations*, (May 1989), p.412.

16. Bin Cheng, Studies in International Space Law, *op. cit.*, p.53.

17. Draft Treaty on the Prevention of the Placement of Weapons in Outer Space, the Threat or Use of Force against Outer Space Objects (PPWT) (submitted on June 10,

2014); Jinyuan Su, Space Arms Control: *Lex Lata* and Currently Active Proposals, 7 *Asian Journal of International Law*, (2017), p.71.

18. Statement by Ambassador Wood: The Threats Posed by Russia and China to Security of the Outer Space Environment, *available at* https://geneva.usmission.gov/2019/08/14/statement-by-ambassador-wood-the-threats-posed-by-russia-and-china-to-security-of-the-outer-space-environment/ (last visited on Jan. 8, 2024).

19. Space junk from 2007 China satellite attack still poses risk, May 7, 2021, *available at* https://asia.nikkei.com/Politics/International-relations/Space-junk-from-2007-China-satellite-attack-still-poses-risk (last visited on Jan. 8, 2024).

20. The Hague Code of Conduct: Multisector Expansion, Vienna Center for Disarmament and Non-Proliferation, *available at* https://vcdnp.org/the-hague-code-of-conduct-multivector-expansion/ (last visited on Jan. 8, 2024).

21. *See* Jack M. Beard, Soft Law's Failure on the Horizon: The International Code of Conduct for Outer Space Activities, 38 *University of Pennsylvania Journal of International Law*, (2017), pp.336~424.

22. Max M. Mutschler, Keeping Space Safe-Towards a long-term strategy to arms control in space-, 2010, p. 17, *available at* https://www.prif.org/fileadmin/HSFK/hsfk_downloads/prif98.pdf (last visited on Jan. 8, 2024).

23. *Available at* https://documents-dds-ny.un.org/doc/UNDOC/GEN/N22/738/92/PDF/N2273892.pdf?OpenElement (last visited on Jan. 8, 2024).

24. A total of 155 nations voted in favor of the resolution while nine, including China and Russia, voted against it. Nine other nations, including India, abstained (Jeff Foust, More countries encouraged to commit to halt destructive ASAT tests, SPACENEWS, June 15, 2023, *available at* https://spacenews.com/more-countries-encouraged-to-commit-to-halt-destructive-asat-tests/, last visited on Jan. 21, 2024).

25. Principles Relating to Remote Sensing of the Earth from Outer Space, U.N Doc. A/RES/41/65 (Dec. 3, 1986).

26. Michael Hoversten, U.S. National Security and Government Regulation of Commercial Remote Sensing from Outer Space, 50 *The Air Force Law Review*, 2001, pp.253, 263–264; Jack M. Beard, Soft Law's Failure on the Horison: The International Code of Conduct for Outer Space Activities, 38 *University of Pennsylvania Journal of International Law*, vol. 2, (2017), pp.350~351.

27. Preamble, UNGA Res. 3232(XXIX), November 12, 1974.

28. US Department of Defense, Law of War Manual (Department of Defense, 2016), pp.940~945.

29. Advisory Opinion on the Legality of the Threat or Use of Nuclear Weapons, ICJ Reports 1996, para.8.

30. The principle of distinction between civilians and combatants and between civilian objects and military objectives.

31. The principle of proportionality in attack.

32. The obligation to take feasible precautions in attack and against the effects of attack.

33. The prohibition of indiscriminate attacks; Jean-Marie Henckaerts, Study on

customary international humanitarian law: A contribution to the understanding and respect for the rule of law in armed conflict, 87 *International Review of the Red Cross*, no 857, (2005), p.14.

34. *Available at* https://law.adelaide.edu.au/woomera/legal-framework (last visited on Jan. 25, 2024).

35. The Womera Manual is an international research project led by University of Adelaide, University of Exeter, University of Nebraska-Lincoln, and University of New South Wales-Canberra.

36. *Available at* https://law.adelaide.edu.au/woomera/about (last visited on Jan. 25, 2024).

37. Cody Scott, Lessons In Risk Management From NASA's Space Security: Best Practices Guide, Jan. 17, 2024, FORRESTER, *available at* https://www.forrester.com/blogs/lessons-in-risk-management-from-nasas-space-security-best-practices-guide/ (last visited on Jan. 25, 2024).

Korean National Assembly's Proposed Legislations Related to Import Ban on Any Seafood from Japan and the World Trade Organization

Min Jung CHUNG
Legislative Research Officer
National Assembly Legislative Research Service

Key Words

Fukushima Daiichi Nuclear Power Plant, Food Sanitation Act, SPS Agreement, World Trade Organization (WTO), International Atomic Energy Agency (IAEA), United Nations Scientific Committee on the Effects of Atomic Radiation (UNSCEAR)

1. INTRODUCTION

On August 24, 2023, the Japanese government began to discharge radioactive material from the Fukushima Daiichi Nuclear Power Plant into the ocean, which heightened the people's anxiety about seafood. In response, the National Assembly of the Republic of Korea (hereinafter, "Korea") proposed two amendments that would establish a legal basis for an import ban on seafood (including processed products) from countries that discharge any radioactive-contaminated water into the ocean to protect health of the people.[1]

Given that the current provision of the Food Sanitation Act allows an import ban based on the hazards of food in a broad sense, the two proposed amendments aim to provide a stronger legal basis more specifically for imposing an import ban on seafood from countries discharging radioactive material into the ocean. While Article 21 of the current Food Sanitation Act allows an import ban based on the hazards of food from a particular country or region, it does not state specific reasons, such as nuclear accidents or contaminated water spills. Meanwhile, the two amendments submitted in 2023 allow an import ban on seafood from countries discharging radioactive materials into the ocean regardless of whether the materials are hazardous.

The National Assembly must review whether the proposed amendments violate international law, including rules set forth by the World Trade Organization (WTO), and the Appellate Body Report: Korea-Import Bans, and Testing and Certification Requirements for Radionuclides (WT/DS495) is the precedent with the most similar and relevant facts and legal issues.[2] While a precedent does not have a binding effect under the WTO dispute settlement framework, a precedent has some influence as it is difficult for a subsequent panel and the Appellate Body to significantly deviate from the legal interpretation or reasoning in the precedent. Note that facts and legal issues relevant to the proposed amendments in 2023 are an extension of the above precedent. This article analyzes the details of the Appellate Body Report, *Korea-Radionuclides*, which serves as a precedent, and examines the potential legal issues that are expected to be argued in Japan's likely complaint to the WTO if the proposed amendments are passed by the National Assembly.

2. BACKGROUND

In the wake of the 2011 Fukushima nuclear accident at the Fukushima Daiichi Nuclear Power Plant in Japan, the Korean government imposed an import ban on 50 products from eight Japanese prefectures in 2012 and required a *radioactive material test certificate* issued by the Japanese government for seafood from 16 other prefectures and a *certificate of origin* issued by the Japanese government for seafood caught in other prefectures besides the 16 aforementioned prefectures. In 2013, mounting concerns were raised in Korea that seafood in the region may have been contaminated with radiation as hundreds of tons of contaminated water flowed into the sea every day from the Fukushima Daiichi Nuclear Power Plant.

On September 6, 2013, the Korean government took provisional measures to ban any seafood imports from eight prefectures around Fukushima.[3] A disagreement between Korea and Japan arose over whether the measures were consistent with the WTO's Agreement on the Application of Sanitary and Phytosanitary Measures (the "SPS Agreement")[4].

On May 21, 2015, the Japanese government requested consultations regarding Korea's import ban on Japanese seafood and other products under the WTO's dispute settlement proceedings.[5] When the consultations did not result in the outcome it wanted, Japan requested a panel be arranged. On September 28, 2015, a panel was established to determine whether Korea's import ban on seafood from Japan was consistent with the WTO SPS Agreement. On February 8, 2016, the panel was arranged and met in a closed session under Appendix 3.2 of the Understanding on Rules and Procedures Governing the Settlement of Disputes (DSU). The Panel released its final report to the state parties in October 2017.[6]

On April 9, 2018, the Korean government filed an appeal against the panel's decision.[7] On April 11, 2019, the Appellate Body released its final report to the state parties. While the panel upheld most of the arguments raised by Japan, the Appellate Body overturned the panel's decision that Korea's measures were not consistent with the SPS Agreement on all key issues.

3. FINDINGS OF THE APPELLATE BODY REPORT, *KOREA-RADIONUCLIDES*

The dispute between Korea and Japan at the WTO is the first case in which the respondent country in a dispute over the SPS Agreement effectively maintained its SPS measures.[8] The Appellate Body found that the panel erred in interpreting and applying the Agreement to most of the issues. Consequently, the panel's decision was overruled on all of the issues except for some procedural issues related to transparency. Japan had raised two types of issues: substantive issues, such as discrimination and unnecessary trade restrictions (Articles 2.3 and 5.6), and procedural issues, such as a breach of obligations to notify measures (Articles 7 and 8).

3-1. Article 5.7 of the SPS Agreement

The Appellate Body accepted Korea's argument that Japan's request for the arrangement of a panel did not include Article 5.7 and, therefore, the panel lacked the authority to hear the case. The panel found that Korea, not Japan, had the burden of proof to demonstrate that it met all of the requirements of Article 5.7. Korea countered by arguing that Japan, the complaining party, had the burden of proof to demonstrate that the requirements of provisional measures had not been met.[9] The Appellate Body found that the panel's decision on Article 5.7 had no legal effect; nor did it make a final determination on the issue of the burden of proof under Article 5.7, which Korea argued.

3-2. Article 2.3 of the SPS Agreement

The Appellate Body found that the product-specific test adopted by the panel contained an error as it omitted a review of territorial conditions under Article 2.3[10]. The panel reached its conclusions by only focusing on the products without considering the territorial conditions that could affect the possible contamination of the food products. The Appellate Body found that the panel did not sufficiently consider territorial conditions when it adopted the product-specific test, simply because the conditions were not manifested in the products.[11] The Appellate Body also found that the territorial conditions of the exporting country where the products were produced must be considered, even if the test results of the final products indicated the same SPS risks within acceptable levels. The Appellate Body's overturn holds significance as it corrects the panel's decision that could potentially limit the importing country's sovereignty regarding SPS based solely on the resulting quarantine of the final products reaching the importing country's borders.[12]

3-3. Article 5.6 of the SPS Agreement

Korea's appropriate level of protection (ALOP) consisted of three qualitative and quantitative factors, and the Appellate Body highlighted that the panel erred in determining a breach of Article 5.6[13] based solely on the quantitative factor of one millisievert (mSv). The appropriate level of protection is a level set by the SPS authorities in the importing country to protect the country's people from specific SPS risks, which is part of the privilege of the importing country as a sovereign state.[14] Therefore, nothing in the SPS Agreement governs the setting of the level, and the panel and the Appellate Body as well as the complaining country cannot set the level on behalf of the importing country or make a determination on the level set by the importing country.

The Appellate Body viewed that Korea's appropriate level of protection has both qualitative ((i) the level present in a normal environment and (ii) as low as reasonably achievable (ALARA)) and quantitative ((iii) one mSv per year) factors.[15] Korea's appropriate level of protection is to maintain the level as low as reasonably achievable under one mSv per year, which exists in a normal environment with no effect of radiation arising from a major nuclear accident. However, under the wrong premise that Korea's appropriate level of protection is only one mSv per year, or the quantitative factor is placed before the qualitative factors, the panel concluded that Korea's SPS measures were more trade-restrictive than required because Japan's alternative measures (cesium testing) could achieve Korea's appropriate level of protection.[16]

3-4. Article 7 and Annex B of the SPS Agreement

The Appellate Body upheld the panel's decision regarding obligations to notify measures under Article 7 and Annex B, and overturned the panel's decision on the establishment of an SPS contact point. The Appellate Body found that the Korean government's press release failed to sufficiently describe the products subject to the measures, and uploading the press release on the website of a ministry (e.g., the Office for Government Policy Coordination, Prime Minister's Secretariat) other than the one responsible for food safety breached transparency obligations.[17] The Appellate Body also found that the panel made an error in determining a violation by Korea based on only two requests made by Japan.[18] The Appellate Body noted that the failure of responding to only two requests does not automatically constitute a violation of Article 7. The Appellate Body determined that the panel should have further reviewed the number of requests received by Korea's contact point during the applicable period and the percentage of the requests, which were not answered.[19]

3-5. Article 8 and Annex C of the SPS Agreement

The Appellate Body upheld the panel's decision not to presume that Japanese and Korean seafood were like products from the perspective that Korea's measures were not based on the origin of food products but on the potential health risks posed by the food products. Article 8 governs the operations of member states' control, inspection, and approval procedures, including obligations to control, inspect, and approve products in a way that is not less favorable than for like domestic products. Japan argued that Korea classified seafood into Japanese or non-Japanese solely on the basis of the origin, and therefore such seafood products were like products. Both the panel and the Appellate Body, however, did not accept Japan's argument. The Appellate Body found that the General Agreement on Tariffs and Trade (GATT), which presumes likeness when a measure discriminates between imported and domestic products based on their origin alone, does not necessarily apply to SPS measures.[20]

4. DISCUSSION

Regarding the above decision, some consider that the Appellate Body did not make a final determination that Korea's measures were inconsistent with the Agreement, and therefore, it was presumably consistent with the Agreement.[21] However, it would be more accurate to argue that the substantive issues of the dispute were not finally determined, and it does not necessarily mean that Korea's measures were consistent with the SPS Agreement.[22]

Although the Appellate Body found flaws in the panel's logic in interpreting and applying the SPS Agreement and overturned its decision on all key issues, it did not review the facts again and make a final determination. More specifically, the Appellate Body dismissed the panel's decision on Article 5.7 because it found that the panel decided on the issue that neither of both parties argued. This does not indicate that Korea's measures were consistent with the SPS Agreement as they met the requirements of Article 5.7 and were considered provisional measures.

The Appellate Body overturned the panel's decision on Article 2.3 because it found that the panel had made an error in reviewing the similarity of Japanese seafood to that of other member states based solely on the risks present in the seafood without considering different territorial conditions. However, it did not review the facts again nor determine that Korea's measures were consistent with Article 2.3.

The Appellate Body overruled the panel's decision on Article 5.6 because it found that the panel understood the appropriate level of protection established by Korea for the country's food safety only based on the quantitative factor, not the qualitative ones, and compared it to the level of protection of Japan's alternative measures. However, it did not review the facts again nor determine that Korea's measures were consistent with Article 5.6 as the level of protection of Japan's alternative measures could not reach the appropriate level of protection set by Korea.

In previous SPS cases, the Appellate Body made its own determination based on the facts contained in the panel's report, considering that there is no remand procedure in the WTO's dispute settlement proceedings. In the dispute over seafood between Korea and Japan, however, the Appellate Body explicitly stated that it only overturned the panel's decision and would not make any determination of facts.[23]

The following two reasons were mentioned regarding why the Appellate Body limited its authority and scope of review: First, some interpreted it as an expression of judicial restraint in deferring to the sovereign right to protect the country's people from psychological anxiety, considering that Korea's measures were taken in the wake of an unusual and exceptional accident at the Fukushima Daiichi Nuclear Power Plant.[24]

Second, some considered that Japan's complaint strategy was not appropriate for a SPS dispute. In previous SPS cases, all of the complaining countries won. However, Japan's complaint strategy was different from the ones used in previous SPS cases.[25] The SPS Agreement requires WTO member states to take SPS measures based on scientific evidence and not to maintain the SPS measures if there is no scientific evidence. However, Japan did not argue that there was no scientific evidence to support any potential risk to seafood posed by environmental contamination from the continued discharge of radioactive materials from the Fukushima Daiichi Nuclear Power Plant into the ocean, and that a risk assessment conducted by Korea was not properly based on science. In other words, Japan did not claim that Korea's measures breached science-based obligations under Articles 2.2, 5.1, and 5.7. Instead, Japan adopted the same approach as that in a GATT dispute by arguing that Korea discriminated against seafood from Japan and imposed unnecessary trade restrictions. In short, Japan only claimed that Korea's measures violated the obligations specified under Articles 2.3 and 5.6, which were less reliant on science. According to this view, after overturning the panel's decision, the Appellate Body intentionally avoided hearing specific facts regarding Articles 2.3 and 5.6 to maintain the integrity of the SPS Agreement, which requires scientific evidence different from the GATT.[26]

5. POSSIBLE COMPLAINT TO BE RAISED BY JAPAN TO THE WTO AND EXPECTED ISSUES

The followings are the potential complaint and issues to be

raised by Japan to the WTO against the Korean National Assembly's proposed amendments for an import ban on any seafood from Japan.

5-1. Possible Complaint to be Raised by Japan to the WTO

A potential violation of the rules of the WTO by the proposed amendments from the Korean National Assembly regarding an import ban on any seafood from Japan will necessarily lead to a complaint raised by Japan to the WTO, and many other variables, including political, diplomatic, and economic interests, will play a certain role. Although China and the United States also adopted an import ban on seafood from Japan after the 2011 Fukushima nuclear accident, Japan filed a complaint with the WTO only against Korea. This is because Korea was the only country that continued to see a sharp decline in seafood exported from Japan to Korea until 2018 after the ban was introduced. China, which banned seafood imported from 10 prefectures in Japan, saw a decline in the imported seafood from 2011 to 2013 but an increase from 2014. The United States, which banned seafood imported from 14 prefectures in Japan, saw no actual decline in the imported seafood (see Table 1).

Japan will also consider that it took nearly four years to proceed from the filing of the dispute to the Appellate Body's decision in the Appellate Body Report, *Korea-Radionuclides*.[27] The WTO's dispute settlement proceedings recognize that *de facto res judicata* is applicable when issues are sufficiently similar between a prior and a subsequent dispute.[28] If the Korean National Assembly enacts a law that provides for an import ban on any seafood from Japan, however, *res judicata* does not apply since the ban constitutes a new dispute that would occur a long time after the proceedings of the panel in the *Korea-Radionuclides* case and could not have been anticipated by the panel.

[Table 1] Seafood exports from Japan

Country	2008-2010	2011-2013	2014-2018
China	249.8	209.6	314.7
United States	173.7	193.8	220.4
Thailand	138.9	181.0	147.9
Vietnam	36.5	155.8	154.0
Hong Kong	112.4	140.3	120.5
Korea	191.7	109.4	115.4
Others	270.1	255.8	340.5
Total	1,173.1	1,245.6	1,413.3

Source: Global Trade Atlas; reprinted *in Jung-Hyun* Yoon & Song Soo Lim, "A Critical Analysis of the SPS Dispute over the Import Ban on Japanese Radioactive Seafood", 44(4), *Korea Trade Review*, (2019), p.29.

5-2. Expected Issues

If Japan files a complaint to the WTO against the Korean National Assembly's legislation regarding an import ban on any seafood from Japan, it is expected to raise different legal issues than those previously addressed in the Appellate Body Report, *Korea — Radionuclides*. As in the Appellate Body Report, *Korea — Radionuclides*, Japan is unlikely to rely solely on Articles 2.3 and 5.6 to argue that Korea discriminates against seafood from Japan and imposes unnecessary trade restrictions. Instead, Japan is expected to argue that Korea's measures breached Articles 2.2, 5.1, and 5.7. In other words, Japan is expected to claim that there is no scientific evidence to support any potential risk to seafood posed by environmental contamination from the discharge of radioactive materials into the ocean, and that a risk assessment conducted by Korea is not properly based on science.

Therefore, Korea needs to prepare evidence and arguments to scientifically support an import ban on any seafood from Japan if the latter files a complaint on different legal grounds. During the panel's fact-finding stage of the previous Appellate Body Report, *Korea — Radionuclides*, Japan successfully supported its claims with scientific analysis based on a vast amount of data, including not only the Japanese government's internal investigation data but also inspection data from international organizations, such as the International Atomic Energy Agency (IAEA) and the United Nations Scientific Committee on the Effects of Atomic Radiation (UNSCEAR), and expert opinions from scientists.[29]

Scientific evidence required under the SPS Agreement should not necessarily be the mainstream view in the scientific community. Even a minority view can be considered consistent with the WTO's SPS Agreement if there is trusted and good-quality scientific evidence for the view.[30] This is true especially when the risks are life-threatening and pose a clear and imminent threat to health and safety of the public.[31]

Risks in a risk assessment refer to not just those in a confined laboratory under strict experimental conditions. Therefore, a risk assessment does not necessarily need to be conducted under strict laboratory conditions.[32] The risks include any potential adverse effect on human health which exists in the real world.

The output of a risk assessment does not necessarily have to be a government report.[33] Furthermore, a risk assessment does not necessarily need to be conducted by the country taking SPS measures. Member states may adopt measures based on not only their own risk assessment but also those conducted by other member states or international organizations as a basis for scientific justification.[34] Instead, a risk assessment needs to be sufficiently specific to justify SPS measures.[35]

In July 2023, the IAEA released its final report indicating that Japan's measures were consistent with international standards and the effect of the measures on people and the environment would be negligible.[36] One of the issues that may be claimed in a subsequent dispute is whether the IAEA's Comprehensive Report on the Safety Review of the ALPS-Treated Water at the Fukushima Daiichi Nuclear Power Station can be accepted as scientific evidence. Assuming that Japan has made the case and proved that the data of the IAEA review is reliable and the evaluation criteria are acceptable, the outcomes of the IAEA review are considered to have scientifically proven that the materials discharged from the Fukushima Daiichi Nuclear Power Plant are identical to those from nuclear power plants under normal operating conditions.

However, considering the IAEA is not an international organization responsible for food safety like the World Health Organization (WHO), it is crucial to continue to review any potential risk to seafood posed by environmental contamination from the discharge of radioactive materials into the ocean despite the findings of the IAEA's review. Hence, it is difficult to expect the WTO's dispute settlement proceedings to recognize the results of the IAEA review as conclusive scientific evidence. Furthermore, the results of the IAEA review in July 2023 are likely weaken as scientific evidence over time. While radioactive materials are discharged into the ocean under strict supervision by the Japanese government and the IAEA, there could be potential errors and changing circumstances during the discharge, and we will continue to see the findings of scientific review and evaluation on such errors and changing circumstances.

6. CONCLUSION

If the Korean National Assembly legislates a law that provides for an import ban on any seafood from Japan, it constitutes a new dispute that could not have been anticipated by the panel during the proceedings of the panel in the *Korea — Radionuclides* case. Furthermore, based on a systematic and comprehensive analysis of the precedents, it is important to collect information required for an objective risk assessment, and argue and prove that legislating a law providing for an import ban on any seafood from Japan owing to the discharge of radioactive materials into the ocean constitutes provisional measures under the WTO SPS Agreement.

Moreover, it is absolutely necessary to take a firm stance that prioritizes health and safety of the Korean people and the operation of risk management procedures for radioactive materials in compliance with radiation risk assessment systems and principles based on scientific evidence to increase international confidence in the legislation of the Korean National Assembly. By recognizing that monitoring radioactive materials in food is an issue which needs to be addressed in the long run until the Fukushima Daiichi Nuclear Power Plant is closed down, Korea, which also has and operates nuclear power plants, should update its inspection and monitoring technology for radioactive materials and its independent information analysis and monitoring capabilities so that the Korean people can feel safe even during a potential nuclear accident. It is important to improve and invest in technology for the internationally defined radioactive materials, for which Korea does not currently have available technology.

Finally, in communicating its final policy decisions on radioactive contamination control in seafood to the public, it is critical for Korea to shift from a one-way risk communication method, in which the government unilaterally informs the decisions and imposes an understanding from the public, to a two-way risk communication method, which allows the public and stakeholders to engage, and promptly and transparently discloses discussions throughout the process. Ultimately, putting the above risk management procedures in place would improve not just the Korean people's trust in applicable laws on food safety passed by the Korean National Assembly but also the international community's confidence.

References

1. Articles

Cho, Youngjeen, "An Analysis of the Korea-Radionuclides Case", 17(2), *Korean Journal of International Economic Law* (2019), pp.7~41.

Chung, Kichang & Kim, Hye Soo, "An Analysis of SPS Dispute in the WTO: Korea - Radionuclides (DS495)," 146, *International Trade Law* (2020), pp.39~93.

Hamada, Taro & Ishikawa, Yoshimichi, "Are Korea's Import Bans on Japanese Foods Based on Scientific Principles? Comments on Reports of the Panel and the Appellate Body on Korean Import Bans and Testing and Certification Requirements for Radionuclides (WT/DS495)," 11(1), *Eur. J. Risk Reg.* (2020), pp.155~176.

Hong, Sung-Kyu & Whang, Hea-Jeung, "A Study on the SPS Agreement and Korea-Radionuclides (Japan) (DS495)," 18(2), *Journal of International Trade & Commerce* (2022), pp.307~327.

Lee, Sung-Hyong & Chun, Cheong-Ghi, "A Study on Major Issue of WTO Korea-Radionuclides (Japan) Case (1)," 15(4), *Journal of International Trade & Commerce* (2019), pp.213~232.

------, "A Study on Major Issue of WTO Korea-Radionuclides (Japan) Case (2)," 15(5), *Journal of International Trade & Commerce* (2019), pp.247~266.

Lin, Ching-Fu & Naiki, Yoshiko, "An SPS Dispute without Science? The *Fukushima* Case and the Dichotomy of Science/Non-Science Obligations under the SPS Agreement," 33(2), *Eur. J. Int'l L.* (2022), pp.651~678.

Seo, Hye Bin, Han, Jung Hyun & Koo, Min Gyo, "Japan's Decision to Release Fukushima's Wastewater into the Ocean and Its Impact on the Environment: Lessons from South Korea's Reponses to the WTO Dispute over Its Ban on Japanese Fishery Imports," 16(3), *Journal of Governance Studies* (2021), pp.197~224.

Yi, Lori, "WTO Korea - Import Bans, and Testing and Certification Requirements for Radionuclides," 32(1), *Kookmin Law Review* (2019), pp.253~295.

Yoon, Jung-Hyun & Lim, Song Soo, "A Critical Analysis of the SPS Dispute over the Import Ban on Japanese Radioactive Seafood," 44(4), *Korea Trade Review* (2019), pp.19~34.

2. Articles in Collections

Voon, Tania, "WTO law and risk factors for non-communicable diseases: a complex relationship," in *Research Handbook on Environment, Health and the WTO*, 390 (G. Calster & D. Prévost eds., Edward Elgar Publishing, 2013).

3. Working Papers and Reports

IAEA, *Comprehensive Report on the Safety Review of the ALPS-Treated Water at the Fukushima Daiichi Nuclear Power Station* (2023), *available at* https://www.iaea.org/sites/default/files/iaea_comprehensive_alps_report.pdf (Accessed on Aug 30, 2023).

4. WTO Dispute Settlement Reports

Appellate Body Report, *Canada/United States ― Continued Suspension of Obligations*, WT/DS320/ AB/R, WT/DS321/AB/R (Nov. 14, 2008).

Appellate Body Report, *European Communities ― Measures Concerning Meat and Meat Products (Hormones)*, WT/DS26/AB/R, WT/DS48/AB/R (Jan 16, 1998).

Appellate Body Report, *Korea ― Import Bans, and Testing and Certification Requirements for Radionuclides*, WT/DS495/AB/R (Apr 11, 2019).

Appellate Body Report, *Japan ― Measures Affecting the Importation of Apples*, WT/DS245/AB/R (Nov 26, 2003).

Panel Report, *Australia ― Measures Affecting Importation of Salmon*, WT/DS18/AB/R (Jun 12, 1998).

Panel Report, *India ― Measures Affecting the Automotive Sector*, WT/DS146/R, WT/DS175/R (Dec. 21, 2001).

5. Internet Sources

Jeong, Jiseon, *Japan vs. Korea – Radionuclides Case (Dispute over Imported Food from Japan)* (2019), *available at* https://disputecase.kr/439, (Accessed on Feb 26, 2024).

Notes

1. Proposed by Member of the National Assembly Lee So-young, Partial Amendment to the Food Sanitation Act, Proposed Bill No. 24031, Aug 28, 2023; Proposed by Member of the National Assembly Yoon Joon-byeong, Partial Amendment to the Food Sanitation Act, Proposed Bill No. 24338, Sep 8, 2023.

2. Appellate Body Report, *Korea — Import Bans, and Testing and Certification Requirements for Radionuclides*, WT/DS495/AB/R (Apr 11, 2019) ("Appellate Body Report, *Korea — Radionuclides*").

3. Office for Government Policy Coordination, Prime Minister's Secretariat, Public Release: Government Bans Imports of "All Seafood" from eight Prefectures Near Fukushima, Sep 16, 2013.

4. *Agreement on the Application of Sanitary and Phyto-sanitary Measures*, Apr 15, 1994, *Marrakesh Agreement establishing the World Trade Organization*, Annex 1A, 1867 U.N.T.S. 493.

5. WTO, *Korea-Import Bans, and Testing and Certification Requirements for Radionuclides*, DS495 (Accessed on Jan 31, 2024), https://www.wto.org/english/tratop_e/dispu_e/cases_e/ds495_e.htm.

6. *Ibid.*

7. Office for Government Policy Coordination, Prime Minister's Secretariat, WTO's Decision on the Appeal Regarding Japanese Imported Food Dispute and the Government's Position, Public Release, Apr 12, 2019.

8. Kichang Chung & Hye Soo Kim, "An Analysis of SPS Dispute in the WTO: *Korea -Radionuclides* (DS495)," 146, *International Trade Law*, (2020), p.83.

9. Lori Yi, "WTO Korea - Import Bans, and Testing and Certification Requirements for Radionuclides," 32(1), *Kookmin Law Review*, (2019), p.289.

10. "Members shall ensure that their sanitary and phytosanitary measures do not arbitrarily or unjustifiably discriminate between Members where identical or similar conditions prevail, including between their own territory and that of other Members...."

11. Appellate Body Report, *Korea - Radionuclides*, para.5.64.

12. *Ibid.*, para.5.91.

13. Article 5.6 states that once the importing country establishes the appropriate level of protection, it must adopt SPS measures only to the extent necessary to achieve the level. Note 3 specifies the criteria to determine whether a measure is more trade-restrictive than required: A measure is not more trade-restrictive than required unless there is another measure, reasonably available taking into account technical and economic feasibility, that achieves the appropriate level of sanitary or phytosanitary protection and is significantly less restrictive to trade.

14. Panel Report, *Australia-Measures Affecting Importation of Salmon*, WT/DS18/AB/R (Jun 12, 1998) ("Panel Report, *Australia-Salmon*"), para.199.

15. Appellate Body Report, *Korea=Radionuclides*, paras.5.26~5.27.

16. *Ibid.*, para.5.28.
17. *Ibid.*, para.5.175.
18. *Ibid.*, para.5.215.
19. *Ibid.*, para.5.214.
20. *Ibid.*, para.5.233.
21. Chung & Kim, *op. cit.*, p.84; Jiseon Jeong, *Japan vs. Korea - Radionuclides Case (Dispute over Imported Food from Japan)* (2019), *available at* https://disputecase.kr/439 (accessed on Feb 26, 2024).
22. Youngjeen Cho, "An Analysis of the Korea-Radionuclides Case," 17(2), *Korean Journal of International Economic Law*, (2019), pp.32~34; Sung-Hyong Lee and Cheong-Ghi Chun, "A Study on Major Issue of WTO Korea-Radionuclides (Japan) Case (1)," 15(4), *Journal of International Trade & Commerce*, (2019), p.230.
23. Appellate Body Report, *Korea - Radionuclides*, paras.5.37.
24. Hye Bin Seo, Jung Hyun Han & Min Gyo Koo, "Japan's Decision to Release Fukushima's Wastewater into the Ocean and Its Impact on the Environment: Lessons from South Korea's Reponses to the WTO Dispute over Its Ban on Japanese Fishery Imports," 16(3), *Journal of Governance Studies*, (2021), p.218; Sung-Kyu Hong & Hea-Jeung Whang, "A Study on the SPS Agreement and Korea-Radionuclides (Japan) (DS495)," 18(2), *Journal of International Trade & Commerce* (2022), p.325.
25. Ching-Fu Lin & Yoshiko Naiki, "An SPS Dispute without Science? The *Fukushima* Case and the Dichotomy of Science/Non-Science Obligations under the SPS Agreement," 33(2), *Eur. J. Int'l L.*, (2022), pp.653~654; Taro Hamada & Yoshimichi Ishikawa, "Are Korea's Import Bans on Japanese Foods Based on Scientific Principles? Comments on Reports of the Panel and the Appellate Body on Korean Import Bans and Testing and Certification Requirements for Radionuclides (WT/DS495)," 11(1), *Eur. J. Risk Reg.*, (2020), p.175.
26. Lin & Naiki, *op.cit*, pp.673~677.
27. Sung-Hyong Lee and Cheong-Ghi Chun, "A Study on Major Issue of WTO Korea-Radionuclides (Japan) Case (2)," 15(5), *Journal of International Trade & Commerce* (2019), p.263.
28. Panel Report, *India-Measures Affecting the Automotive Sector*, WT/DS146/R, WT/DS175/R (Dec. 21, 2001), paras.7.54~7.66.
29. Cho, *op.cit.*, p.31.
30. Appellate Body Report, *Canada/United States — Continued Suspension of Obligations*, WT/DS320/ AB/R, WT/DS321/AB/R (Nov. 14, 2008) ("Appellate Body Report, *US/Canada — Continued Suspension*"), para.677.
31. Appellate Body Report, *European Communities — Measures Concerning Meat and Meat Products (Hormones)*, WT/DS26/AB/R, WT/DS48/AB/R (Jan 16, 1998) ("Appellate Body Report, *EC — Hormones*"), paras.193~194.
32. *Ibid.*, para.187. In this case, the EU argued that the WTO's Dispute Settlement Body should consider not only scientific justification but also non-scientific factors, including consumer concerns, political circumstances, and social values.

But the argument was not accepted.

33. Panel Report, *Australia-Salmon*, paras.8.136~8.137.

34. Appellate Body Report, *EC-Hormones*, para.190; Panel Report, *EC-Approval and Marketing of Biotech Products*, para.7.3024; Tania Voon, "WTO law and risk factors for non-communicable diseases: a complex relationship," in *Research Handbook on Environment, Health and the WTO*, 390 (G. Calster & D. Prévost eds., Edward Elgar Publishing, 2013), p.407.

35. Appellate Body Report, *EC-Hormones*, para.200; Appellate Body Report, *Japan-Measures Affecting the Importation of Apples*, WT/DS245/AB/R (Nov 26, 2003) ("Appellate Body Report, *Japan-Apples*), para.202.

36. IAEA, *Comprehensive Report on the Safety Review of the ALPS-Treated Water at the Fukushima Daiichi Nuclear Power Station*, 2023 (Accessed on Aug 30, 2023), https://www.iaea.org/sites/default/files/iaea_comprehensive_alps_report.pdf ("IAEA, Comprehensive Report on the Safety Review of the ALPS-Treated Water at the Fukushima Daiichi Nuclear Power Station").

An Overview of Recent ISDS Cases Involving Korea

Sok Young CHANG
Assistant Professor
Incheon National University, Faculty of Law, Incheon, Korea

Key Words

ISDS, Investor-State Dispute Settlement, Elliott v. Korea, Lone Star v. Korea, annulment proceeding

1. INTRODUCTION

The Republic of Korea (hereinafter, "Korea") has been involved in a number of Investor-State Dispute Settlement (hereinafter, "ISDS") cases so far, and while most of them are still pending, one of them, *Elliott v. Korea*, was settled in 2023.[1] Moreover, *Lone Star v. Korea*, which was settled in 2022, is drawing much attention until lately as annulment proceedings are still ongoing.[2]

2. BRIEF SUMMARY OF CASES

2-1. *Lone Star v. Korea*

Lone Star v. Korea is a case that has attracted a fair amount of attention for more than a decade in Korea for being the first ISDS case brought against Korea, and for causing an "eat and run" controversy when the US private equity fund sold the Korean Exchange Bank with large profits after holding the shares only for a short term. *Lone Star v. Korea* was initiated on November 21, 2012, and it took almost 10 years for the tribunal to render an award on August 30, 2022.[3]

Soon after the International Center for Settlement of Investment Disputes (hereinafter, "ICSID") rendered an award on this case, the Korean government submitted a request for rectification of the award pursuant to Article 49(2) of the ICSID Convention. According to the provision of Article 49(2), the State party that wishes to request rectification should make it within 45 days after the date on which the award was rendered, and the request of the Korean government was made within 45 days after August 30, 2022, on October 14, 2022. The Korean government pointed out that there were errors in the amount of the total loss resulting from the Hana transaction and in the amount of the overall damages. The Claimants also requested not only to rectify the errors the Respondent identified but also to correct the foreign exchange rates applied in the calculation. The Tribunal concluded that an error had occurred in adding interests to the amount of the total loss for the period from May 24, 2011, to December 2, 2011, which predated the date of injury, and corrected the total loss resulting from the Hana transaction from USD 432,037,364 to USD 433,000,000. Accordingly, due to this decision on rectification, the amount that the Respondent should pay the Claimants was reduced from USD 216,500,000 to USD 216,018,682.[4]

Moreover, the parties filed an application for annulment of the award respectively, and in the case of Korea, the application was submitted on September 1, 2023, after a thorough consideration of whether there are grounds for annulment since the list of grounds provided in Article 52 of the ICSID Convention is exhaustive.

Among the five grounds for annulment, the Korean government's request for annulment was based on the grounds that there was a manifest excess of powers by the Tribunal, a serious departure from a fundamental rule of procedure, and a failure to state reasons. First, the Korean government claimed that the Tribunal had exceeded its powers by failing to apply the general international law principles of state responsibility when finding Korea responsible for breach of an international obligation. Regarding the Tribunal's departure from the rule of procedure, the principal issue raised by the Korean government was that the Tribunal had disregarded the rules of evidence and decided in favor of the Claimants without sufficient evidence. Lastly, the Korean government argued that the Tribunal had failed to state reasons with regard to how the Lone Star Funds could have reasonable expectation of profits and to the conclusion acknowledging state responsibility of Korea.

Under Article 52(5) of the ICSID Convention, a party to annulment proceedings may request a stay of enforcement of the award until the final decision of the Tribunal, and thus Korea asked for the stay of enforcement of the award when applying for the annulment. After reviewing the parties' positions, the Tribunal decided to postpone the enforcement of the award until the decision on annulment on   December 15, 2023.[5]

2-2. *Elliott v. Korea*

Elliott v. Korea was initiated on July 12, 2018, when Elliott (Elliott Associates, L.P.) sent a notice of arbitration and statement of claim against Korea under the Korea-US Free Trade Agreement (hereinafter, "KORUS FTA") and the Arbitration Rules of the United Nations Commission on International Trade Law (hereinafter, "UNCTRAL Rules"). The dispute arose concerning the merger of two Korean companies, Samsung C&T Corporation and Cheil

Industries Incorporated in 2015, and the Claimant (Elliott) was a US hedge fund that owned 7.1 percent of Samsung C&T Corporation's shares. Elliott opposed the merger and claimed that, because of the Korean government's intervention, it lost its money. In this regard, Elliott submitted its claim to arbitration, and the Permanent Court of Arbitration acted as a registry. The Tribunal handed down an award on June 20, 2023, after five years of litigation.[6]

During the arbitral proceedings, the Claimant argued that Korea had breached the minimum standard of treatment obligation and the national treatment standard stated in the KORUS FTA by improperly intervening in the shareholder vote in this event. On the other hand, the Respondent claimed that the Tribunal lacked jurisdiction over the Claimant's claim and also argued that the Claimant failed to prove that the Claimant had suffered a substantial loss.

After the review, the Tribunal ruled in favor of the Claimant and decided that Korea had failed to afford the minimum standard of treatment to Elliott and violated Article 11.5 of the KORUS FTA. First, the Tribunal found that the conduct of the National Pension System (hereinafter, "NPS") was attributable to Korea as the NPS is a *de facto* State organ. The Tribunal came up with this conclusion as the NPS was created by a statute; it is functionally and financially closely linked to the Korean State; its officials are appointed by the Minister of Health and Welfare; and it is subject to annual audits by the National Assembly. Then, in the merits, the Tribunal looked at the Korean courts' decisions on the criminal proceedings regarding the NPS's approval of the merger of the two companies. According to the courts' decisions, the Respondent intervened in the event and influenced the vote to make sure that it would be in favor of the merger. As a result, the Tribunal concluded that Korea had breached international obligations and ordered to pay damages to Elliott with interest and also to pay part of the legal costs incurred by the Claimant, which in sum amounts to approximately USD 107.8

million.

Shortly after the award was rendered, Korea requested the correction and interpretation of the award under Articles 37 and 38 of the UNCITRAL Rules on July 18, 2023, and, two days later, Elliott submitted its request for correction of the award as well. Both of the parties submitted their response to the other party's request. With regard to these requests, the Tribunal accepted the errors the Respondent questioned and clarified the errors regarding in which currency pre-award interest should be calculated in the decision on requests for correction and interpretation of the award.[7]

Moreover, Korea, being unsatisfied with the result, decided to challenge the award by filing a lawsuit in London on July 18, 2023. It was submitted to the court in the United Kingdom as the seat of arbitration was the UK. While Korea maintained that it was quite rare for a government to be ordered to pay damages arising from exercising shareholder's voting rights by a public agency, Elliott made some remarks against Korea for pursuing further legal proceedings on this matter and asked the Court to dismiss the case without hearing. However, the Court did not accept Elliott's request and declined the request for summary dismissal of the case.[8] The reason why the UK Court did not dismiss the case was that the jurisdictional claim raised by the Korean government was an important issue related to the interpretation of the KORUS FTA, and whether exercising minority shareholders' voting rights could be regarded as government's acts was an issue that should be carefully examined. Therefore, the Court ordered Elliott to pay 50 percent of the legal costs incurred by the Korean government.

3. CONCLUSION

As seen above, Korea challenged the awards of the two recent cases, and there are still several cases pending. Among them, the final results of these two cases would be particularly important. First, *Lone Star v. Korea* has received more attention than any other case in Korea, and thus the final result of the case would not be any different. Moreover, the result of *Elliott v. Korea* would have a crucial effect on a case with a similar background, *Mason v. Korea*, which was pending until recently and on which the Tribunal ruled in favor of Mason in April 2024.[9]

Notes

1. Elliott Associates L.P. v. Republic of Korea, PCA Case No. 2018-51.

2. LSF-KEB Holdings SCA and others v. Republic of Korea, ICSID Case No. ARB/12/37.

3. LSF-KEB Holdings SCA and others v. Republic of Korea, ICSID Case No. ARB/12/37, Award, August 30, 2022.

4. LSF-KEB Holdings SCA and others v. Republic of Korea, ICSID Case No. ARB/12/37, Decision on Rectification, May 8, 2023.

5. LSF-KEB Holdings SCA and others v. Republic of Korea, ICSID Case No. ARB/12/37, Decision on Stay of Enforcement of the Award, December 15, 2023.

6. Elliott Associates L.P. v. Republic of Korea, PCA Case No. 2018-51, Award, June 20, 2023.

7. Elliott Associates L.P. v. Republic of Korea, PCA Case No. 2018-51, Decision on Requests for Correction and Interpretation of the Award, September 1, 2023.

8. Ministry of Justice, "Elliott case, Elliott's request for summary dismissal without hearing dismissed in its entirety", Press release, October 19, 2023.

9. Mason Capital L.P. and Mason Management LLC v. Republic of Korea, Case No. 2018-55.

Domestic Implementation of the HCCH 1993 Adoption Convention

Gyooho LEE
Professor of Law
Chung–Ang University School of Law, Seoul, Korea

Key Words

HCCH 1993 Adoption Convention, International Adoption Act of 2023, Special Act on Domestic Adoption of 2023, Ministry of Health and Welfare, Child Rights Protection Agency

1. BACKGROUND OF THE IMPLEMENTATION OF THE HCCH 1993 ADOPTION CONVENTION

1.1 Enactment of the International Adoption Act of 2023

The *Convention of 29 May 1993 on Protection of Children and Co-operation in Respect of Intercountry Adoption* (hereinafter, the "HCCH 1993 Adoption Convention"), which entered into force on May 1, 1995, aims at the protection of "children and their families against the risks of illegal, irregular, premature or ill-prepared adoptions abroad."[1] As of November 14, 2022, the number of Contracting Parties to the HCCH 1993 Adoption Convention was 33. The Republic of Korea (hereinafter, "Korea") signed up for this Convention on May 24, 2013, but has yet to ratify it.

Nonetheless, the Bill Related to International Adoption[2] was submitted to the Health and Welfare Committee of the Korean National Assembly on December 9, 2022, and referred to the Legislative and Judiciary Committee of the Korean National Assembly on February 23, 2023. Finally, it was passed at the Plenary Session of the National Assembly on June 30, 2023. It purports to enact a domestic law consistent with the HCCH 1993 Adoption Convention prior to ratifying it. The Act Related to International Adoption (hereinafter, the "International Adoption Act")[3] was enacted on July 18, 2023, and will become effective on July 19, 2025.

1.2 The Comprehensive Revision of the Special Act on Domestic Adoption of 2023

Adoption is a form of protection that provides a permanent home for children subject to protection, and the adoption process should be child-centered. In most countries, including advanced countries, the adoption system is centered on the central and local governments, but, in Korea, due to the special circumstances of the three year-long Korean War, which occurred in 1950, the adoption system centered on private adoption agencies was established and has lasted so far. In order to ensure that adoptions are carried out based on the best interests of the child subject to protection, the government aims to promote structural changes to the adoption system, including strengthening the responsibility of the State throughout the adoption process. In addition, in order to implement the HCCH 1993 Adoption Convention, the international adoption system will be regulated separately under the newly enacted International Adoption Act, limiting the scope of application of the current Special Act on Adoption[4] to the domestic adoption. Thus, the Special Bill Related to Domestic Adoption[5] was introduced to the

Health and Welfare Committee of the Korean National Assembly on June 29, 2023, and referred to the Legislative and Judiciary Committee of the Korean National Assembly on February 23, 2023. The Bill was passed at the Plenary Session of the Korean National Assembly on June 30, 2023. In sum, the Special Act Related to Domestic Adoption (hereinafter, the "Special Act on Domestic Adoption")[6] was comprehensively revised on July 18, 2023, and will take effect on July 19, 2025.

2. AN OVERVIEW OF ITS IMPLEMENTATION

2.1 The Main Contents of the International Adoption Act

(i) International adoption is the transfer of a child's habitual residence from the Republic of Korea to a foreign country or from a foreign country to the Republic of Korea in order to be adopted or as a result of adoption (Article 2 of the International Adoption Act).

(ii) International adoption may be permitted only when it is in the best interests of the child, including providing a permanent home for a child who has not found an adoptive family in Korea, and no organization or person involved in international adoption shall acquire an unfair financial advantage as a result of an adoption under this Act (Articles 3 and 4 of the International Adoption Act).

(iii) The central authorities in the Republic of Korea shall be the Ministry of Health and Welfare (Article 5 of the International Adoption Act).

(iv) A child eligible for international adoption under this Act shall be a child determined by the Minister of Health and Welfare to be eligible for international adoption or the

biological child of a married couple in the case of a spouse
seeking to adopt the biological child of the spouse alone
(Article 7 of the International Adoption Act).

(v) The Minister of Health and Welfare shall match the child to
be adopted with a person deemed qualified to be an adoptive
parent after deliberation and resolution by the Adoption
Policy Committee (Article 10 of the International Adoption
Act).

(vi) The International Adoption Act stipulates the procedure for
consultation between central authorities in international
adoptions (Articles 11 and 21 of the International Adoption
Act).

(vii) The Ministry of Health and Welfare, in co-operation with
the central authorities of the adopting country, shall receive
and verify the child's adaptation report after the
international adoption is established and ensure that the
child has acquired the nationality of the adopting country
(Article 16 of the International Adoption Act).

(viii) A person who intends to become an adoptive parent shall
apply to the Minister of Health and Welfare, and the
Minister of Health and Welfare shall conduct counseling
and a home environment investigation on the person who
intends to become an adoptive parent (Article 20 of the
International Adoption Act).

(ix) If the adoption of a child adopted from a foreign country is
cancelled, the Minister of Health and Welfare shall
cooperate with the central authorities of the adoptive country
to take protective measures, including returning the child to
Korea (Article 26 of the International Adoption Act).

(x) The State may enter into bilateral or multilateral agreements
with States Parties to the HCCH 1993 Adoption Convention
or with non-State Parties as necessary (Article 31 of the

International Adoption Act).

2.2 The Main Contents of the Special Act on Domestic Adoption

(i)   The title of the former Special Act on Adoption was modified to the Special Act on Domestic Adoption, and it establishes special exceptions to the requirements and procedures for domestic adoption of children subject to protection, as well as matters necessary to support such adoption, in order to promote the rights, interests, and welfare of adoptees and adoptive families, and to facilitate domestic adoption of children subject to protection in accordance with the principle of the best interests of the child.

(ii) The Minister of Health and Welfare shall establish and implement a basic plan for the promotion of domestic adoption every five years based on the results of a survey on adoption in order to promote domestic adoption (Article 10 of the Special Act on Domestic Adoption).

(iii) The Adoption Policy Committee shall be established as a special committee of the Child Policy Coordination Committee to deliberate and resolve major matters related to the policy of promoting domestic adoption and matters related to adoption (Article 12 of the Special Act on Domestic Adoption).

(iv) The child to be protected must be a child subject to protection who is determined to be in the best interests of the child by the governor of a city or province, or the mayor or head of county or of district office (Article 13(1) of the Special Act on Domestic Adoption).

(v)   The State and local government may entrust the child to be adopted to a childcare facility under the Child Welfare Act for care and protection and may subsidize the costs of childcare (Articles 13(3) and 39 of the Special Act on Domestic Adoption).

(vi) A person who intends to become a foster parent must apply to the Minister of Health and Welfare, and the Minister of Health and Welfare must conduct counseling and a home environment survey on the person who intends to become a foster parent and prepare a report on the same (Article 19 of the Special Act on Domestic Adoption).

(vii) The Minister of Health and Welfare shall match the prospective adoptive parents with the child to be adopted after deliberation and resolution by the Adoption Policy Committee (Article 20 of the Special Act on Domestic Adoption).

(viii) The Minister of Health and Welfare shall provide regular counseling and necessary welfare services for the mutual adjustment of the adoptive parents and the adopted child for one year after the adoption is established and shall prepare a report on the child's adjustment (Article 31 of the Special Act on Domestic Adoption).

(ix) A person who has been adopted under the Special Act on Domestic Adoption may request the Director of the Child Rights Protection Agency to disclose adoption information relating to him or her (Article 33 of the Special Act on Domestic Adoption).

(x) The Minister of Health and Welfare may entrust some of the tasks under the Special Act on Domestic Adoption to the Child Rights Protection Agency and other social welfare corporations and organizations that have the necessary facilities and employees to carry out the entrusted tasks (Article 37 of the Special Act on Domestic Adoption).

3. COMMENTS

The International Adoption Act of 2023 and Special Act on Domestic Adoption of 2023 will become effective on July 19, 2025. It is expected that the Korean government will ratify the HCCH 1993 Adoption Convention before July 19, 2025.

Notes

1. https://www.hcch.net/en/instruments/conventions/specialised-sections/intercountry-adoption (last visit on January 30, 2024).
2. Bill No. 2122990.
3. Act No. 19553. It was enacted on July 18, 2023, and will become effective on July 19, 2025.
4. Act No. 20108. It was revised on January 23, 2024, and became effective since the same date.
5. Bill No. 2122992.
6. Act No. 19555. It was comprehensively revised on July 18, 2023, and will become effective on July 19, 2025.

CONTEMPORARY PRACTICE AND
JUDICIAL DECISIONS

Resolutions Relating to International Law Adopted by the 21st National Assembly of Korea in 2023

Min Jung CHUNG
Legislative Research Officer
National Assembly Legislative Research Service

Key Words

resolutions, National Assembly, East Sea, Joint Development Zone, Sado Gold Mine

The National Assembly of the Republic of Korea (hereinafter, "Korea") gathers and expresses its positions regarding the government's foreign policy in the form of resolutions. Such resolutions commonly urge the Korean government, foreign governments, or the international community to implement specific measures related to Korea. To facilitate international cooperation, the resolutions use commonly accepted international communication channels (international agreements, charters, etc.). Resolutions can be viewed as an effective tool by which the constitutional authority of the National Assembly can be protected while also guaranteeing a democratic process domestically. Given the growing importance of public diplomacy, the role of the National Assembly as a flexible form of diplomacy is also growing, and greater weight is expected to be placed on the National Assembly's resolutions.

As of December 31, 2023, there were a total of 14 resolutions related to international law adopted at the plenary session by the 21st National Assembly in 2023 (Table 1). In general, resolutions related to international law are adopted by the Foreign Affairs and Unification Committee. One of the characteristics of the 2023 National Assembly resolutions related to international law is a significant increase in quantity. In 2023, there were fourteen resolutions, compared to only five in 2022. In addition to this quantitative increase, in 2023, there was a qualitative change from 2022 in that the proportion of human rights resolutions increased (from one out of five cases in 2022 to five out of fourteen cases in 2023), while, in 2022, there were fewer resolutions declaring the will to realize justice by applying human rights, a universal value of international law, equally to all countries.

The year 2023 saw an increase in the percentage of resolutions calling for Japan to correct some of its behaviors. In 2022, there was one resolution calling out and condemning Japan, which Korea has been at odds with historically, while there were six resolutions in 2023. This is because members of the National Assembly should act very sensitively to the direction of public opinion. Whenever there is any conflict in the country's relations with Japan, the Korean people tend to react very strongly and emotionally, and members of the National Assembly adopt a strategy of jumping on the bandwagon of these emotions, instead of calming them down. It is in part because their biggest goal is to win the next election. Every time anti-Japanese sentiment outbursts among the Korean people, members of the National Assembly adopt resolutions demanding corrective actions from Japan, visit Japanese officials to protest, or otherwise engage in highly pretentious activities to deliver the people's anger. These activities are likely to be covered and highlighted by the media, which may increase awareness about such politicians among the people, and, in turn, make a difference in an election. By contrast, if members of the National Assembly try to persuade the people to react reasonably and bring relations between Korea and Japan back to normal, it may have negative consequences on their re-election. In this context, whenever there is any conflict or confrontation between Korea and Japan, members of the National Assembly are incentivized to stir up the conflict rather than cooling it down.

In 2023, the National Assembly proposed establishing an inter-parliamentary union with the United States, the United Kingdom, and Canada to reinforce exchanges on the shared issues that the countries were currently facing. While diplomacy, in principle, is conducted exclusively by the administration as a part of the executive power, it is becoming increasingly challenging for the administration to handle all diplomatic activities in today's diplomacy as diplomatic issues are becoming more diverse and complex. Considering the broad scope of exchanges between countries and the transboundary nature of current issues, parliamentary diplomacy may contribute to widening the exchanges led by the administration and offer some support to resolve issues when government-driven exchanges do not work as intended. This is why parliamentary diplomacy is becoming increasingly useful and necessary in today's diplomacy.

In 2024, it is expected that the Korean National Assembly will identify a number of agendas that reflect the universal perspective of international law (promotion of international peace, global environment, global economic order, and democracy) and adopt resolutions on them. Hopefully, the National Assembly will serve as a bridge in relations between Korea and Japan by reminding the people of the strategic value and potential of the relations.

[Table 1] Resolutions Related to International Law Adopted by the 21st National Assembly in 2023

(As of December 31, 2023)

Bill Number	Bill Name	Responsible Committee	Date of Adoption at the Plenary Session
2125870	Resolution Calling for the Protection of Civilians and a Peaceful Resolution to the Israel-Hamas Armed Conflict	Foreign Affairs and Unification Committee	December 8, 2023
2125646	Special Resolution for the Continued Development of Bilateral Relations on the 140th Anniversary of Diplomatic Relations between the Republic of Korea and the United Kingdom	Foreign Affairs and Unification Committee	December 8, 2023
2125542	Special Resolution for the Continued Development of Bilateral Relations on the 140th Anniversary of Diplomatic Relations between the Republic of Korea and Germany	Foreign Affairs and Unification Committee	December 8, 2023
2125113	Resolution Calling for an End to Arms Trade and Technical Collaboration for Weapons between the Russian Federation and the Democratic People's Republic of Korea in Violation of United Nations Security Council Resolutions	Foreign Affairs and Unification Committee	December 8, 2023
2124297	Resolution Calling for the Designation of the East Sea	Foreign Affairs and Unification Committee	December 8, 2023
2125661	Resolution Calling on the People's Republic of China to Cease Forced Repatriation of Defectors from the Democratic People's Republic of Korea	Foreign Affairs and Unification Committee	November 30, 2023
2124426	Resolution Calling on the	Foreign Affairs	November 30,

	Government of Japan to Reveal the Truth and Apologize for the Massacre of Koreans during the Great Kanto Earthquake	and Unification Committee	2023
2121884	Special Resolution for the Continued Development of Bilateral Relations on the 60th Anniversary of Diplomatic Relations between the Republic of Korea and Canada	Foreign Affairs and Unification Committee	November 30, 2023
2120611	Resolution Calling on the Government of Japan to Promptly Implement the Agreement between the Republic of Korea and Japan Concerning the Joint Development of the Southern Part of the Continental Shelf Adjacent to the Two Countries and Prepare Practical Implementation Measures	Foreign Affairs and Unification Committee	November 30, 2023
2125087	Resolution Reaffirming the Republic of Korea's Undisputed Sovereignty over Dokdo and Condemning Japan's Claim to Dokdo and Historical Revisionism in Textbooks	Foreign Affairs and Unification Committee	November 9, 2023
2122922	Resolution Calling for Withdrawing the Fukushima Daiichi ALPS Treated Water Discharge Plan and Preparing Measures to Ensure Seafood Safety and Protect Fishermen	Agriculture, Food, Rural Affairs, Oceans and Fisheries Committee	June 30, 2023
2120073	Special Resolution Calling for the Sustainable Development of Bilateral Relations on the 70th Anniversary of the Republic of Korea-United States Alliance	Foreign Affairs and Unification Committee	April 12, 2023
2119672	Resolution Calling on the	Culture, Sports and	February 27, 2023

	Government of Japan to Withdraw Its Reapplication for the Inscription of Sado Gold Mine on the World Heritage List and Implement UNESCO's Recommendations for Modern Industrial Facilities in Japan	Tourism Committee	
2119997	Resolution Honoring the Victims of Turkey-Syria Earthquakes and Calling for Support for Recovery	Foreign Affairs and Unification Committee	February 14, 2023

Source: National Assembly Bill Information System (last accessed on January 31, 2024), http://likms.assembly.go.kr/bill/BillSearchResult.do.

1. RESOLUTION CALLING FOR THE PROTECTION OF CIVILIANS AND A PEACEFUL RESOLUTION TO THE ISRAEL-HAMAS ARMED CONFLICT

Since Hamas, a Palestinian militant group, attacked Israel on October 7, 2023, the Israel-Hamas armed conflict has continued with increasing consequences on both sides. The number of civilian and foreign casualties has been growing, and Israel's blockade has resulted in hunger, thirst, disease, and a severe public health crisis in Gaza.

On December 8, 2023, the National Assembly adopted a resolution expressing its deepest concerns over the growing civilian suffering in Gaza in the wake of the armed conflict between the two sides and calling for humanitarian aid in Gaza and a peaceful resolution to the conflict as early as possible to prevent further civilian suffering. More specifically, the National Assembly condemned Hamas for indiscriminately killing civilians, and called on Israel and Hamas to cease indiscriminate attacks on civilians and agree on a humanitarian ceasefire. It also called for the immediate and unconditional release of all civilians detained unlawfully by either side. The National Assembly urged the Korean government to work with countries that respect international human rights and humanitarian law to accelerate a resolution to the conflict.

The National Assembly called on Israel and Hamas to agree on an immediate ceasefire and create humanitarian corridors to allow safe entry and exit of humanitarian aid and aid workers in the Gaza Strip, which is under a comprehensive blockade, based on international humanitarian law and United Nations Security Council Resolution (S/RES/2712) adopted on November 15, 2023. The National Assembly, however, took a more cautious approach in officially supporting the two-state solution for governance in post-war Gaza. To begin with, it is a matter over which Israel has sovereign discretion as it is a security measure, considering the diplomatic relations between Korea and Israel. It is Israel that holds the key to the solution. Israel needs to withdraw 700,000 Jewish people living in the West Bank and East Jerusalem. Israel, however, doubled down on its hardline stance on Gaza. On November 10, 2023, Israeli Prime Minister Benjamin Netanyahu stated that Israel will continue to control Gaza even after the war ends and that the country will not rely on United Nations peacekeepers. Considering that the United States administration has been quite consistent in its policy towards the Israeli–Palestinian conflict, it remains to be seen which side the administration will lean more towards on the spectrum between the two extremes.

2. SPECIAL RESOLUTION FOR THE CONTINUED DEVELOPMENT OF BILATERAL RELATIONS ON THE 140TH ANNIVERSARY OF DIPLOMATIC RELATIONS BETWEEN THE REPUBLIC OF KOREA AND THE UNITED KINGDOM

Korea and the United Kingdom established diplomatic ties by

signing the Korea-United Kingdom Treaty of 1883 on November 26, 1883, and the year 2023 marks the 140th anniversary thereof. The United Kingdom is a longtime ally of Korea, which fought and bled together during the Korean War. During the war, the United Kingdom decided to deploy its military forces within just two days of the outbreak of the war and sent some forces of the Far East Fleet stationed in Hong Kong, the 29th Infantry Brigade, and No. 41 (Royal Marine) Commando from its mainland. Until the Korean Armistice Agreement, the United Kingdom sent 81,084 troops in total, of which1,106 killed in action, 2,674 wounded, and 1,060 taken as prisoners of war. Today, the United Kingdom continues to protect peace on the Korean Peninsula as part of the United Nations Command. The UK is also a future-facing partner with Korea, which shares common values, such as democratic principles, fundamental human rights and freedom, open and fair trade, global economic security, and tackling climate change around the world.

On November 22, 2023, the leaders of both countries reaffirmed their commitment to upholding these shared values and agreed to remain committed to protecting international norms and order in the face of any unlawful acts of aggression and provocation. On December 8, 2023, the National Assembly adopted a resolution welcoming the Korea-United Kingdom relations elevated to a global strategic partnership and declaring its full support for bilateral security, economic, and energy cooperation. With this resolution, the National Assembly said it would never forget the noble sacrifices made by the United Kingdom veterans and proposed establishing a bilateral inter-parliamentary union for practical consultations on bilateral issues.

3. SPECIAL RESOLUTION FOR THE CONTINUED DEVELOPMENT OF BILATERAL RELATIONS ON THE 140TH ANNIVERSARY OF DIPLOMATIC RELATIONS BETWEEN THE REPUBLIC OF KOREA AND GERMANY

Korea and Germany established diplomatic ties by signing the Korea-Germany Treaty of 1883 on November 26, 1883, and the year 2023 marks the 140th anniversary thereof. Korea dispatched nurses and miners to Germany in 1963 at the request of West Germany, and the year 2023 also marks the 60th anniversary of the dispatch. Korea and Germany have a very unique sense of solidarity towards each other due to their shared historical experience of going through the wounds of division and accomplishing remarkable economic growth and democracy in a short period of time.

On October 19, 2023, the German Bundestag adopted a resolution celebrating the 140th anniversary of the establishment of diplomatic ties between Germany and Korea. In this resolution, the Bundestag stated that as democracies and value partners, Germany and Korea support peace, security, respect for human rights, and international order based on the rule of law. It also recognized Korea as one of Germany's important economic partners in Asia, which plays a crucial role in the German federal government's and the EU's strategy in the Indo-Pacific. The Bundestag also declared that, as both countries share a common experience, Germany will support the efforts of the Korean government to stop North Korea's nuclear threats and achieve a peaceful reunification on the Korean Peninsula.

On December 8, 2023, the National Assembly adopted a similar resolution in response to the German Bundestag's adoption of a resolution commemorating the 140th anniversary of the establishment of diplomatic ties between the two countries. In the resolution, the National Assembly celebrated the 140th anniversary of the establishment of diplomatic ties between the two countries and the 60th anniversary of the dispatch to Germany, calling on both countries to work together to tackle global conflicts and seek shared prosperity for humanity, to act proactively to greatly increase bilateral economic and trade relations and stabilize supply chains, and to expand people-to-people exchanges. Back in 2013, the National Assembly adopted the Resolution Calling for Promoting Bilateral Friendship and Cooperation on the 130th Anniversary of Diplomatic Relations between the Republic of Korea and Germany and the 50th Anniversary of the Dispatch of Korean Workers to Germany.

4. RESOLUTION CALLING FOR AN END TO ARMS TRADE AND TECHNICAL COLLABORATION FOR WEAPONS BETWEEN THE RUSSIAN FEDERATION AND THE DEMOCRATIC PEOPLE'S REPUBLIC OF KOREA IN VIOLATION OF UNITED NATIONS SECURITY COUNCIL RESOLUTIONS

United Nations Security Council Resolutions strictly prohibit any arms import from North Korea and any technology transfer to North Korea. On September 13, 2023, however, there was a summit between Russian President Vladimir Putin and North Korean leader Kim Jong Un, during which the two countries presumably made an arms deal, and North Korea received military reconnaissance satellite launch technology, warship and submarine technology, and nuclear and ballistic missile technology from Russia in exchange for providing weapons.

On October 26, 2023, the foreign ministers of Korea, Japan, and the United States issued a joint statement strongly condemning the arms deal between Russia and North Korea. On December 8, 2023, the National Assembly also adopted a resolution condemning the

Russian Federation for receiving weapons and military supplies from North Korea. In the resolution, the National Assembly called on the Russian Federation to cease any arms deal with North Korea, while urging the South Korean government to make every effort, including independent sanctions, to prevent the arms deal between the Russian Federation and North Korea.

5. RESOLUTION CALLING FOR THE DESIGNATION OF THE EAST SEA

The name of the East Sea has been used for more than 2,000 years and is still used by 75 million Koreans and holds such significance to the Korean people that it is included as the first word of the country's national anthem. Due to the unique historical background between Korea and Japan, however, the name of the Sea of Japan has been spread in the international community. In 1929, the International Hydrographic Organization (hereinafter, "IHO") published the Limits of Oceans and Seas to clarify the names of oceans and seas. Japan requested that the sea east of the Korean Peninsula be called the Sea of Japan, and it was accepted by the IHO. Since Korea was under Japanese colonial rule at that time, Korea was not able to make a fair case for the designation of the East Sea in the international community.

Korea, which joined the IHO in 1957, argued at the 1997 General Assembly of the IHO that the designation of the Sea of Japan was not fair, and the Sea of Japan and the East Sea should be designated together or the third edition (S-23) of the Limits of Oceans and Seas should be revoked. The issue was put on hold at the 2012 and 2017 General Assemblies. In the 2020 General Assembly, however, the IHO decided to adopt a digital nautical chart, which used a numerical identifier for the sea, instead of the existing international standard nautical chart (S-23), which exclusively designated the Sea of Japan.

Even though the existing nautical chart, which exclusively designated the Sea of Japan, had already been revoked by the General Assembly of the IHO, the United States Department of Defense, which had interchangeably used the Sea of Japan and the East Sea in Korea-Japan-United States military drills, announced that it would officially designate the sea as the Sea of Japan in 2023. On December 8, 2023, the Korean National Assembly adopted a resolution calling on the United States Department of Defense to withdraw its decision to designate the sea as the Sea of Japan, the Japanese government to accept the legitimacy of the designation of the East Sea, and the Korean government to make diplomatic efforts to ensure that the East Sea is designated exclusively in the international community.

6. RESOLUTION CALLING ON THE PEOPLE'S REPUBLIC OF CHINA TO STOP THE FORCED REPATRIATION OF DEFECTORS FROM THE DEMOCRATIC PEOPLE'S REPUBLIC OF KOREA

North Korean defectors staying abroad are considered South Korean citizens under the South Korean Constitution and refugees under international law. China is a party to multilateral international conventions, including the Convention Relating to the Status of Refugees and the Convention against Torture and Other Cruel, Inhuman or Degrading Treatment or Punishment. However, China prioritized the 1960 Criminal Extradition Agreement, the 1986 Mutual Agreement on Illegal North Korean Defectors, and the 1993 Jilin Province Border Management Ordinance, which it signed with North Korea, to forcibly repatriate North Korean defectors living in

China.

On November 30, 2023, the Korean National Assembly adopted a resolution calling on the Chinese government not to forcibly repatriate North Korean defectors in China and to allow them to go to a third country or South Korea of their own choosing. In the resolution, the Korean National Assembly urged international organizations, such as the United Nations High Commissioner for Refugees, to strongly demand that the Chinese government comply with international conventions and called on the South Korean government to work with the international community to make diplomatic efforts to protect the human rights of North Korean defectors, who are citizens of the Republic of Korea under the South Korean Constitution.

7. RESOLUTION CALLING ON THE GOVERNMENT OF JAPAN TO REVEAL THE TRUTH AND APOLOGIZE FOR THE MASSACRE OF KOREANS DURING THE GREAT KANTO EARTHQUAKE

The Great Kanto Earthquake was a 7.9 magnitude earthquake, which took place on September 1, 1923, in Kanto, Japan. According to the White Paper on Disaster Management published by the Japanese government, more than 105,000 people were killed or missing during the earthquake, and estimated economic damages accounted for approximately 37% of Japan's gross domestic product (GDP) at that time. As the Japanese people were in distress in the aftermath of the Great Kanto Earthquake, Japan declared martial law and deployed the military. As rumors spread that Koreans had poisoned wells to kill the Japanese people at that time, thousands of Koreans were massacred. Nonetheless, without revealing the truth or making any official apology, the Japanese government maintained that there was no official record supporting the massacre of Koreans.

On the 100th anniversary of the Great Kanto Earthquake in 2023, however, the Japanese parliament and media began to channel the voice of self-reflection to correct injustice regarding the massacre of Koreans. On November 30, 2023, the Korean National Assembly adopted a resolution calling on the Japanese government to reveal the truth and officially apologize for the massacre of Koreans during the Great Kanto Earthquake. More specifically, it called on the Japanese government to officially apologize for the massacre of Koreans directly or indirectly involving the Japanese military and police during the Great Kanto Earthquake, to make public all documents related to the massacre, and to investigate the truth thoroughly. It also called on the Korean government to make public the progress of discussions with the Japanese government and demand that the Japanese government reveal the truth and apologize.

8.   SPECIAL RESOLUTION FOR THE CONTINUED DEVELOPMENT OF BILATERAL RELATIONS ON THE 60TH ANNIVERSARY OF DIPLOMATIC RELATIONS BETWEEN THE REPUBLIC OF KOREA AND CANADA

Relations between Korea and Canada began with Canadian missions in the late 19th century, and diplomatic ties were formally established in January 1963. Long before establishing formal diplomatic ties, the two countries were allies, which fought and bled together on the battlefield. During the Korean War, Canada sent more than 26,000 troops to the Korean Peninsula, the third largest number after the United States and the United Kingdom, 516 of whom were killed in action. After establishing official diplomatic ties, Canada and Korea have continued to develop robust and friendly cooperative relations in the economic sector by signing the

Korea-Canada Free Trade Agreement (FTA) and the Science and Technology Cooperation Agreement. In recent years, the two countries increasingly expanded their cooperation to other sectors for the future, such as economic security, climate change, and advanced science and technology, which also include people-to-people exchanges.

On November 30, 2023, the National Assembly adopted a resolution commemorating the 60th anniversary of the establishment of diplomatic ties between Korea and Canada, calling on the two governments to cooperate across many different sectors for future prosperity, including minerals, energy, and science and technology, to expand people-to-people exchanges, and to conduct a wide range of education and public relations activities related to the Korean War. In the resolution, the Korean National Assembly declared that it would provide its full support for developing a comprehensive strategic partnership between the two countries. It also proposed establishing an inter-parliamentary union to allow the two parliaments to expand interactions on shared issues.

9. RESOLUTION CALLING ON THE GOVERNMENT OF JAPAN TO PROMPTLY IMPLEMENT THE AGREEMENT BETWEEN THE REPUBLIC OF KOREA AND JAPAN CONCERNING THE JOINT DEVELOPMENT OF THE SOUTHERN PART OF THE CONTINENTAL SHELF ADJACENT TO THE TWO COUNTRIES AND PREPARE PRACTICAL IMPLEMENTATION MEASURES

The Agreement between the Republic of Korea and Japan Concerning the Joint Development of the Southern Part of the Continental Shelf Adjacent to the Two Countries (hereinafter, "Agreement") was signed in 1974, took effect in 1978, and will remain in effect for at least 50 years until 2028. Although the two countries conducted two joint explorations up to the 1990s under the Agreement, both countries returned the mining concession in 1993 for economic reasons. In 2001, the two countries signed a memorandum of understanding for joint exploration at a meeting of Korean and Japanese industry ministers, under which the two countries conducted a three-dimensional geological survey and found some potential oil reserves. Japan, however, unilaterally stopped exploration activities saying that it had poor economic profitability. After that, the Korean government designated the mining concession holder in 2009 and 2020, and notified the Japanese government. The Japanese government, however, has not designated its mining concession holder, which prevents the exploration and development of resources in the Joint Development Zone (hereinafter, "JDZ").

Claiming that it is not economically profitable, Japan has not implemented the Agreement. Nonetheless, China is currently developing a gas field in waters just 860 m from the JDZ, and, with advances in oil field exploration and mining technology in the past three decades, during which there has been no significant exploration in the JDZ, economic profitability for the project could be different this time. Even if Japan declares the end of the Agreement after June 2025, Korea will not simply agree to any boundary delimitation based on the midline principle for which Japan claims. If the Agreement comes to an end and the JDZ becomes non-delimited waters, it is likely to exaggerate a conflict over the delimitation of the continental shelf between Korea, China, and Japan in the East China Sea. The most realistic option that can benefit the two countries at this moment is for Japan to designate the mining concession holder for joint development in the JDZ, and for Korea and Japan to resume the Joint Committee.

On November 30, 2023, the Korean National Assembly adopted a resolution expressing regret over the Japanese government's failure to implement the Agreement and strongly calling on Japan to implement the Agreement. In the resolution, the Korean National Assembly urged the two governments to figure out practical implementation measures to ensure the sustainable development of the JDZ, while calling on the Korean government to proactively develop its own domestic resources in waters near the JDZ. Of course, it would be better if commercially profitable resources were identified and jointly developed within the framework of the Agreement. If it is not feasible, however, it would be worth considering exploring and developing waters on the Korean side outside the JDZ. It is because it may prompt Japan to jointly develop the JDZ with Korea out of concern that potential resources could be sucked up through connected geological structures.

10. RESOLUTION REAFFIRMING THE REPUBLIC OF KOREA'S UNDISPUTED SOVEREIGNTY OVER DOKDO AND CONDEMNING JAPAN'S CLAIM TO DOKDO AND HISTORICAL REVISIONISM IN TEXTBOOKS

On March 28, 2023, the Japanese government reviewed and approved social studies textbooks for elementary schools, which designated Dokdo as Japan's territory. Furthermore, the textbooks' map of Japan's territorial land, waters, airspace, and exclusive economic zone (EEZ) designates Dokdo as Takeshima and draws a boundary line between Ulleungdo and Dokdo, presenting Dokdo as if it were part of Japan's territory. In addition, the *Diplomatic Bluebook*, *Defense of Japan (Annual White Paper)* and *National Security Strategy of Japan* published by the Japanese government have repeatedly claimed that Dokdo is part of Japan's territory and Korea is illegally occupying the islets.

One of the options to respond to Japan's provocations to

officially protest on behalf of the Korean people without escalating the Dokdo issue into a territorial dispute is the adoption of a resolution by the Korean National Assembly. If the issue over Dokdo escalates into a territorial dispute, Korea would need to resort to a peaceful means of resolving it, including referring to the International Court of Justice (hereinafter, "ICJ"), to minimize the potential impact. The most prudent strategy Korea can adopt for Dokdo, however, is to handle the international situation in a way that makes referring to the ICJ unnecessary. Of course, if Korea wins and the ICJ makes a legally binding ruling in favor of Korea, Japan would never be able to claim territorial rights over Dokdo again. Nevertheless, it is hard to say that things have gotten much better, objectively considering the current situation. Moreover, there is no guarantee that Korea would not lose if Japan and Korea refer the Dokdo issue to the ICJ. If Korea loses, there would be no way for Korea to reclaim Dokdo unless the international order is reshaped. Hence, it is not reasonable for Korea to give up the strategic advantage of its current occupation of Dokdo and agree to refer to the ICJ, in which the benefits of a potential victory do not necessarily outweigh the costs.

On November 9, 2023, the Korean National Assembly adopted a resolution calling on the Japanese government to revoke its approval of social studies textbooks for elementary school, which misrepresented Dokdo, and to withdraw its unfounded claims to Dokdo, which are repeated in official documents issued by the Japanese government. In the resolution, the Korean National Assembly urged the Japanese government to honestly reflect in the textbooks the Neighboring Country Clause, which the Japanese government promised to the international community in 1982, and to sincerely reflect on and apologize for its past wrongdoings in history. It also called on the Korean government to step up and make every diplomatic effort to clearly correct Japan's false territorial claims and historical revisionism in textbooks.

11. RESOLUTION CALLING FOR WITHDRAWING THE FUKUSHIMA DAIICHI ALPS TREATED WATER DISCHARGE PLAN AND PREPARING MEASURES TO ENSURE SEAFOOD SAFETY AND PROTECT FISHERMEN

On April 13, 2021, the Japanese government set forth a basic policy to release contaminated radioactive water stored at the Fukushima Daiichi Nuclear Power Plant. In the policy, Japan said the country will dilute tritium, which is technically impossible to remove through purification equipment, in seawater until it becomes less than 1,500 Bq per liter (becquerel, the activity of a quantity of radioactive material in which one nucleus decays per second), one-fortieth of the country's regulatory limit. However, concerns remain that contaminated water stored at the Fukushima Daiichi Nuclear Power Plant was already produced with damaged nuclear fuels and in fact contains many unknown radionuclides even if Japan repeatedly reprocesses radionuclides below the discharge threshold. Furthermore, it is difficult to recover even a trace amount of radioactive material once discharged into the sea, and it may accumulate in the ecosystem and cause irreversible harm.

The standing committees of the Korean National Assembly highlighted that Korea should engage in multilateral negotiations to ensure that contaminated water from the Fukushima Daiichi Nuclear Power Plant is disposed of by a method that meets international safety standards and transparency (e.g., releasing into the atmosphere). The standing committees also discussed that the International Atomic Energy Agency (IAEA) should serve as an expert as an objective and fair third party in the process of verifying the safety of contaminated water discharges from the nuclear power plant and disclosing the results, that the United Nations (UN) and other international organizations, such as the World Health Organization (WHO), should publicly discuss the potentially negative impact of contaminated water discharges from the nuclear power plant on the marine environment, and that Korea should call for international cooperation with not just neighboring countries, such as China and Russia, but also regional stakeholders, such as the European Union (EU) and other countries in the Pacific. These discussions in the standing committees led to the adoption of two consecutive resolutions over the course of 2020 and 2021. In late June 2023, however, the IAEA published its final report noting that Japan's measures meet international standards, and the impact on people and the environment would be negligible.

In response, the Korean National Assembly adopted a resolution on June 30, 2023, strongly condemning the Japanese government's unilateral decision to discharge contaminated water from the Fukushima Daiichi Nuclear Power Plant into the sea and calling on the Japanese government to roll back the decision. It urged the Korean government to file a lawsuit with, and request provisional measures from, the International Tribunal for the Law of the Sea. The Korean National Assembly also called for the participation of a third-party expert group, independent of the IAEA, in any scientific verification of the safety of Japan's contaminated water treatment.

12. SPECIAL RESOLUTION CALLING FOR THE SUSTAINABLE DEVELOPMENT OF BILATERAL RELATIONS ON THE 70TH ANNIVERSARY OF THE REPUBLIC OF KOREA-UNITED STATES ALLIANCE

The year 2023 marks the 70th anniversary of the Korea-United States alliance. The presidents and senior defense leaders of Korea and the United States have defined the alliance as "a global comprehensive strategic alliance," "an alliance that takes action and moves forward into the future," or "the most capable alliance in the past 70 years of history." The current coordination between the United States and Korean military authorities is stronger than ever, and it is considered to show the alliance's capability, readiness, and willingness to respond to any threat posed by North Korea. However, some have a concerning view about the current situation on the Korean Peninsula that both North Korea and the Korea-Untied States alliance are stuck in a security dilemma due to an arms race. According to this view, dialogue between North and South Korea is still critical to ease tensions on the Korean Peninsula.

Furthermore, economic security and technology are also crucial for Korea and the United States. The global supply chain is directly linked to national security. The ongoing technological revolution across various fields, such as microelectronics, artificial intelligence (AI), biotechnology, and supercomputing, is becoming a source of modernizing a country's defense and obtaining its economic competitiveness. In addition to securing the countries' critical supply chains and technological capabilities, it is an equally important challenge for Korea and the United States to create the most dynamic economic framework in the Indo-Pacific. To do so, the two countries need to reinforce bilateral communication through a wide range of channels, including parliaments, to ensure that industrial and technological policies do not shift towards extreme nationalism and to take a step towards a future-facing comprehensive alliance.

On February 24, 2023, the Korean National Assembly adopted a resolution calling for further strengthening the Korea-United States alliance on the 70th anniversary of the alliance, which includes not only a security alliance on the level of the Korean Peninsula but also an economic and security alliance on the global level. First, the National Assembly declared that the alliance means reciprocal expansion and development for the shared prosperity of both countries. Second, the National Assembly said it will remain committed to legislatively and institutionally supporting the implementation of the Korea-United States alliance in good faith, which has been elevated to a global comprehensive strategic alliance. Third, the National Assembly honored the sacrifices and dedication made by United States and United Nations troops in the Korean War, which served as the starting point for the alliance. Fourth, the National Assembly called on the United States and Korea to work together to deter North Korea's nuclear and missile threats while making efforts to establish peace through dialogue with North Korea. Fifth, the National Assembly defined the Korea-United States alliance as an economic security alliance and a technological alliance and called on the two countries to solidify cooperation in the fields of stable global supply chains, emerging technologies, and cybersecurity. Finally, the National Assembly highlighted the importance of bilateral communication and cooperation in building regional order and tackling global challenges and proposed establishing an inter-parliamentary union.

13. RESOLUTION CALLING ON THE GOVERNMENT OF JAPAN TO WITHDRAW ITS REAPPLICATION FOR THE INSCRIPTION OF THE SADO GOLD MINE ON THE WORLD HERITAGE LIST AND IMPLEMENT UNESCO'S RECOMMENDATIONS FOR MODERN INDUSTRIAL FACILITIES IN JAPAN

When a country's facilities are inscribed on the World Heritage List, it increases the country's cultural pride. Japan is trying to apply for the inscription of modern Meiji industrial facilities, including the Sado Gold Mine, on the World Heritage List. These facilities, however, are the site of horrific violations committed against human rights. During World War II, the Japanese government and corporations mobilized hundreds of thousands of Koreans, prisoners of war from Allied forces, Chinese people, and Southeast Asians into harsh forced labor at this site in violation of international law. The Korean National Assembly is deeply concerned about Japan's efforts to inscribe the site on the World Heritage List.

In 2015, the UNESCO World Heritage Committee (hereinafter, "Committee") already decided to inscribe other Japanese Meiji modern industrial facilities, a site of forced labor against Korean victims during the Japanese occupation, on the World Heritage List. At that time, the Committee recommended that Japan provide a commentary to visitors to understand the full historical context of the facilities, and Japan promised to follow the recommendation, which it has not done yet properly.

In July 2015, the 39th session of the Committee decided to inscribe 23 Meiji modern business facilities in Japan on the World Heritage List, including seven facilities where tens of thousands of Koreans were forced into labor during World War II, such as Hashima (Gunkanjima) Coal Mine, Miike Coal Mine, Takashima Coal Mine, Yahata Steel Works, and three facilities in Mitsubishi Shipyard, and recommended that Japan develop an interpretive strategy to help visitors understand the full historical context of the facilities. In response to the recommendation, Kuni Sato, Permanent Delegate of Japan to UNESCO, said that Japan will set up an information center to inform visitors of the fact that many Koreans were forced into labor against their will under harsh conditions at some of the facilities in the 1940s and take appropriate measures to honor the victims to fully implement the Committee's recommendation. This statement by the Japanese delegate was included in the Committee's inscription decision (WHC Decision 39 COM 8B.14).

The subsequent progress report submitted by the Japanese

government, however, did not include any information on measures to inform of forced labor or honor the victims. In addition, an exhibition at the Japan Industrial Heritage Information Center in Tokyo, which was made public on June 15, 2020, did not include any measures to honor the victims of forced labor, and only offered testimonies and documents denying that Koreans were forced to labor. Despite two resolutions adopted by the Korean National Assembly on December 9, 2020, and September 16, 2021, Japan continued to hide or cover up the forced labor of Koreans in its modern industrial facilities, and it also decided to apply for the inscription of the Sado Gold Mine on the World Heritage List in 2022. After Japan's application in 2022 was rejected for the lack of documentation, Japan filed a reapplication in January 2023.

On February 27, 2023, the Korean National Assembly adopted a resolution calling on the Japanese government to reflect on and take responsibility for what it did in its war of aggression and withdraw its application for the UNESCO inscription of the Sado Gold Mine. The National Assembly noted that Japan's push for the inscription of Meiji modern industrial facilities on the World Heritage List while hiding the fact that the facilities were a site of forced labor directly runs counter to universal human rights norms, such as the United Nations Charter and the International Labour Organization Conventions, and international criminal law, which punishes war crimes and crimes against humanity. Appealing to international law, and the universal values and conscience of humanity, the Korean National Assembly made a resolution on the following three points: First, the National Assembly called on the Japanese government to withdraw its application for the inscription of the Sado Gold Mine on the World Heritage List. Second, the National Assembly urged the Japanese government to fully implement the Committee's recommendation and follow-up measures, which it promised to do, regarding the decision to inscribe Sites of Japan's Meiji Industrial

Revolution (Iron and Steel, Shipbuilding, and Coal Mining) on the World Heritage List. Finally, the National Assembly called on the Korean government to actively respond to such attempt of Japan so that UNESCO would refuse to inscribe the Sado Gold Mine on the World Heritage List.

14. RESOLUTION HONORING THE VICTIMS OF TURKEY–SYRIA EARTHQUAKES AND CALLING FOR SUPPORT FOR RECOVERY

On February 6, 2023, a 7.8 magnitude earthquake and subsequent aftershocks caused massive causalities in Turkey and Syria. The international community continued to provide efforts to support those in the areas affected by the earthquake. Greece, despite not usually being on friendly terms with Turkey, immediately dispatched a rescue team, and Armenia opened its border for the first time in 35 years. Israel, which was also at odds with Turkey over the Palestinian issue, also sent a rescue team, saving 19 people. In Northeast Asia, Japan dispatched a medical team to Turkey and sent emergency relief supplies, such as tents and blankets, to Syria through civilian airplanes.

On February 14, 2023, the Korean National Assembly also adopted a resolution calling on the Korean government to join the international community's support efforts, and make every effort to provide emergency relief and recovery support. After expressing its deepest condolences to the people of Turkey and Syria, the National Assembly urged the Korean government to make its best effort to provide emergency relief and recovery support for those affected by the earthquake. The National Assembly committed itself to making every effort to ensure that the Korean government provides humanitarian aid and emergency relief activities in line with its international status, not only for the earthquake disaster in Turkey and Syria but also for potential disasters in the future around the world.

Judicial Decisions in Public International Law (2023)

Eungi HONG
Judge
Seoul Central District Court (Seoul, Korea)

Key Words

state immunity, sovereign act *(acta jure imperii)*, sovereign activity, Vienna Convention on Diplomatic Relations, Convention Relating to the Status of Refugees, Refugee Convention, Article 31.1, comfort women victims, customary international law, United Nations Committee on the Elimination of Discrimination Against Women, UN CEDAW

Supreme Court Judgment No. 2019DA247903
Rendered on April 27, 2023

Main Issues

1. Whether state immunity can be applied in a lawsuit arisen from a private activity of a foreign State in the Korean territory
2. The factors to consider when determining if a foreign State's use of land for consular purposes constitutes a sovereign act *(acta jure imperii)*, thereby potentially limiting the jurisdiction of Korean courts

Facts

1. The defendant, State of Mongolia, purchased a plot of land and a building in Seoul in 1998 (hereinafter, "the Defendant's Building"). Since then, the defendant has used the property as the Embassy of Mongolia in the Republic of Korea (hereinafter, "Korea").

2. The plaintiff, a private Korean company, purchased land adjacent to the defendant's property around 2015. Subsequently, it was discovered that a portion of the defendant's building encroached 11m² onto the plaintiff's land, and approximately 19.9m² of the plaintiff's land (Both of the portions are hereinafter, "the Disputed Land") was used as accessory space of the Defendant's Building, such as warehouse.

3. The plaintiff filed a lawsuit against the defendant, seeking the removal of the encroaching portion of the Defendant's Building, the delivery of the Disputed Land, and the return of any unjust enrichment derived from the Disputed Land.

Reasoning

1. APPLICATION OF STATE IMMUNITY IN PRIVATE ACTIVITIES

According to customary international law, sovereign acts of a State are generally immune from the jurisdiction of foreign domestic courts. However, there are exceptions. Unless there are specific circumstances where a State's private activity is part of, or closely related to, sovereign activity – and where exercising jurisdiction over it could unduly interfere with the sovereign activities of the foreign State – Korean courts may assert jurisdiction over cases involving a private act conducted by a foreign State (Supreme Court Judgment No. 97DA39216, No. 2009Da16766).

When addressing issues arising from a foreign State's occupation of property, it cannot be assumed that the foreign State automatically enjoys exemption from the jurisdiction of the domestic court where the property is located, merely because the occupant is a foreign country. Property falls under the realm of territorial sovereignty. Currently, there is no international treaty or customary international law that explicitly grants an exemption based solely on the foreign ownership of property.

Moreover, the reasons behind a foreign State's occupation of property can vary widely, encompassing different causes, purposes, and forms. It is not necessarily the case that a foreign State's use of domestic property always constitutes private activities that are either inherently sovereign or closely related to sovereign activities.

However, diplomatic missions, which represent a country abroad, engage in diplomatic relations, protect nationals, and handle consular affairs, present a distinct scenario. The use of property by a foreign State for such diplomatic missions is closely aligned with sovereign activities and purposes. According to Article 22 of the Vienna Convention on Diplomatic Relations, the premises of diplomatic missions are inviolable, and the host State is under an obligation to protect them.

Therefore, when lawsuits are initiated against a foreign State concerning its occupation of property for diplomatic missions, Korean courts' ability to exercise jurisdiction may be limited to prevent hindrance to the diplomatic functions of the mission. In assessing whether a lawsuit poses a risk of interfering with these diplomatic functions, it is crucial to consider various factors. These include the nature of the plaintiff's claims and their legal grounding, the potential impact of any judgments that prevail, and how these claims or judgments might relate to, or affect, the diplomatic mission and its operations.

2. CLAIM ON THE REMOVAL AND DELIVERY OF THE DISPUTED LAND

The appellate court concluded that the defendant's use of buildings and land in the diplomatic area has a direct or indirect impact on the execution of diplomatic duties, and therefore, it is deemed to be relevant to sovereign activities. Hence, the court ruled that the jurisdiction of the Korean courts is limited. The Supreme Court confirmed the reasoning.

3. CLAIM ON THE RESTITUTION OF THE UNJUST ENRICHMENT

The appellate court determined that, due to the reasons previously mentioned, the jurisdiction of Korean courts does not extend to the plaintiff's claim for unjust enrichment. However, the Supreme Court provided a contrasting viewpoint, arguing that seeking restitution for unjust enrichment from the foreign State, in cases of property rights infringements, does not inherently affect its occupation of diplomatic premises. The Court expressed difficulty in identifying a direct connection between such claims or judgments and the diplomatic mission's execution of its duties.

Unless specific circumstances suggest a risk of impeding the diplomatic mission's functions, monetary claims such as these cannot be deemed a threat. Consequently, the Supreme Court overturned the appellate court's decision on this aspect of the claim and remanded the case for further review.

Comments

No comprehensive international treaty specifically addresses the applicability of State immunity in real estate lawsuits involving diplomatic missions. Article 9 of the European Convention on State Immunity (ECSI) states that state immunity does not extend to proceedings related to immovable property within the forum State's jurisdiction. The determination of this issue is therefore subject to each country's judicial and legislative frameworks.[1]

The court recognized that, while Korean courts generally hold jurisdiction over civil suits concerning the occupation of real estate by foreign States for diplomatic purposes, this jurisdiction is curtailed when such proceedings could interfere with the sovereign functions of the State. It is important to note that factors influencing the determination of these exceptional cases include the legal foundation of the claim, the potential outcomes of a prevailing judgment, and its repercussions on the operations of diplomatic missions.

Supreme Court Judgment No. 2021Do3652 Rendered on March 13, 2023

Main Issue

Whether the Convention relating to the Status of Refugees (hereinafter, "the Refugee Convention") Article 31.1. on the prohibition of imposing penalties on refugees for their illegal entry can be a ground for the exemption of criminal penalties.

Facts

1. The defendant, a foreigner of Iran nationality, entered Korea on Mar. 13, 2016, upon the issuance of visa in the guise of invitations for business purposes, while the genuine intent was to file a claim for refugee status in Korea.

2. On Mar. 21, 2016, the defendant filed an application for

refugee status in the Seoul Immigration Office, and it was denied by the Office on Aug. 27, 2017. He filed a lawsuit in the Seoul Administrative Court for the cancellation of the decision in 2018. The court found that the defendant is a refugee under the Refugee Convention as he is a foreigner who has well-founded fear of persecution due to his conversion from Islam to Christianity once he returns to Iran and accepted his claim by reversing the decision in 2019. The judgment was confirmed by the appellate court and the Supreme court.

3. The defendant was arrested on July 17, 2018, on charges of violating the Immigration Act through a false application for a visa and the Criminal Act by obstructing official duties through fraudulent means and was indicted on the same accounts.

Reasoning

1. THE APPLICABILITY OF THE REFUGEE CONVENTION

The Constitution of Korea Article 6.1. states, "Treaties duly concluded and promulgated under the Constitution and the generally recognized rules of international law shall have the same effect as the domestic law of the Republic of Korea." The Refugee Convention was referred to the State Council for deliberation on May 28, 1992, approved by the National Assembly on May 28, 1992, whereby an instrument of accession was deposited with the Secretary-General of the United Nations on Dec. 3, 1992, and took effect in Korea from Mar. 3, 1993.

The Refugee Convention, being a treaty ratified upon consent of the National Assembly, holds the same effect as domestic law. Depending on the content and nature of individual provisions, it can be applied directly in adjudication.

2. THE REFUGEE CONVENTION AS A GROUND FOR EXEMPTION OF PENALTIES

Regarding the criminal punishment of illegal entry by refugees, Article 31.1 of the Refugee Convention states, "The Contracting States shall not impose penalties, on account of their illegal entry or presence, on refugees who, coming directly from a territory where their life or freedom was threatened in the sense of Article 1, present themselves without delay to the authorities and show good cause for their illegal entry or presence."

Considering that the provision directly states that the Contracting States shall not impose penalties on refugees who have met specific requirements, this provision may serve as the applicable basis for the exemption from punishment in a criminal trial in Korean courts, which has acceded to and ratified the Refugee Convention.

The term "illegal entry" subject to the exemption of punishment refers to an act of entering the state in violation of procedures stipulated in immigration laws and statutes that are directly and indivisibly related thereto, hindering the State's conduct of immigration duties. Therefore, not only an act constituting a violation of the Immigration Act by either entering the country without entry permission or a visa, or upon obtaining entry permission or a visa illegally, but also a criminal act under the Criminal Act consisting of the said act as a constituent element of a crime, are included in the "illegal entry."

Conclusion

Therefore, the appellate court's judgment, which exempted the defendant from criminal punishment on the grounds that the defendant satisfied the requirements under Article 31.1 of the Refugee Convention, was justifiable, and the Supreme Court dismissed the prosecutor's appeal.

Seoul High Court Judgment No. 2021Na2017165 Rendered on November 23, 2023

Main Issues

1. In cases where Korean nationals file a civil lawsuit against Japan in Korean courts for damages resulting from unlawful acts, the question is whether state immunity can be recognized for the defendant.

2. The elements to consider in deciding whether the Korean Courts have international jurisdiction over cases with foreign elements.

3. The applicable law and the existence and scope of liability for damages

   (Ed. Only the first issue will be dealt with here.)

Facts

1. There are 16 plaintiffs in this case, among whom three are themselves comfort women victims, while the remaining plaintiffs are heirs of comfort women victims. These victims were recognized and registered as comfort women between 1932 and 1945 under the Act on the Protection, Support, and Memorial Services for the Victims of Japanese Military Sexual Slavery, due to being subjected to forced sexual acts while confined in comfort stations established by Japan for the benefit of its military personnel during that period.

2. The plaintiffs filed a lawsuit against the defendant, Japan,

seeking compensation of 200 million won (equivalent of 150,000 USD) per comfort woman victim for mental suffering due to the defendant's recruitment of comfort women.

3. The defendant governed the Korean Peninsula after signing the Korea-Japan Annexation Treaty in 1910. Subsequently, through events such as the Manchurian Incident in 1931, the Second Sino-Japanese War in 1937, and the Pacific War in 1941, the frontlines expanded. During these events, the defendant established and managed comfort stations for the management of its military personnel.

4. Upon the military's request, the defendant mobilized comfort women using administrative organizations including the police, transferred Korean comfort women outside the Korean Peninsula, and managed the health and hygiene of comfort women through military personnel.

5. Among the plaintiffs, comfort women were either coerced or recruited through job placement into becoming comfort women. They were forcibly subjected to sexual acts with military personnel while confined in comfort stations in countries such as China, Japan, Thailand, and Myanmar, and in the process, they were subjected to torture and violence.

6. As the defendant could not be served with the summons, the first-instance court proceeded with the case through service by public notice.[2] It found that state immunity can be applied to the defendant and dismissed the plaintiffs' claims.

Reasoning

1. LEGAL BASIS FOR STATE IMMUNITY

1-1. Legal Basis

This case involves Korean nationals filing a lawsuit for damages against Japan due to illegal acts in the Korean courts. Korea has not enacted any laws regarding the scope of State immunity in civil litigation against foreign States by its courts, nor has it entered into any treaties with Japan or other countries regarding the recognition of mutual civil jurisdiction. Therefore, the determination of whether State immunity is recognized for the defendant in this case should be based on customary international law, which serves as a source of law for courts.

1-2. Requirements for Customary International Law

For customary international law to be established, the existence of a general practice of States and a sense of legal obligation (*opinio juris*) are generally required. In determining the existence of the "general practice" of States, consideration may be given to the content of "state practice," including legislation, judgments, administrative measures of individual states, resolutions of international organizations, among others. "*Opinio juris*" refers to the recognition by individual States that they are legally bound to adhere to the established practice, as described above.

2. CUSTOMARY INTERNATIONAL LAW REGARDING STATE IMMUNITY

2-1. State Immunity Relevant to This Case

The actions of the defendant originated from the illegally occupied Korean Peninsula, specifically within the territory of Korea and extended to various foreign countries. These actions constitute unlawful acts against the bodies of comfort women victims, who are Korean nationals. The plaintiffs in this case seek compensation for the damage suffered by the victims due to such actions by the defendant. The court examined the existence of customary international law related to State immunity within the necessary scope to resolve this case and considered its content.

2-2. Legal Materials

2-2-1. International Conventions Ratified by the Defendant at the Time of the Actions and Relevant Provisions of Criminal Law

By the end of the 2nd World War, Japan ratified the Convention with Respect to the Laws and Customs of War on Land, International Convention for the Suppression of the White Slave Traffic, International Convention for the Suppression of the Traffic in Women and Children (While reserving its application to the colonies including Korean peninsula), Slavery Convention, and Forced Labour Convention (ILO, No. 29).

Under the domestic law applicable to the Korean Peninsula at the time, as stipulated in the Korean - Japanese Annexation Treaty, Article 226 of the former Criminal Law of the defendant (Law No. 45, enacted in 1907) regulated the crime of "abduction, enticing, or selling for the purpose of transfer abroad."

2-2-2. Relevant International Conventions and Laws of Individual
Countries

The court considered the following international conventions and regulations of individual countries: United Nations Convention on Jurisdictional Immunities of States and Their Property (Articles 5, 6, and 12, to date, the Convention has not yet met the requirements for enforcement), European Convention on State Immunity (Article 11, 31), US Foreign Sovereign Immunity Act (28 U.S.C., hereinafter, "US FSIA," Article 1605), Japan's "Law on Civil Jurisdiction over Foreign Countries" (Article 3, 10), and UK State Immunity Act 1978 (hereinafter, "UK SIA," Articles 1, 5, and 16).

In addition to the aforementioned countries, there are other countries such as South Africa, Canada, Australia, Singapore, Argentina, Israel, Pakistan, and Malawi, etc., which do not recognize State immunity for unlawful acts committed within their own territories. The provisions of these countries' laws regarding unlawful acts within their territories are generally similar to Article 5 of the UK SIA.

2-2-3. Traditional Theories and Customary International Law on
State Immunity

State immunity is explained by customary international law as the principle that domestic courts do not have jurisdiction over lawsuits against foreign States, and that States are not subject to the jurisdiction of foreign courts regarding their acts and property. This principle is based on the fundamental principle of equality and independence among sovereign States, or the principle that "an equal has no authority over another equal (par in parem non habet imperium)."

The legal theory of state immunity historically began with an absolute immunity where courts of one country could not exercise jurisdiction over acts of another country, regardless of whether the acts were sovereign, authoritative, or public *(acta jure imperii)* or non-sovereign, non-authoritative, or private *(acta jure gestionis)*. Subsequently, this legal theory evolved from an absolute immunity to a restrictive immunity, where state immunity is not recognized for non-sovereign acts of foreign states. In 1812, the United States Supreme Court declared that state immunity was in accordance with generally accepted customary international law, adopting the doctrine of absolute immunity [The Schooner Exchange v. McFaddon, 11 U.S. 116, 137(1812)].

Starting from the mid-19th century, courts in countries such as Belgium, Italy, and Greece began to issue judgments based on the doctrine of restrictive immunity. However, even until around the time of the 2nd World War, courts in countries like the UK and Poland continued to issue judgments based on the doctrine of absolute immunity. After the 2nd World War, as courts in countries like the UK and the US adopted the doctrine of restrictive immunity, it became recognized as a general practice in the international community.

2-2-4. Relevant Foreign Judicial Precedents

Regarding acts during the 2nd World War, Italian Supreme Court rendered the Ferrini judgment (No. 5044 of Nov 6, 2003, registered on Mar 11, 2004) and Greek Supreme Court rendered the Distomo judgment (No. 11/2000, May 4, 2000), both of which denied Germany's State immunity and awarded compensation for individual damages. In response, the German government claimed that Italy violated international law concerning State immunity by issuing the Ferrini judgment and approving the enforcement of the Distomo judgment by Greek courts, and subsequently filed a lawsuit against Italy at the International Court of Justice (ICJ) [Jurisdictional Immunities of the State (Germany v. Italy: Greece intervening)

Judgment, I.C.J. Rep. 2012, 99, hereinafter, "the ICJ judgment"]. The ICJ, by a majority opinion, found that Italy had violated its obligation to respect Germany's State immunity privileges.

Subsequently, the Italian Parliament enacted Law No. 5 of 2013 on Jan. 29, 2013, requiring Italian courts to reject jurisdiction for cases falling within the scope of the ICJ judgment and to reconsider or review judgments already recognizing jurisdiction. However, the Italian Constitutional Court ruled on Oct. 22, 2014, that Law No. 5 of 2013 was unconstitutional for the following reasons: (i) the legal interpretation of State immunity in the ICJ judgment completely nullifies the right of victims of crimes against humanity and violations of fundamental rights to have their cases heard; and (ii) denying judicial remedies for crimes against humanity ultimately results in justifying State immunity.

After the ICJ judgment, the following cases have ruled that state immunity does not apply to foreign States in cases of damages incurred by civilians during wartime: the Brazilian Federal Supreme Court's Changri-la judgment of 2021 (ARE 954858/RJ), the Ukrainian Supreme Court's judgment of 2022 (308/9708/19: Civil Cases), and the High Court of England and Wales' Al Masarir v Kingdom of Saudi Arabia judgment of 2022 [EWHC 2199 (QB)].

2-3. Content of Customary International Law Regarding State Immunity

Customary international law concerning state immunity is neither fixed nor permanent. As previously noted, there has been a shift from the doctrine of absolute immunity to that of restrictive immunity. Moreover, when examining the existence of customary international law concerning state immunity, it is crucial to consider the dynamic nature of customary international law through the lens of state practice and *opinio juris*. Even during the transition from absolute to restrictive immunity, there was inevitably a period during which judgments based on both doctrines coexisted within various countries. Thus, it cannot be assumed that judgments based on restrictive immunity up to a certain point violated customary international law. Given the evolution of customary international law, it is imperative to consider not only state practice and *opinio juris* but also the direction and trend of such law.

It is also significant to note that numerous instances of state practice have been observed where state immunity is not recognized for unlawful acts committed by foreign States within the territory of the forum State, beyond reasons such as commercial transactions.

(i) Although it has not yet come into force, international conventions like the UN Convention on Jurisdictional Immunities of States and Their Property and the European Convention on State Immunity, signed by 28 countries and ratified by 22 countries, respectively, as well as domestic laws enacted by several countries including the US FSIA, Japan's relevant legislation, and the UK SIA, explicitly regulate similar provisions. These do not distinguish between sovereign acts and non-sovereign acts when determining conditions under which state immunity is not recognized for unlawful acts within the territory. It's challenging to find judgments explicitly stating the unlawful acts in question were sovereign and thus not subject to relevant laws. However, the High Court of England and Wales' ruling in Al Masarir v Kingdom of Saudi Arabia, determined that the UK SIA does not differentiate between sovereign and non-sovereign acts. The commentary by the International Law Commission (ILC) on Article 12 of the UN Convention on Jurisdictional Immunities of States also suggests that this provision's scope is broad enough to apply to intentional bodily harm, damage to property, arson, politically motivated assassinations, and even attempted murder (ILC, "Draft articles on Jurisdictional Immunities of States and their Property, with commentaries 1991," Yearbook of the International Law Commission, 1991, vol. II Part Two, 13).

(ii) Recent judgments, such as the Changri-la judgment by the Brazilian Federal Supreme Court and the judgment by the Supreme Court of Ukraine on Apr. 14, 2022, fundamentally deny the application of state immunity to claims for damages due to unlawful acts committed by foreign military forces within the forum State's territory. Despite these acts being considered sovereign, these judgments align with the provisions of the aforementioned Conventions on state immunity and legislative content of individual countries.

Furthermore, such state practices have been carried out by a considerable number of countries. However, comparing the number of countries engaged in such practices to the total number of UN member States (193) to ascertain the existence of a customary practice is not appropriate. Additionally, these state practices, formed through national legislation or supreme court judgments, are endowed with legal certainty.

Moreover, considering the historical progression from absolute to restrictive immunity doctrine, along with the trend of many countries denying state immunity for unlawful acts within their territory, it suggests the international legal framework concerning state immunity is moving towards protecting individuals' rights to redress.

Taking into account the identifiable state practices, the legal certainty surrounding them, and the dynamic nature of customary international law indicating the current direction of change, even the most conservative interpretation of customary international law regarding state immunity suggests that, at the very least, within the territory of the forum State, state immunity is not recognized for unlawful acts committed against the nationals of the forum State, regardless of whether such acts are deemed sovereign acts.

    (iii) However, regarding actions of armed forces, there are discrepancies between the content of the UN Convention on Jurisdictional Immunities of States, and the individual legislations of countries such as the US and Japan, as well as the European Convention on State Immunity and the UK SIA. The European Convention on State Immunity, for instance, does not affect the state immunity privileges enjoyed by a contracting State concerning acts or omissions of its armed forces on the territory of another contracting State. Meanwhile, the UK SIA excludes application to actions of foreign armed forces while they are in the UK, particularly those covered by the 1952 Visiting Forces Act.

    In the ICJ judgment, Italy argued that Germany's actions constituted unlawful acts within the territory of the forum State, thus state immunity should be denied. However, this argument was rejected by the ICJ. It's noteworthy that this judgment specifically addressed state immunity concerning "acts committed in the course of conducting an armed conflict" within the territory of the forum State. Given that the situation at hand did not involve an actual armed conflict in the traditional sense, but rather actions related to the mobilization of "comfort women," it's difficult to consider these actions as falling within the broader interpretation of "armed conflict" contemplated by the judgment. Considering the evolution of customary international law regarding state immunity, there's no basis to interpret "armed conflict" in this case more broadly than its ordinary meaning, making it challenging to consider the actions in question, specifically the deceptive recruitment, abduction, and detention of comfort women, as occurring "in the course of conducting an armed conflict" as contemplated by the ICJ judgment.

3. APPLICATION TO THIS CASE

The acts of the defendant in this case, as previously discussed, constitute unlawful acts perpetrated against the nationals of the forum State within the territory of the forum State. Therefore, based on the current valid customary international law as confirmed above, the defendant's state immunity is denied in this case.

Furthermore, in the context of the application of customary international law as outlined above, it raises a question whether state immunity is denied even if only "part" of the unlawful acts in question occurred within the territory of the forum State. This introduces an issue of interpretation regarding the content of state practices recognized by treaties or individual legislations, specifically concerning "unlawful acts occurring within the territory of the forum State." Article 12 of the UN Convention on Jurisdictional Immunities of States and Article 10 of the aforementioned Japanese legislation, for instance, specify that state immunity is denied even if only "part" of the actions in question occurred within the territory of the forum State. When considering the denial of state immunity concerning unlawful acts occurring within the territory of the forum State, there is no compelling reason to require that the entirety of the actions in question occur within the territory of the forum State. Additionally, the judgment of the UK Wales High Court in Al Masarir v Kingdom of Saudi Arabia also noted that Section 5 of the UK SIA does not require all unlawful acts to occur within the UK.

4. CONCLUSION

Applying the aforementioned customary international law to this case, it can be inferred that state immunity is not recognized for the defendant in this case. Therefore, the Courts of Korea have jurisdiction over the defendant. Furthermore, the said courts determined that the defendant has an obligation to pay damages of 200 million won to each comfort woman plaintiff after recognizing their claims.

Consequently, the courts nullified the first-instance court's judgment that recognized state immunity over the defendant and recognized the defendant's liability for damages. This judgment was not appealed and became final.

5. COMMENTS

This case proceeded with service by public notice to the defendant, who did not respond, resulting in its closure. Consequently, the court did not further explore the potential implications of the 1965 Korea-Japan Claims Agreement or the 2015 Korea-Japan Agreement on the Comfort Women Issue as possible defenses for the defendant.

On the other hand, in a case involving forced laborers from Korea from the 2nd World War suing Japanese companies for damages, the Supreme Court of Korea ruled in 2012 that the claims for damages by the forcibly mobilized victims were not extinguished by the 1965 Korea-Japan Claims Agreement (Case No. 2009Da22549, 2009DA68620 rendered on May 24, 2012). Subsequently, in cases where forced labor victims sued the State of Japan for damages, the Seoul Central District Court in 2014 (Case No. 2013Gahab11596 rendered on Oct. 30, 2014)[3] and the Seoul High Court in 2019 (Case No. 2014Na48797 rendered on Jan. 18, 2019) accepted the plaintiffs' claim using the same reasoning. These judgments were upheld by the Supreme Court of Korea (Case No. 2019Da3226 rendered on Jan. 25, 2024).

**Supreme Court Judgment (En Banc) No. 2018Do13877
Rendered on September 21, 2022**

Main Issues

In the context of the offense of forcible indecency as outlined in Article 298 of the Criminal Act, the legal question focuses on two key issues:

1. Whether the assault and threat must be to a degree that renders the victim unable to resist (negative perspective).
2. Whether it suffices to establish the offense if the perpetrator exercises illegal physical force or induces a level of fear sufficient to impair the victim's ability to resist significantly (positive perspective).

Facts

1. The defendant asked the victim, his 15-year-old female cousin, if he could hug her. He then hugged her, laid her on the bed in his house, and climbed on top of her. He asked the victim if he could touch her breast, placed his hand inside her shirt, and touched her breasts for about 30 seconds. When the victim tried to leave the room, he followed her and hugged her for one minute.
2. The appellate court found it challenging to regard the defendant's words to the victim as inducing fear in her and difficult to determine that the degree of physical force exerted by the defendant significantly impeded the victim's ability to resist. Therefore, the court concluded that the requisite assault or threat for the crime of forcible indecency was absent and acquitted the defendant.

Reasoning

1. THE MAJORITY OPINION

1-1. Precedents Regarding Assault and Threat in the Crime of Forcible Indecency

Article 298 of the Criminal Act stipulates that anyone who commits indecent acts against a person through assault or threat shall be punished with imprisonment for up to ten years or a fine of up to 15 million won. The Supreme Court has indicated that assault or threat in this context should reach a level that makes it difficult for the victim to resist.

1-2. Interpretation Criteria for Assault or Threat

Considering the following circumstances, assault or threat should be interpreted as exercising unlawful force against the victim's body or causing harm sufficient to induce fear in the victim:

(a) The Criminal Act does not explicitly define the degree of assault or threat in the context of forcible indecency, but the term "forcible" implies compelling someone to do something against their will using power or force.

(b) The protected interest in the crime of forcible indecency is the right to sexual self-determination, and when sexual acts are performed against the victim's will through assault or threat, their passive right to sexual self-determination is violated.

(c) The assault or threat in the crime of forcible indecency should be recognized to the same extent as in assault or threat crimes under the Criminal Act. Doing so reflects recent changes in judicial practice and ensures legal stability and predictability of judgments.

All previous Supreme Court rulings (Including Case No. 2011Do8805 rendered on Jul. 26, 2012) that specified the degree of assault or threat with the perspective which does not align with this judgment will be revised.

1-3. Application to This Case

In light of the facts admitted, there is sufficient reason to consider that the defendant exercised unlawful force against the victim and committed forcible indecency. However, the lower court's acquittal based on the absence of assault or threat to the extent of making it difficult for the victim to resist, according to the existing precedents, is a misinterpretation of the law. Therefore, the lower court's judgment is hereby reversed and remanded.

2. THE SEPARATE OPINION OF JUSTICE Dong-Won Lee

In this case, while I concur with the majority opinion's conclusion to set aside and remand the trial on the grounds that, even under the legal principles of precedent, the defendant's actions can be sufficiently regarded as constituting forcible indecency.

However, the existing interpretation regarding assault or threat in the crime of forcible indecency should be maintained, and the expansive interpretation of the scope of punishment for forcible indecency should be addressed through legislative action by the National Assembly, as suggested by the majority opinion (Ed. Only relevant parts are excerpted below).

The United Nations Committee on the Elimination of Discrimination Against Women (hereinafter, "CEDAW") issued General Recommendation No. 19 on Jan 29, 1992, stating, "States parties shall take all appropriate measures to eliminate gender-based violence, whether by public or private actors, ensuring that legislative measures taken to prevent gender-based violence encompass all women and guaranteeing their dignity and self-worth." While this recommendation is critical in shaping laws to protect women adequately, it does not possess binding force in this case as directly applicable international human rights standards. Furthermore, even considering this recommendation, it does not necessarily imply that assault or threat must be met with significant resistance.

3. THE CONCURRING OPINION TO THE MAJORITY OPINION OF JUSTICE Jung-Hee Rho

The majority opinion's decision to change the traditional legal principles in precedent regarding the interpretation of assault or threat in the crime of forcible indecency is a progressive step towards implementing the principle of legality in substantive criminal law (Ed. Only relevant parts are excerpted below).

The laws and jurisprudence of major countries regulating sexual offenses are transitioning from requiring the victim's "resistance" to recognizing the absence or lack of "consent" as its fundamental criterion. It is necessary to consider that the essence of the crime of rape and forcible indecency, which aims to protect sexual freedom or sexual self-determination, lies in the absence or lack of "consent" of the victim, even in interpreting the elements of "assault or threat," which are the constitutive elements of the crime, under the current law.

As mentioned in the separate opinion, the UN CEDAW Committee, following General Recommendation No. 19 in 1992, issued General Recommendation No. 35 in 2017, stating that the definition of sexual offenses should be based on the absence of freely given consent and should take into account coercive environments. The CEDAW Committee has expressed particular concerns about the constitutive elements of assault or threat in Article 297 (rape) of the Criminal Act. While these recommendations do not have direct binding force, considering the spirit of these recommendations and the global trend reflected in the legislative examples of major countries, it can be said that the traditional legal principles in precedent, which require resistance from the victim and narrowly interpret the meaning of "assault or threat" as defined in the current Criminal Act and the Special Act on Sexual Crimes, are increasingly difficult to justify and rationalize within the entire legal order.

Notes

1. Kyounrok Ahn, *The Jurisdiction of the Korean courts over civil lawsuits regarding Foreign States occupation of properties*, Supreme Court Case Review Vol.135, Supreme Court Library of Korea (2023), p.281.

2. Civil Procedure Act

   Article 191 (Method of Service in Foreign Country)

   Service to be effected in a foreign country shall be entrusted by the presiding judge to the Korean ambassador, minister or consul stationed therein or the competent government authorities of such country.

   Article 194 (Requirements for Service by Public Notice)

   (1) Where the domicile, etc. or the work place of a party is unknown, or where it is impossible to comply with the provisions of Article 191 in regard to a service to be effected in a foreign country, or it is deemed ineffective even if such provisions are complied with, a junior administrative officer, etc. of a court may, either ex officio or upon request from the parties, make service by public notice.

3. This decision was introduced in Lee Keun-Gwan, *Major Judicial Precedents of Public International law* in 2014, KYIL Vol.2, Ilchokak (2015), pp. 350~357.

Judicial Decisions in Private International Law (2023)

Jiyong JANG
High Court Judge at Suwon High Court

Key Words

international jurisdiction, applicable law, CISG, public order, mandatory provision, sovereign immunity

1. JURISDICTION

1-1. Sovereign Immunity

Supreme Court Decision 2019Da247903 Decided on April 27, 2023 〔Removal of Building, etc.〕

〔Facts〕

Plaintiff filed a lawsuit claiming that the defendant, Mongolian government, infringed plaintiff's ownership of real property by occupying Mongolian diplomatic mission.

〔Summary of Decision〕

[1] According to customary international law, sovereign acts of the State are exempted from jurisdiction of another country in principle.

However, unless there are extenuating circumstances where there is a concern that as any judicial act committed by a foreign country within the territory of the Republic of Korea (hereinafter, "Korea") falls under sovereign activities or is closely related thereto, the exercise of jurisdiction over such act may be deemed unjustifiable interference with a foreign country's sovereign activities, a court of Korea may exercise jurisdiction against the corresponding foreign country. [2] Viewing that on the sole ground that a subject of the occupancy of real property, which is an object of territorial sovereignty, is a foreign country, the foreign country's act of occupying real property should be exempted from jurisdiction of a court of the country in which said real property is located is difficult, and in occupying real property, diverse causes, purposes, and types can exist, and thus a foreign country's occupancy of real property within the territory of Korea can be seen to correspond to any judicial act falling under sovereign activities or closely related thereto. However, a diplomatic mission is an institution established in a foreign country for a country to do diplomatic activities, protect its nationals residing in a foreign country, and administer consular affairs, etc. on behalf of the country, and thus a foreign country's act of occupying real property as a diplomatic mission abroad can be seen to be closely related to sovereign activities in light of its nature and purpose, and as the area used for diplomatic and consular missions in a foreign country under international law is inviolable territory in principle, the host State has an obligation to protect such area. Therefore, in relation to a foreign country's occupancy of real property as a diplomatic mission abroad, where there is a concern that a lawsuit filed against the corresponding foreign country is deemed likely to interfere with the performance of official duties of diplomatic missions, the exercise of jurisdiction of a court of Korea over such lawsuit is limited, and in such a case, whether the above lawsuit may be deemed likely to interfere with the performance of official duties of diplomatic missions should be determined in comprehensive consideration of the grounds and details of claim alleged by the Plaintiff, the effectiveness of the judgment favorable to the Plaintiff based thereon, and the degree of the relevance between such claim or judgment and diplomatic missions abroad or duties of public officials belonging thereto.

1-2. Agreement on Exclusive International Jurisdiction

Supreme Court Decision 2017Da219232 Decided on April 13, 2023 【Damages, etc.】

【Facts】

Plaintiffs using service provided by the defendant, Google Inc, requested the process of information obtained by the defendant. Whether the exclusive international jurisdiction agreement designating federal or state court of Santa Clara County, California, USA has a reasonable connection to the dispute and was not manifestly unreasonable, unfair, or contrary to public policy was in question.

【Summary of Decision】

[1] For an agreement on exclusive international jurisdiction, excluding jurisdiction of the court of Korea and designating a foreign court as a competent court, to be valid, the corresponding case should not belong to exclusive jurisdiction of the court of Korea; a foreign court designated should have jurisdiction in relation to the corresponding case under the foreign law; and the corresponding case is required to have a reasonable connection with the foreign court, and unless an agreement on exclusive international jurisdiction as such is markedly unreasonable and unfair and thus corresponds to any juristic act against public order and good morals, such agreement on jurisdiction should be valid.

[2] Article 27 of the former Act on Private International Law (wholly amended by Act No. 18670, Jan. 4, 2022; hereinafter, the "former Private International Law") regulates that where a customer concluded a customer contract, falling under any subparagraph of Article 27(1), for a purpose besides his/her occupation or business activities, the customer may file a lawsuit against the other party to the customer contract in the country where his/her habitual residence is located (Article 27(4) of the former Private International Law). In addition, Article 27(1)1 of the former Private International Law regulates, as a type of customer contract, a case where, prior to the conclusion of the contract, the other party of the consumer engages in occupation or business activities such as solicitation of transactions by an advertisement in the country of the habitual residence or toward the country from outside and the consumer took all the steps necessary for the conclusion of the contract in that country. This is to protect the reasonable expectation for the application of the provisions on the protection of customers in the country where his/her habitual residence is located that a passive customer who conducted any act necessary for the conclusion of a contract in that country attracted to an advertisement of the opposite party that can be confirmed in the country of the habitual residence has and to substantially guarantee the right of the customer who has difficulty filing a lawsuit with a foreign court to be tried. Accordingly, when considering the purpose and purport of Article 27 of the former Private International Law, it should be careful in interpreting this unfavorably to the customer, and thus where the other party creates profits by using information on the age, gender, location, and behavioral pattern of the customer, the customer cannot be excluded from the customer contract in accordance with Article 27(1)1 of the former Private International Law on the sole basis of such reason unless there are special circumstances even if there is no price such as a usage fee, etc. that the customer should directly pay to the

opposite party under the contract.

Meanwhile, the parties of the customer contract may also agree on international jurisdiction in writing, but such agreement shall be effective only where the agreement is concluded after a dispute already occurred (Article 27(6)1 of the former Private International Law) or where the agreement allows a consumer to file a lawsuit not only to the court, but also to a foreign if the agreement was concluded before the occurrence of a dispute (Article 27(6)2 of the former Private International Law). This is to restrict the effectiveness of such agreement in order for the protection that the former Private International Law grants to the customer not to be easily deprived by such agreement on international jurisdiction between the parties by having the parties agree on international jurisdiction under the condition that the customer accurately grasps the significance and results thereof after a dispute specifically occurred and merely allowing any additional agreement on international jurisdiction favorable to the customer prior to the dispute. Therefore, even if the parties entered into an agreement on international jurisdiction, where the agreement was reached before the occurrence of a specific dispute and the details of the agreement also correspond to an agreement on exclusive jurisdiction, not an agreement on additional jurisdiction, such agreement should be seen to be not effective in relation to the customer contract, and thus the customer may file a lawsuit against the opposite party with the court in the country where the habitual residence of the consumer is located pursuant to Article 27(4) of the former Private International Law despite such agreement on international jurisdiction.

[3] Article 25 of the former Private International Law allows the party's autonomy with respect to the choice of the law applicable to contractual obligations by stipulating that a contract shall be governed by the law which the parties choose explicitly or implicitly, and such principle is likewise applicable to the customer contract.

However, where a customer contract, falling under any subparagraph of Article 27(1) of the former Private International Law, is concluded, the protection that the mandatory provisions of the country of the habitual residence give to the customer shall not be deprived despite the parties' choice of the applicable law (Article 27(1) of the former Private International Law). This is to restrict the effectiveness of such agreement on the applicable law in order for the protection that the former Private International Law grants to the customer not to be easily deprived by the choice of the applicable law between the parties. Therefore, even where the parties of the customer contract choose the law of the country other than the one where the habitual residence of the consumer is located as the applicable law, the application of the mandatory provisions of the country where the habitual residence of the consumer is located shall not be excluded. Meanwhile, Article 30(2) and (4) of the former Act on Promotion of Information and Communications Network Utilization and Information Protection (wholly amended by Act No. 16955, Feb. 4, 2020; hereinafter, the "former Information and Communications Network Act"), as the provision to guarantee the right on the personal information of the users of information and communications services, specifies the right to self-determination of personal information under the Constitution, and when comprehensively considering the purpose and purport of the former Information and Communications Network Act, the function and role of the above provisions for the protection of personal information, and the sanctions imposed on the provider of the information and communications services for breaches of the former Information and Communications Network Act, viewing that the above provisions correspond to mandatory provisions is reasonable.

[4] The right to self-determination of personal information is a constitutional right that has a data subject make his/her own decision in relation to when, to whom, and to which extent his/her personal

information can be allowed to be known and used. The former Act on Promotion of Information and Communications Network Utilization and Information Protection (wholly amended by Act No. 16955, Feb. 4, 2020; hereinafter, the "former Information and Communications Network Act"), by specifying the right to self-determination of personal information as such, stipulates that if a provider of information and communications services was requested to let a user of an information and communications services access, or to provide him/her with, data including the status of the use of his/her personal information or the provision of such personal information to a third party, the provider shall take necessary measures without delay (Article 30(2)2 and (4)). However, the fundamental rights under the Constitution should be exercised to the extent of enabling a person to live communally with others within the national community and not undermining other constitutional values or the national law and order, and the user's right to request for accessing and providing information guaranteed by Article 30(2) of the former Information and Communications Network Act has intrinsic limits in that such right may be also restricted by Act only when necessary for national security, the maintenance of law and order, or public welfare in accordance with Article 37(2) of the Constitution of Korea, and the exercise of such right should be just without any violation of the constitutional order. Article 30(4) of the former Information and Communications Network Act, to the same effect, stipulates that a provider of information and communications services, who received a request for the access to, or the provision of, information, shall take necessary measures to the necessary extent. Accordingly, a provider of information and communications services may limit or deny the access to, or the provision of, information after notifying the user of the said ground when there is any justifiable ground such as where the access to, or the provision of, information requested by a user is prohibited or restricted by any other statute, or where if it is allowed, it is likely to cause harm to

the life or body of any other person or unfairly damages the property
and other interests of any other person. Meanwhile, where a provider
of information and communications services, with no domicile or
place of business in Korea, who should observe other foreign statutes
or regulations as well as those of Korea, refuses to access or provide
such information on the grounds that foreign statutes or regulations
limit the release of the related information, any justifiable ground
cannot be seen to exist immediately on the sole basis of the fact that
foreign statutes and regulations including such details exist, and such
details of foreign statutes and regulations should be seen to be also
able to be considered in determining whether any justifiable ground
exists to limit or deny access to such information. This is because
forcing the provider to permit the perusal or provision of any
information whose release should be prohibited by foreign statutes
and regulations is to coerce the provider of information and
communications services into committing any contradictory act,
which has a harsh aspect; and in particular, such matter pertains to
national security, criminal investigation, etc., and if it is disclosed, it
is deemed likely to seriously undermine the interests of the
corresponding nation, and thus it cannot be seen desirable even in
light of the comity of nations. Eventually, whether a provider of
information and communications services who should observe other
foreign statutes or regulations as well as those of Korea has taken all
necessary measures in accordance with Article 30(4) of the former
Information and Communications Network Act should be determined
after comprehensively taking into account the following matters:
whether the non- disclosure obligation based on the corresponding
foreign statutes or regulations is consistent with the details and
purpose of the Constitution and law of Korea; whether the need to
respect such foreign statutes and regulations is remarkably superior to
the need to protect personal information; and as the requirements for
the non-disclosure required by the corresponding statutes and
regulations are fulfilled with respect to any information that a user

demands to peruse or provide, whether a provider of information and communications services should substantially bear a non-disclosure obligation. Moreover, examining in light of the purpose and purport of users' right to request for perusing and providing information in accordance with Article 30(2) of the former Information and Communications Network Act, by having users make a follow-up confirmation as to whether the corresponding information was provided according to due process and whether such information was used in accordance with the purpose of provision, having the users control any unlawful or unfair use of their personal information is reasonable. Therefore, where any justifiable ground is recognized to exist based on the aforementioned circumstances, a provider of information and communications services should notify the user of the reason for restriction or refusal by specifying such matters, and even if the provider provided any information for foreign investigation agencies on the grounds of national security, criminal investigation, etc., unless the collection of the above information is an obstacle to its purpose as the said ground has already ceased to exist, the provider should let the user peruse the fact that the corresponding information was provided or should inform the user of such fact.

2. APPLICABLE LAW

2-1. CISG

Supreme Court Decision 2021Da255655 Decided on September 27, 2023【Damages, etc.】

【Facts】

The plaintiff, which was a corporation established by the laws of Italy, engaged in the business of textile wholesaling, and the defendant is a company established by the commercial laws of Korea. The Plaintiff claimed that the optical brightener was added to the product supplied by the defendant, which violated the delivery terms of the original contract.

Although the United Nations Convention on Contracts for the International Sale of Goods 1980 (hereinafter, the "CISG") does not expressly provide for the limitation of liability, the Korean law, which is supplementary to the CISG, may limit the debtor's liability was in question.

【Summary of Decision】

[1] There is a similarity between the duty to mitigate the loss stipulated in Article 77 of the CISG and limitation of liability in that where a party who relies on a breach of contract failed to take reasonable measures to mitigate the loss, a party in breach may claim a reduction in the damages in the amount by which the loss should have been mitigated; however, the duty to mitigate the loss cannot be seen to be identical to limitation of liability under which the amount corresponding to a certain proportion of the total loss amount is reduced. There is no specific provision concerning limitation of liability in the CISG other than Article 77, contributing to a defect in the regulation of limitation of liability, which constitutes an internal gap. According to Article 7(2) of the CISG, an internal gap, i.e., questions concerning matters governed by the CISG that are not expressly settled in it, should be settled in conformity with the general principles on which it is based or, in the absence of such principles, in conformity with the law applicable by virtue of the rules of private international law. Article 77 of the CISG stipulates to the effect that avoidable losses cannot be compensated for, and Articles 79 and 80 of the CISG also state to the effect that where a breach of contract is attributable to external circumstances uncontrollable by a party in breach or a nonbreaching party's act or

omission, a party in breach is exempted from liability. Comprehensively taking into account the purpose and intention of the CISG provisions, the principle of fair distribution of losses, which is intended for the adjustment of interests of parties based on the principle of equity, can be seen to constitute the general principles of the CISG, and thus liability may be limited according to the CISG general principles on a fair distribution of losses, despite an internal gap within the CSIG concerning limitation of liability.

[2] Article 74 of the CISG states that damages for breach of contract consist of a sum equal to the loss, including loss of profit, suffered by the other party as a consequence of the breach, while also limiting the amount of damages by stating that such damages may not exceed the loss which the party in breach foresaw or ought to have foreseen at the time of the conclusion of the contract, in the light of the facts and matters of which he then knew or ought to have known as a possible consequence of the breach of contract. Foreseeability must be determined on the basis of not only a person in breach but also the same kind of a reasonable person placed under the same circumstances, by comprehensively considering the background and process leading up to the conclusion of contract and the content of contract.

2-2. Japanese Law: Public Order

Supreme Court Decision 2023Da215590 Decided on October 26, 2023 【Delivery of Movables】

【Facts】

A Buddhist statue was stolen from the Japanese temple, defendant-assistant, and it was forfeited by the Korean government, defendant. The plaintiff claimed that the statue was originally owned by the plaintiff and the defendant-assistant argued that the possession period for acquiring ownership was completed.

Whether the old Act on Conflict of Laws was in force on the date of completion of period for acquiring ownership of the Buddhist statue, and the applicable law for determining whether the defendant-assistant participant acquired ownership of the Buddhist statue should be the Japanese Civil Act, where the Buddhist statue was located at the time of completion of period was in question.

【Summary of Decision】

[1] Article 3 of the Addenda to the Act on Private International Law (entered into force on January 4, 2022) provides that the governing law applicable to matters arising before the enforcement date shall be governed by the previous Act on Private International Law, and the former Act on Private International Law constitutes that the matters arising before the enforcement date (July 1, 2001) shall be governed by the old Act on Conflict of Laws. Therefore, the governing law to be applied to the legal relationship that existed when the former Act on Conflict of Laws Private International Law Act (hereinafter referred to as "the old Act") was in force shall be determined in accordance with the old Act.

[2] Article 12 of the old Act stipulates that real rights, or other rights subject to registration, with regard to movable or immovable property shall be governed by the law of the place in which the property is situated, and the acquisition or loss of, or changes in those rights shall be governed by the lex situs at the time of the completion of the causal act or fact. Therefore, the governing law for determining whether the possessor of immovable property has acquired ownership upon the completion of the possession period is the law of the place where the object is situated at the time of the completion of the period, and unless there are special circumstances, the fact that the property has historical, artistic, or academic significance does not make difference.

[3] Article 5 of the old Act stipulates that "The provisions of a foreign law shall not apply, if the provisions are clearly contrary to good morals and other public order of Korea." However, it should be cautious about excluding the application of foreign law as the applicable law to legal relations with foreign elements, as it may render conflicts of law norms such as private international law or conflict of laws meaningless. In particular, if the substance of the foreign law designated as the applicable law is not significantly different from the law of Korea, which is the lex fori, and the result of its application does not make a substantial difference compared to the result of applying Korean law, it is difficult to conclude that the application of the foreign law is contrary to good morals and other public order that the Korean legal system seeks to protect, so the application of the foreign law should not be easily excluded unless there are any other special circumstances.

Treaties/Agreements Concluded by the Republic of Korea

Treaties/Agreements
Concluded by the Republic of Korea

The Editorial Board
ILA Korean Branch

1. MARINE ENVIRONMENT MANAGEMENT ACT

https://elaw.klri.re.kr/eng_service/lawView.do?hseq=64109&lang=ENG

2. ACT ON THE MANAGEMENT OF SPECIFIC SUBSTANCES FOR THE PROTECTION OF THE OZONE LAYER

https://elaw.klri.re.kr/eng_service/lawView.do?hseq=61379&lang=ENG

3. IMMIGRATION ACT

https://elaw.klri.re.kr/eng_service/lawView.do?hseq=61640&lang=ENG

INDEX

AUTHOR GUIDELINES AND STYLE SHEET

I. SUBMISSION

Manuscripts should be submitted in Microsoft Word and electronically sent to ilakoreanbranch@gmail.com

II. GENERAL TERMS AND PEER-REVIEW SYSTEM OF PUBLICATION

All manuscripts are subject to initial evaluation by the KYIL Editorial Board and subsequently sent out to independent reviewers for a peer review. The Editorial Board accepts manuscripts on a rolling basis and will consider requests for an expedited review in appropriate cases.

III. FORMATING

1. ABSTRACT

Please include an abstract (no more than 150 words) at the beginning of an article.

2. TEXT

Main Text: Times New Roman, font size 12, 1.5 spacing
Endnotes: Times New Roman, font size 12, single spacing

3. CITING REFERENCE

The KYIL requires endnotes with subsequent numbering; the initial endnote should be indicated with '*,' if it is necessary to provide explanatory information about the manuscript.

Please include a reference list for all works the are cited at the end of the manuscript.

IV. NOTES

1. BOOKS

P. Malanczuk, *Akehurst's Modern Introduction to International Law*, 7th ed. (New York: Eoutledge, 1997), p. 1.

2. ARTICLES

Chao Wang, *China's Preferential Trade Remedy Approaches: A New Haven School Perspective*, Vol.21 No.1, Asia Pacific Law Review, (2013), p. 103.

3. ARTICLES IN COLLECTIONS

J. Paulsson & Z. Douglas, *Indirect Expropriation in Investment Treaty Arbitrations, in* Arbitration Foreign Investment Disputes 148 (N. Horn & S. Kroll eds., Kluwer Law International, 2004).

4. ARTICLES IN NEWSPAPER

YI Whan-Woo, *Korea, New Zealand embrace free trade pact*, Korea Times, November 14, 2014.

5. UNPUBLISHED MATERIALS

PARK Jung-Won, *Minority Rights Constraints on a State's Power to Regulate Citizenship under International Law*, Ph.D thesis (2006), on file with author.

6. WORKING PAPERS AND REPORTS

OECD, *'Indirect Expropriation' and the 'Right to Regulate' in International Investment Law*, OECD Working Paper, 2014/09.

7. INTERNET SOURCES

C. Schreuer, The Concept of Expropriation under the ETC and Other Investment Protection Treaties (2005), http://www.univie,ac,at/ intlaw/pdf/csunpuyblpaper_3pdf. [Accessed on September 22, 2015]

V. GUIDELINE FOR AUTHORS

1. ARTICLE

Manuscripts must be in the form of a regular paper including endnotes and references. The length for an articles should not exceed 10,000 words in English excluding notes and references.

2. SPECIAL REPORT

Manuscripts for Special Report must be in the form of a descriptive report which covers the international law issues related to Korea in the past 5 years. Special Report must include author's comments with less than 10 endnotes and 5 references. The length for a special report should be no more the 5,000 words.

3. RECENT DEVELOPMENT

Manuscripts must cover the trends in international law related to Korea in the preceding year. Recent Development must be in the form of a short report, including less than 5 endnotes. The length for Recent Development should be no more than 2,000 words.